SCIENCE FOR THE PEOPLE is a loosely knit national organization of scientific workers. Through many local chapters, its basic goal is to redirect the priorities of American science away from "following the logic of profit." The organization grew out of a campus-based group formed to oppose classified war research, but later expanded its concern to such other areas as de-professionalizing science; developing materials for teaching science in a social-political context; providing critiques of present science curricula, methods, and school structure; and raising crucial women's issues within the scientific community.

CHINA:
SCIENCE WALKS ON
TWO LEGS
A Report from
SCIENCE FOR THE PEOPLE

 DISCUS BOOKS/PUBLISHED BY AVON

AVON BOOKS
A division of
The Hearst Corporation
959 Eighth Avenue
New York, New York 10019

First Discus Printing, October, 1974

DISCUS TRADEMARK REG. U.S. PAT. OFF. AND
FOREIGN COUNTRIES, REGISTERED TRADEMARK—
MARCA REGISTRADA, HECHO EN CHICAGO, U.S.A.

Printed in the U.S.A.

CONTRIBUTORS

DELEGATION: Mary Altendorf, Minneapolis, Minnesota
David Aronow, Worcester, Massachusetts
John Dove, Brookline, Massachusetts
Minna Goldfarb, Port Jefferson, New York
Ginger Goldner, New York, New York
Judy Greenberg, San Francisco, California
Marvin Kalkstein, East Setauket, New York
Frank Mirer, Cambridge, Massachusetts
Geri Steiner, Brookline, Massachusetts
Vinton Thompson, Chicago, Illinois

EDITORS: Dan Connell, Truro, Massachusetts
Dan Gover, Boston, Massachusetts

To the eternal friendship and the continuing struggle of the Chinese and American peoples.

After several decades, the victory of the Chinese people's democratic revolution, viewed in retrospect, will seem like only a brief prologue to a long drama. . . . The Chinese revolution is great, but the road after the revolution will be longer, the work greater and more arduous.

—Mao Tse-tung,
Selected Readings (1949)

ACKNOWLEDGMENTS

It would have been impossible to produce this book without the help of many other people. Our warmest thanks go to the people of China for making our visit one of the most memorable months of our lives. Lack of space prevents us from naming all those whose tireless work, good humor, and patient explanations helped us to learn more in a month than we thought possible, but we must at least single out our official host, Chou P'ei-yüan, and our comrades from the Foreign Affairs Bureau of the Scientific and Technical Association: Pang Chan, Chu Yung-hang, Su Fung-ling, Ten Ting-yü, Ch'ien Gao, Chu Ching-ning, and Ch'iang Ch'i.

Thanks go also to Ethan Signer, Ernest Kovacs, Norval Welch, the Chinese Embassy in Ottawa, the China Travel Service office in Hongkong, and the U.S.-China People's Friendship Association in San Francisco for their help prior to the trip.

While we were in China, Wang You-hua, Ann Tompkins, Joan Hinton, Sid Engst, Norman Schulman, and Dr. George Hatem took time to discuss and explain some of the things we were seeing from a western perspective.

On our return we were assisted by countless friends who read, corrected, and criticized early drafts of the book, with special help from Peter Mayer. Nancy Hodes and Kathy Lazarus did their best to clear up the Chinese spelling. The finished manuscript was produced by Gina Abeles, Arlene Barron, Phyllis Connell, and Ellen Kelley.

Finally, we wish to thank the members of SESPA/Science for the People, especially the collectives in Boston, New York, Chicago, Minneapolis, Berkeley, and St. Louis, who helped us prepare for the trip and, when we returned, helped us to understand some of what we had seen.

CHINA:
SCIENCE WALKS ON TWO LEGS

INTRODUCTION

China is suddenly at the center of attention in the United States. Why? For nearly twenty-five years most Americans were cut off from first-hand information about the People's Republic. The Chinese people, about a quarter of the world's population, were a faceless mass to us. Whatever negative image we had of China, it was mostly a blank.

Then all at once the door to travel was open and reports of travelers—reporters, scholars, and ordinary people—began to appear and were very surprising. As an image of New China formed, it was opposite to our view of the Third World as a uniform place of poverty, ignorance, exploitation, and disease. We got reports of a functioning society where food was adequate, disease limited, health care available, crime at a minimum, the children in school: a society that was making great strides in industry, agriculture, science, and military strength. A picture of the social organization of the People's Republic of China began to form and it appeared to be one of a radically different system, a developing socialist nation. And as the picture became clearer and more complete, many wondered if the Chinese experience might suggest approaches to some of the pressing problems of American society.

Why should we, authors of this book and members of an organization called Science for the People, be so interested in science in China? Think for a moment about the ways in which science and technology enter our daily lives as Americans. We read about fabulous developments in medical science, but it's hard to get emergency care no matter how much we can pay, and most of us fear the enormous cost of prolonged illness. Instead of marveling at the productivity of advanced scientific agriculture, we worry about pesticide contamination, try to cope with spiraling rises in food prices, and read about famine in the Third World. Products of industry roll out of the factories, providing the basis for our material wellbeing, but at the same time industry pollutes and degrades the environment around us and work remains repetitive and dehumanizing. Advances in transportation leave us with airport noise and traffic jams. A fuel shortage leaves us with colder houses and slower cars but little or no attention given to mass transportation. Developments in psychology result in the massive use of amphetamines to control the behavior of "hyperactive" children. The computer, touted as an almost magical thinking machine, is used to fight an absentee war in Southeast Asia, and here at home it compiles lists of hundreds of thousands of people opposed to that war. The laser, a significant scientific tool, is used to guide bombs to the targets selected by these computers, and yet a primitively armed force of guerrilla fighters is able to outfox it. Lasers and computers are popularly known for their nonmilitary uses, but the research and development of laser and computer technology had their first inspiration and initial funding within the context of military capabilities, as so most scientific and technological advances in our society. The list is endless. All around us experts with academic degrees and white coats come up with the answers, trying to force us to accept their advice without understanding it, but they seem to lead us out of one crisis only to confront a new one. No wonder more and more people working in the sciences have become dissatisfied with the misuse of their own work. The Science for the People organization grew up as all kinds of scientific workers and other people affected by the results of technology began to analyze and respond to these contradictions.

Originally known as Scientists and Engineers for Social and Political Action, SESPA first surfaced with an attempt to pass a "No War Research" resolution at a meeting of the American Physical Society. (See Appendix 1 for a more detailed profile of the organization.) The organization developed out of a campus-based group opposing the classified nature of war research and grew to include over a dozen chapters and many more individuals around the country who were united by a commitment to redirect science to serve human needs. Members became active in the movement against the war in Indochina and went on to question the use of science and technology in American policy toward the Third World as a whole.

As scientific workers, we began to analyze and respond to the many conflicts between the potential value of science and its actual effects. It became obvious to us that the real accomplishments of Western science are obscured by the aim of making profits and by a system that doesn't plan rationally. SESPA began to think of itself as "Science for the People" when individuals and groups outside the technical community started raising these issues of scientific abuse. Fundamentally, we have come to view the problems of science as flowing from the basic problems of political and economic control in the society. We have learned that technology follows the logic of profit and that control of funding dominates the direction of scientific work. In short, scientific activity is not value-free in this or any other society.

On university campuses SESPA members have set up courses to explore the political control of scientific work and have also criticized the practice of science in the universities themselves. On the secondary-school level we have organized workshops, critiqued curricula, and developed original materials that deal with science in its social and political context. Off campus we have focused on the environment, food additives, occupational health, psychosurgery, and pollution control, among other issues. In the workplace, where scientific workers face the same problems of job security, pay scales, and discrimination as other workers, SESPA members have tried to form organizations to connect these workplace issues to a concern with the overall direction of the corporation or laboratory. In our own work we try to practice humane values and collective decision making.

Our basic aim is to debunk the myth of an apolitical, benevolent science that prevails in America. We felt that the Chinese were also struggling to develop another way of doing things, and we became increasingly interested in getting a first-hand look at their progress in these areas. As exchange visits started to take place a few years ago, we thought it might be possible to send a delegation to China, and we wrote to the Academy of Science in Peking. We also formed a collective in the Boston area to begin studying China and to coordinate a nationally selected group. Notices were mailed to SESPA chapters around the country and printed in the bimonthly *Science For The People* magazine, but we waited for a response from the Chinese before making formal arrangements. A full year later we received an invitation to send a delegation of ten people. On short notice (two weeks) the group was selected from SESPA chapters in Boston, New York, Chicago, St. Louis and Minneapolis. Its members included a chemist, three psychologists, a welfare mother who had been doing science-related organizing, a college science teacher, a computer programmer, a graduate student in biology, a medical student, and a nurse. The members were politically active in the areas of occupational health, prison reform, Science for Vietnam (affiliated with SFTP), day care, community mental health, survival programs, workplace organizing, the environmental movement, and restructuring education.

The full group assembled for the first time in San Francisco in February 1973 and flew to Hongkong. We entered the People's Republic of China at Shumchun on February 21. In the next four weeks, spent as guests of the Chinese Scientific and Technical Association, we visited the cities of Canton, Peking, and Shanghai, and parts of Honan, Shansi, and Hunan provinces. We saw research institutes, schools and universities, factories and agricultural communes, clinics and hospitals; and we talked with scientific workers, teachers, political cadres, students, doctors, and ordinary workers and peasants.

Unfortunately, no one in the group was fluent in Chinese, although one of us, John Dove, had an elementary knowledge of the language and was able to teach the rest of us simple phrases. Overall, however, we depended on interpreters throughout the trip. The reader should understand that within the limitations of our visit there was no way that we could make this a comprehensive study of science in China. Because of time, geography, and our own lack of knowledge, we saw far too little in four weeks to possibly profess such an accomplishment. What we did see, though, was a substantial cross-section of scientific activity that reflected the particular interests of our group.

We saw China as the Chinese presented it to us and readily admit that we believed what we saw and heard. The reader may feel that our presentation lacks an element of objectivity or skepticism. If so, it is probably because we were deeply impressed by New China, and our impressions are no doubt based in part on a clear political bias.

The experience of being part of an official delegation was totally new to us. As the novelty wore off we felt that we were among friends and colleagues who were doing their best to give us the information we wanted to bring back about China. The general theme of our hosts was that "there are some successes, but there are also some shortcomings. If you tell only what is good about China, people will find out the truth and become disillusioned." Following this advice, we have tried to be fair in reporting our observations of China in relation to our experience as scientific workers in America.

But it is also important to view our experiences in the broad context of Chinese society rather than to make direct comparisons of specific differences between science in China and in the United States. China is still a very poor country materially and is just now going through the equivalent of our industrial revolution of the nineteenth and early twentieth centuries. The point to emphasize, however, is that what took us a century and a half to accomplish, the Chinese have done in scarcely twenty-five years. They have a long way to go before their overall level of science and technology surpasses ours, but at the rate they are advancing such a possibility is not nearly so remote as it may seem. Our attention and our enthusiasm, therefore, are not so much directed at the concrete accomplishments of the Chinese—although the Chinese are rightly excited about them—but rather at the rate of development and at the particular social and political context that fosters such an accelerated rate of change. Science in China, in its sense of systematically investigating and solving problems, is becoming the property of the entire people, and is integrating all problems into a scientific methodology: problems of production, technology, education, medicine, social relations, basic research, planning, and so on. In Chinese theory science is not the exclusive domain of those with special training, nor is its development limited to advancing only that sector of the economy which is already at a high level without involving most of the workers and peasants in the process. This approach to science, which is practiced in most of the western world, is something China is determined to avoid.

Science "walks on two legs" in China. Her ancient traditional knowledge together with more modern advances made through regular scientific channels are one leg. The broad masses of ordinary people who had always been denied access to scientific developments have become the other leg. Basically, the idea of walking on two legs means to exercise the underdeveloped one, rather than putting all resources into the stronger one. It does not mean cutting the stronger one off in favor of the weaker, as some western observers have implied.

Examples of such misinterpretation occur in many foreign reports on the state of higher education since the Cultural Revolution. We had heard before we went that there had been a general closing of all institutions of higher learning, that faculty and students had been sent out into the factories and the countryside to be "educated" by the workers and peasants, that universities were only very gradually reopening, with limited student enrollment, and that there would be a seven- or eight-year hiatus before any graduates would again be produced. There are facts underlying some of these statements, but the implication that education completely stopped could not be further from the reality we found.

Much of what we saw and heard during our trip was described in terms of the way things were done since the Cultural Revolution. Scientists we spoke to told us how their work and their relationships with colleagues, students, workers, and peasants were changed by it. We came to see this great political movement, which flared into open conflicts during the years 1966 to 1968, as the most profound struggle in Chinese society since Liberation in 1949. Its consequences affected people at all levels of society: in factories, schools, communes, research institutes, health care facilities, the government, and the Communist Party.

As we heard it discussed, the Cultural Revolution seemed to question the general direction China was moving in on the road to development. It reoriented the relationship of the political leadership to ordinary people and exposed fundamental disagreement at the highest level of the Communist Party. This disagreement arose over the question of whether the Party leadership had drifted away from the masses. Some Party cadres had started to use their positions to secure privileges for themselves and their families, and the Party itself was on its way toward becoming a management elite. This part of the leadership became known as "Party people in authority taking the capitalist road"; it favored the use of economic incentives instead of political mobilization, and emphasized the development of heavy industry located near the urban centers. Eventually it became identified with Liu Shao-ch'i, then president of the People's Republic and vice-chairman of the Communist Party.

As early as 1962 and 1963 Mao Tse-tung had warned against the restoration of capitalism in the economy and

attacked the growth of a Party cadre elite, establishing the
position in the leadership that became known as the "socialist road." By 1966 students at Peking University were
responding to the failure of city authorities to criticize an
anti-Maoist play by openly demonstrating against office-
holders. The Red Guards, formed by militant students in
the universities and schools, began to denounce elitist
Party cadres. They were officially received by Chairman
Mao, who called on them to "bombard the headquarters
of Party power holders who take the capitalist road."

Important political changes took place during this time.
Liu Shao-ch'i was eventually removed from power and the
"capitalist road" lost its influence in the Party leadership.
In Shanghai a mass organization led by workers seized
control of the municipal government. Struggles between
established authorities and workers and students flared
throughout the country. To resolve them, revolutionary
committees were set up in 1968 to consolidate and unify
contending political forces on all levels of society. Workers
formed an average of 50 percent of these committees; political cadres made up another 36 percent; and People's
Liberation Army representatives averaged 14 percent.
These revolutionary committees oversaw the restructuring
of most social institutions and the reformation of Party
committees. At the time of our trip, the revolutionary
committees were still very much in existence and were
usually responsible for the daily running of institutions.

The scientific workers we talked to often described their
work and their lives in relation to the larger changes in society that had been wrought by the Cultural Revolution.
In general, it seemed to be a movement against elitist
forms of expertise and specialization, back to a clearer reliance on the initiative of the masses of people. It shifted
emphasis away from urban concentration, toward the development of production and social facilities in the countryside where the vast majority of the population lives.
With regard to science, the Cultural Revolution led to an
emphasis on the applications of research and directed research toward meeting immediate needs. It implemented
structural changes in the way scientific activity is carried

out. Scientists told us that they now engage in more direct productive work than they formerly did. They go out of their laboratories and institutes to meet with people in industry and agriculture whom their work affects. On the other hand, workers and nonprofessionals come into the scientific institutions and participate in their decision-making processes. Scientific education seems to have become more practical, less professional, and more directly involved in production. The aim is for students in all fields to have a background of factory or farm work so that they will have a better understanding and common feeling with the people whom their work will serve.

At Tsinghua (People's) and Peita (Peking) Universities in Peking, and at Futan University in Shanghai, we talked with many faculty members and students who had been connected with their institutions throughout the Cultural Revolution. Their stories sounded similar to stories of the American student movement of the same period, but with strikingly different results. At the onset of the Cultural Revolution the universities were alive with demands for student power, open admissions, fewer examinations, and a more relevant curriculum. The university system still had its roots in the old class structure of educating an elite according to special texts and methods. But, we were told, this was not consistent with the policies of socialism in China and the students, even though they were privileged, rebelled.

The Cultural Revolution did not aim to eliminate "the old guard" but to transform each of its members into a new type of socialist scientist or professor. Many of these professionals had a difficult time achieving their "transformation," but those we met seemed to be better suited to their new roles as servants of the people rather than competitive careerists.

One of our first questions as we toured scientific institutes and universities was a common one among American intellectuals trying to make sense of the Chinese experience: Wasn't it difficult for Chinese scientists to give up their research to meet scientific priorities, to be removed from their labs and reassigned to work in agriculture or industry? The response we received was generally one of great amusement. Professor Tan Chia-chen, a geneticist in Peking, told us that his work had never been as exciting as it is now. His research revolves around the theoretical genetics of crossing different plant species. When he was sent to the countryside he discovered that "the peasants were ahead of the theoreticians." Spurred by the need to increase production, they had succeeded in crossing the castor bean and the cotton plant, both oil-producing crops. Theoretical geneticists would have advised them not to waste time trying: in theory it should not have worked. Now Professor Tan spends part of each year out with the peasants learning from them so that he can take new information back to the laboratory. Sometimes peasants come back to the lab with him to teach and work with students, and students in turn go to the countryside to work with the peasants. Professor Tan remains a prominent scientist, but he has developed an ability to work with practical aspects of agriculture that has made his own research more effective and beneficial.

In the Shanghai Machine Tool Factory ordinary workers study calculus at midday, so that they will eventually understand the entire production process, including the theoretical levels. Other workers set up small shops in the universities to build electronic equipment, and teach students and professors how to build it for their own research purposes.

Housewives who organized themselves into small local factories to produce paper boxes have moved on to more complex things like flashlight batteries and even transistors. Inspired by parables like "The Foolish Old Man Who Removed the Mountains," they have spurred themselves on to even greater tasks. Now there are street factories that build computers.

Peasants in Linhsien, a large, once arid valley, designed and built an enormous irrigation canal after experts had advised them against it. They built hundreds of tunnels and aqueducts along the 70-kilometer route that winds over rough mountain peaks, and it was their self-reliance and determination that pushed the task through to its completion. The Red Flag Canal serves as a monument to their efforts and an inspiration to people throughout China.

Science, in short, is being demystified in China. According to the Marxist conception, it is the summation of the laboring people's experience and properly belongs to them. The idea of science as the private property of scientists, as being something too deep for ordinary people to understand, must be abolished. In its place, a vast exercise in sharing knowledge is being carried out through the length and breadth of China, to make science a part of the mass culture.

At our formal reception in the Great Hall of the People in Peking, Liu Hsi-yao, head of the Science and Education Group of the State Council, told us that China is building up a huge contingent of scientific workers at the same time it is bringing the broad masses into the development of science. What we saw first-hand bore this out. Universities, factories, communes, and other institutions are all involved, under the leadership of the Chinese National Academy of Sciences. Our host group, the National Science and Technology Association, has the special task of organizing discussions and seminars for the masses of the people. At every level of society, from the Central Committee to the grass roots, special technical bodies exist to insure that science, one of the primary building blocks of a socialist society, is learned and used by everyone.

New methods for sharing and spreading scientific knowledge, both formal and informal, require an atmosphere of mutual trust and respect among professionals and nonprofessionals. This is not a natural state of affairs once any elite has been given the privilege attendant upon specialized training. Doctors do not naturally trust old women to carry out public health work, nor do professors readily take advice from their students or from simple peasants. That is why what we saw of the practice of science in China was so impressive. In the widest possible range, it tries to combine the efforts of specialists and nonspecialists alike for the common effort. Gradually we came to understand some of the methods used to effect a transformation in human nature and motivation. We hope to convey them in the pages to follow as we trace what we learned about the reeducation of intellectuals and the growth of self-reliance among the peasants and workers. Surely no underdeveloped country has ever initiated such a broad integration of all its people toward the solution of problems through the use of a scientific and human method, a method that is both a tool for unifying the society and for utilizing its resources to serve the entire people. We begin our book with an account of the construction of the Red Flag Canal because of the unique insight it offers into the Chinese experience and the ways political strengths are used to overcome scientific and technological obstacles. As such, it is a kind of extended parable that informed our entire visit.

Following the essay on the Red Flag Canal, we begin our substantive discussion of science in China with a chapter on agriculture, which remains the backbone of the Chinese economy and the focus of much of Chinese applied science. From there we move into the other major area of applied science—industry—and then into the more theoretical area of research science as we observed it in Chinese research institutes. The next chapter, on schools, is a transitional chapter showing how science is integrated into the mass culture through its educational system. Chapters on the health care system and the mental hospital in Shanghai go on to illustrate the extent of the interconnectedness of science and politics in the everyday lives of the Chinese people. Finally there is a chapter on planning, to demonstrate the use of scientific method in the general area of social organization. We close with a brief summing up of the political theory behind the practice of Chinese science, and leave the reader to evaluate its relevance to his or her experience here in America.

Although much of the following material is a collection of our impressions—in some cases better backgrounded than in others—we have not sought to achieve a single style. Each chapter incorporates the first-hand observations and the subsequent revisions of several different members of the group, in some instances as many as seven, so we have intentionally avoided attributing specific authorship to any of the sections. Like the Chinese, we choose to stand or fall together.

None of us being proficient in the Chinese language, we are sure to have made some mistakes in the spelling of Chinese names of people and places. In transliterating Chinese we have followed as consistently as possible the Wade-Giles System for the sake of familiarity for American readers, although the Chinese themselves have devised and use a more phonetic system known as *pinyin.*

1 THE RED FLAG CANAL

*There is an ancient Chinese fable called "The
Foolish Old Man Who Removed the Mountains." It tells
of an old man who lived in northern China long, long ago
and was known as the Foolish Old Man of North
Mountain. His house faced south and beyond his doorway
stood the two great peaks, T'aihang and Wangwu,
obstructing the way. With great determination, he led his
sons in digging up these mountains hoe in hand. Another
greybeard, known as the Wise Old Man, saw them and
said derisively, "How silly of you to do this! It is quite
impossible for you few to dig up these two huge
mountains." The Foolish Old Man replied, "When I die,
my sons will carry on; when they die, there will be my
grandsons, and then their sons and grandsons, and so on to
infinity. High as they are, the mountains cannot grow any
higher and with every bit we dig, they will be that much
lower. Why can't we clear them away?" Having refuted the
Wise Old Man's wrong view, he went on digging every
day, unshaken in his conviction. God was moved by this,
and he sent down two angels, who carried the mountains
away on their backs. Today, two big mountains lie like a
dead weight on the Chinese people. One is imperialism, the
other is feudalism. The Chinese Communist Party has long
made up its mind to dig them up. We must persevere and
work unceasingly, and we, too, will touch God's heart. Our*

God is none other than the masses of the Chinese people. If they stand up and dig together with us, why can't these two mountains be cleared away?

—Mao Tse-tung, "The Foolish Old Man Who Removed the Mountains" (1945), *Selected Works*, Vol III

Our caravan of jeeps and buses, loaded with ourselves, our hosts and interpreters, members of the Hsikou Brigade we had just visited, and our professional drivers, careened around sharp curves through the snowy blue T'aihang Mountains. The steep striated mountainsides of sheer rock reminded us of the Big Horn Mountains of Utah, and it was easy to picture the flash floods springtime would bring down the dry, stony gulches. Often, coming around a curve of rocky road propped against the cliff with hand-hewn stone retaining walls, we would encounter a few peasants tilling a tiny plot of winter wheat they had some-how managed to fit between road and cliff. Occasionally a mountain village appeared in a valley below, and we saw many cave homes dug into the mountainsides with Gothic arch face walls of unbaked brick matching the surrounding brown earth.

Pictures were difficult to take from the bouncing jeeps, but none of us will ever forget the image of sun- and wind-burned peasants pitted optimistically against this massive and forbidding landscape.

Not many years ago, high in these mountains, young men armed with pickaxes and a common goal swung on long ropes from the sheer cliffs to chip out toe holds in the solid rock. In a film we watched with some of these same peasants, we saw their bodies silhouetted against the sky in a slow ballet as each pushed off in turn to gain dis-tance for a new attack on the stone face. With simple tools and homemade dynamite they gradually chipped and blasted a winding rock shelf around 70 kilometers of for-midable peaks. Occasionally there was no way around, and they had to burrow straight into the mountain, cutting tunnels up to half a mile in length. As they worked, thousands of other peasants chipped out other parts of the mountains and slowly shaped many millions of blocks of stone with pickaxes and cold chisels. The laboring peasants on the cliffs and in the valley below had a common vision and were determined to carry out what must now be among the world's great engineering feats. They call it the Red Flag Canal; its hand-built masonry, if formed into a wall a meter high and a meter thick, would stretch halfway around the earth at the equator.

These peasants live in a valley called Linhsien (Lin County), in the northwest corner of Honan Province. For many centuries the more than five hundred little villages of this great valley had been plagued by endless drought. The far-off Chang River descended rapidly from its source and dissipated on the other side of the mountains. In the valley a few rivers poured down gorges in flash floods once or twice a year, tearing down everything in their path and drying up overnight before their lifeblood waters could be put to any use. For more than two hundred of these villages, even drinking water was 10 or more kilometers' walk away, and the peasants tell many tales of death from thirst and suicide. Irrigation was out of the question. In the worst seasons people left their homes in droves, returning only when the little seasonal rain filled a few wells. They had tried everything to capture water here and there—to no avail. Well bits 80 meters deep came up dry; catch basins for rain and snow water were soon exhausted. Only the Chang River taunted from afar as their impossible hope. It flowed the year round. After Liberation, the Chinese people set out to achieve goals that had been beyond the reach and even the imagination of the old society. In 1958, the year of the Great Leap Forward, masses of ordinary people all over the country had achieved extraordinary feats in large-scale construction. Why not the peasants in Lin County? Everyone had studied Chairman Mao's famous tale of "The Foolish Old Man Who Removed the Mountains," a story of painstaking chipping away at a herculean task. The young people, among them one with a few years of engineering education, talked about a canal through the mountains and tramped for months to survey the possibilites. At last, they presented a plan to the county officials, and a team of experts was called in from the cities to repeat the survey.

These engineers came back shaking their heads at the peasants' notions and announced that the project could not be done. Were the peasants to give up their last hope because the "experts" called them foolish? Or were they to become like thousands of "foolish old men" and move their own mountains? Debate raged, and at last the County Party Committee was won over to back the project. At that time China's economy had suffered a temporary setback, and two "lines" emerged all over the country as possible solutions: Mao Tse-tung advocated self-reliance among the people as the way to overcome difficulties, but many people in high positions, following Liu Shao-ch'i (then president of the People's Republic of China), wanted to restore economic tactics of private enterprise and reliance on professional expertise. These people considered the canal a hopeless and wasteful economic venture, yet the peasants decided to pursue their project in opposition to this view. During the four years it took to build the canal's 70-kilometer main trunk, four orders to stop work were given by officials later considered "capitalist roaders." All supplies were withheld and inspection teams came to make sure work had stopped. The people refused to be held back, however, and young volunteers blasting tunnels would hide in the mountains until the teams had gone away. During growing and harvest seasons, most of the peasants worked in the sparse fields, but all who were not needed worked tirelessly at the great canal as it slowly took shape. In off seasons everyone joined in, and the tales of heroism on the high cliffs multiplied and spurred the peasants on.

For a time the women of Lin County were relegated to the more menial tasks of feeding and supporting the men. They were not allowed near the canal site itself, as it was considered too dangerous. When we visited the various parts of the Red Flag Canal, which includes not only 1500 kilometers of trunks and branches into the valley, but also hundreds of reservoirs, dams, aqueducts, and power stations, our tour guide was a beautiful, bright-eyed young woman of twenty-three. Her name is Han Yung-ti, but she is known far and wide in China as "Iron Girl," leader of a thirty-woman "Iron Girl Team." As we drove the bumpy roads of Linhsien from one canal point to another, she told us her story:

In 1968 we were building a very important tunnel. All the men and women wanted to join in the work, but the leaders only allowed the men to go; they did not allow the women near the site. The women and girls thought that was a feudalist idea! At that time I organized the women and girls to study Chairman Mao's works and eventually became leader of the Iron Girl Team. Chairman Mao teaches us that women are equal to men; what men can do, women can also do. We applied to the leaders again. We were determined to go down the shafts [which had been dug vertically down into the mountain to create more faces from which to cut the tunnel and to provide air shafts] and do the blasting with dynamite. Finally the leaders allowed the women into the shafts to join the men.

We women had recalled our miserable lives before Liberation. There was a saying in the country that men could go all around the country, but women could go all around the courtyard. We had no rights politically or economically. After Liberation, we poor and lower-middle peasants became masters of our own country. If we women did not do the work, who *would* do all the work to be done? Chairman Mao told us that women hold up half the sky and men the other half. We women all thought building the canal was for the revolution and in the interest of all the people in this county, so we were determined to join the work—and that is what we did.

At the beginning, our team was not called the Iron Girl Team. Many men, many people, did not think we could do everything just like men, but we put our ideas into practice and went to watch what the men

did: swinging hammers, holding the chisels, and
later, how to place dynamite and detonate it. Finally
the men believed us. At first we couldn't actually
do many of these things, but with the help of men we
learned. We went out with them and we stood back
and watched to see how things were done, and when
we had questions we just asked the men until we
learned how to do all these things. In about four or
five days we mastered the skills, and then we participated.

The Iron Girl Team was small—only about thirty
women with an average age of twenty-two—but after
hard work the peasants gave us the honor of this
title: Iron Girls. We got some of our knowledge
reading science books, but most of it came from
direct practice. For example, how did we learn the
blasting work? We had asked the leaders to be allowed to do this work, but they didn't believe we
could do it. When we were allowed to try, one girl
would have to go down and place five charges at
once before coming up out of the shaft. I went down,
but I cried, "Let me up!" after lighting only four of
them because I was afraid to stay longer. I told the
work crew that only four of the charges were good.
Then the girls wanted to know why only four of the
five were useful. As they went off, and there were
really only four explosions, I was asked again why only
four had been good. Then I explained that I was
afraid to stay down longer, and had only lit four of
them. The men and the other workers praised me
and said "You not only can do the other kinds of
work, but also the work of blasting." I replied, "But
I didn't do well, I only fired four charges, and not
five. Chairman Mao teaches us to fear neither hard-
ship nor death. Why didn't I dare fire the fifth charge?"
In order to change my wrong thinking, I went down
the shaft again to fire the fifth charge, because if I
didn't I thought it might endanger the other workers.

The smoke had not dissipated and it was very dark
in the deep shaft. As I went down, I couldn't open

my eyes and my lantern went out. I was afraid, but I thought of Chairman Mao's words and the safety of the other workers. Finally I got the lantern lit again and also lit the last fuse. Only then did I come up. From this experience, all the girls learned that only by linking practice with Chairman Mao's teachings can we accomplish everything! With the guidance of Mao Tse-tung thought and the help of the men workers, all the girls learned to swing hammers and do blasting. We met many difficulties on the work site, but whenever new difficulties came along we organized ourselves to study Chairman Mao's work, "The Foolish Old Man Who Removed the Mountains," and the fine qualities of many of our heroes.*

As we heard Iron Girl's story we were impressed by the conviction with which she, like so many other people in China, used the works of Mao Tse-tung in daily application to very concrete problems. The "Foolish Old Man" is far more than an ordinary parable. It has been used over and over in many different situations to overcome the feelings of incompetence that most people have if they have never had formal education and the respect that comes with it. When the peasants were told by their highest leader that their own common sense, their ability to analyze their own life conditions, and their patient hard work could achieve seemingly impossible goals, they found a new confidence. It wasn't just a good feeling, it was something to hold on to and make real. Every stone mortared into the canal, every new kilometer completed, shows that the story which inspired them was real. It seemed to us that almost every person we met in China had felt the reality of that story in a concrete way by applying it to some task that seemed impossible at first. The

---

*Throughout this book, extended quotations are transcriptions of tapes recording both the Chinese speaker and our interpreters' translation. The translations are used here, sometimes leading to awkward or stilted passages when a series of comments is strung together as a single quotation.

stories we heard convinced us that every new achievement brings with it a new sense of freedom and confidence: freedom to do the things the people want to do for their collective advance out of feudalism. To them, freedom is not the absence of restraints, except in the sense that they have broken the chains of ignorance and submission. Freedom in China is seen as the power of understanding concrete conditions in order to achieve ever greater accomplishments, to solve the problems of the past.

Every new landmark on the canal brought this lesson home to us. Taoyüan Aqueduct spans one of the dry gulches through which the flash-flood rivers pass. The work crews had originally planned an open channel aqueduct across a series of tall Romanesque arches, but the local peasants, seeing the plans, argued that the deep riverbed was difficult to cross and asked why a roadbed could not be built on top of the aqueduct to serve as a bridge. Plans were revised accordingly, and the doubly useful structure stands as an impressive monument to its peasant planners, builders, and users.

As we crossed back over the valley from Taoyüan Aqueduct, following the water down to the level valley floor, we noticed how the smaller branch irrigation canals were built to flow through each field and then drop down about three to eight feet into the next trough. At a number of these dropoffs the peasants had harnessed the water power to produce electricity. We stopped off to visit the smallest of these hydroelectric stations; a one-room brick building with a single generator turning out just 40 kilowatts. A straw-and-mud-thatched roof on rough-hewn log beams stood over the dials and meters of the electrical equipment. High up on the center beam, inconspicuously dabbed in black paint, an inscription read: "Built by the Revolutionary Committee [of the local commune] July 1, 1971." The beaming young man who watched over this generator told us how each brigade had sent one representative to a county school for a month to learn how to build and run such a plant. The largest of the thirteen on this stretch turns out 3000 kilowatts, he said, and the goal is twenty-six stations to make full use of this branch canal.

Here was a peasant who had become an engineer in his own right, encouraged by his fellows to overcome backwardness.

As we climbed back into our two little buses, Iron Girl talked about her own life before and after the building of the canal:

Before I became a part of the Iron Girl Team, I had only a primary school education. You see, things were very difficult at that time. You had to walk more than 10 kilometers just to get water. I was determined to give up going back to school and to go to work instead, since work was really the main task of the people in Lin County. Now that the canal is done, I still work in its management. We are planning to build many more small reservoirs. In the summer we can store much water in them to discharge later in the season when the flow is less. Through the experience of building Red Flag Canal, we developed many technicians in the local communes, and now they design the small reservoirs. I participated in this designing work and also in the labor of building them. Every brigade has its own small reservoir, with enough water to irrigate its own fields. Usually this is 200,000 to 400,000 cubic meters of water. [Lin County has fifteen communes, with thirty to forty brigades in each.]

We asked Iron Girl to tell us a little about her personal life. Her rosy cheeks blushed rosier and her answer was frequently punctuated by laughter which caught Ch'iang Ch'i, our young woman interpreter, until the two melted in laughter together and we wondered if the full translation was coming through.

Last year I got married. My husband is a worker from my village, but he works in an iron and steel factory. We usually see each other every week or two. [Here the laughter became irrepressible.] It isn't very regular, sometimes we only see each other once in a month. I have much work in organizing the women. Every brigade, commune, and county has women's organizations. I work in both brigade and county women organizations. Every month or two the county group meets, but the brigade meetings are often—every three to five days. Depending on the tasks at hand, we discuss different things. Since the Cultural Revolution our consciousness has been raised in several ways. Before, we women could only do certain kinds of light work, but during the Cultural Revolution we liberated our minds and trained ourselves to do everything men can do.

I joined the Party in 1969. Five or six of the women in the Iron Girl Brigade are also Party members now. Many young people want to do more work for the Party and the people, so they apply for membership. Then the masses in the county give their opinions about who should join. If we work very hard and study very hard, the masses will support our applications. Then the Party organization will have their own discussions about us, and some of us will be accepted. The Party committee itself organizes the masses to discuss such things and draws opinions from them. If the application is rejected, the Party Committee and other comrades will work with us until we make more progress, in the hope that we may be accepted at a later time. Being in the Party means working harder for the people. After joining the Party, I studied more about its policies and went more among the masses to listen to their opinions and to carry out Party policies among the people. I try to set a good example and listen to all their opinions—right or wrong—to take them to the Party Committee for discussion. Our leading body, with six men and three women, averages about twenty-eight years, ranging from twenty-five to forty-five. We meet almost every evening, to sum up the day's experiences. At the commune level we meet about once every two weeks, and at the county level, about every two or three months. During the Cultural Revolution we often organized in three-in-one committees of the old, middle-aged, and young. The average Party age is much younger now, and more women are included because we paid attention to the political equality of women.

In this way continuous discussion, planning, and summing up of opinions is carried on between the Party and the people. Every man, woman, and child is part of the whole collective as it struggles toward ever greater achievements. Revolutionary committees are made up of about half Party members and half locally elected non-Party people. These committees plan, guide, and otherwise organize economic, cultural, and educational activities, and are the formal liaison between the Party and the people. Such a structure, practising self-reliance and struggling against nonrepresentative leadership, was able to design and build Red Flag Canal, so that Lin County is now a lush green valley producing far more wheat, vegetables, meat, and fruit than its people can consume.

When we sat with these peasants to see the film made of the building of the canal, it was impossible not to be caught up in their joy at seeing old peasants who had lived a lifetime of thirst dipping their cups into the first waters that flowed down the canal branches into the valley. Where else in the world could we have experienced the true meaning of liberation more clearly than in sharing the pride and pleasure of the people of Lin County?

Water is indeed the "lifeblood of agriculture," as the peasants had often repeated. Harnessing the Chang River through this gigantic network of canals, tunnels, aqueducts, lock systems, and bridges had made both irrigation and electricity possible. Electricity in turn had made possible lights, communications, fertilizer factories, and other new forms of production. To us, the most important fact was that local peasants, for thousands of years victims of a hostile terrain and the elements, had overcome seemingly impossible conditions with little technical assistance. The most powerful tools were the people themselves, inspired and guided by the writings and encouragement of Mao Tse-tung and those among the leadership who followed his teachings. The confidence thus gained had enabled vast numbers of previously illiterate peasants to discover science for themselves and to become, in a very real sense, working scientists.

2 SCIENCE IN AGRICULTURE

The Red Star Commune. China is still a peasant country. More than 80 percent of the Chinese people cultivate the land to make their living and more than 90 percent live in rural areas. The Chinese Revolution grew up in the countryside and received steadfast support from the bulk of old China's impoverished and exploited peasantry. Throughout the Chinese Revolution, both before and after the military and political victory of 1949, conflicting strategies for consolidating socialism in the countryside have set the backdrop for crucial struggles within the Chinese Communist Party. The disputes within the Party have in turn reflected underlying social developments in the countryside and in the cities. Especially since 1949, scientific and technical developments and the uses to which they are *or could be* put in agriculture have played a key role in these struggles. Many branches of science, particularly biological science, as they are practiced in China today, must be understood in terms of Chinese agriculture and the political milieu in which it is undertaken.

During our stay in China we visited two agricultural communes. The first, the Red Star Sino-Korean Friendship People's Commune, is about half an hour's drive from Peking. It is a suburban commune, close to a large city and devoting a significant part of its agricultural effort to supplying city dwellers' day-to-day needs for fresh vegetables, poultry, and the like. In this sense it is not typical of China's people's communes. The suburban communes tend to have more light industry, more tractors and farm machinery, and higher family incomes than more remote communes.

Perhaps significantly, we were taken to visit Red Star Commune on our third full day in China, before we saw so much as the vestibule of a university or research institute. In China today applied science takes precedence over more abstract laboratory research and, intentionally or unintentionally, our itinerary mirrored national priorities. Our hosts also let it be known that familiarity with a relatively well-developed flat-land commune world enhance our understanding of Hsikou, the mountain commune we were to visit later.

We drove in a caravan of sedans from our hotel in central Peking out toward Red Star Commune on a clear cold morning, first crossing Tien An Men Square and then winding through narrow, twisting streets lined with small shops and thronged with people going to work. Farther toward the edge of the city the streets widened and straightened. Small and medium-sized factories appeared, with occasional queues of workers lined up in front of factory dining halls for their morning meal. As homes and factories gave way to fields, we reached a check point beyond which visitors are not permitted to go without permission. Our drivers halted briefly while our escorts showed our pass to soldier guards.

Then we drove down roads lined with leafless trees to take our first look at the North China countryside. Two impressions struck us first: it was terribly barren and there were people everywhere. The landscape stretched out flat and dull brown into the distance with virtually no ground cover, broken only by rows of trees and occasional cornstalk windbreaks. For some reason, there are no lawns in North China, not even strips of unmown grass along the roads. Someone mentioned to us that the country people think the grass breeds bugs, and so they pull it up. At any rate, only unremitting bare ground meets eyes cast in any direction.

In sharp contrast to this physical background, the land was everywhere alive with people. Along the roadside flowed a thick stream of horse carts, bicycles, handcarts, and pedestrians. Our drivers honked constantly, swerving this way and that to narrowly avoid accidents. Almost all the other motor vehicles were buses or slow-moving trucks crammed to overflowing with people or goods. The heavy animal traffic left a valuable trail of manure which youngsters swept up in specially constructed dust pans as they patrolled by bicycle.

Out in the fields in every direction clusters of people worked together at building fences, digging ditches, and preparing the land for spring planting. People were rarely working alone. By contrast, riding in rural American areas in the winter and even in the summer, you're often led to wonder where in the world everyone's gone. Our rural areas are sparsely populated and getting more so. But everywhere we went in China we were to be deeply impressed by the density of people who can and do live well on the land.

Arriving at Red Star Commune, we were ushered into a long reception room with sofas (a word which has been adopted by the Chinese), armchairs, and tea and cigarettes for everyone. At the head of the room hung a portrait of Kin Il Sung, premier of the Democratic People's Republic of Korea, next to a portait of Mao Tse-tung. A Korean banner decorated one wall and a small glass case held momentos of Sino-Korean friendship. Mr. Sen, a lively-mannered, friendly man, middle-aged, and vice-chairman of the commune's revolutionary committee, welcomed us and noted that we were all very young (we ranged in age from twenty-three to forty-four). He proceeded to introduce us to Red Star Commune.

At this point we may remind ourselves that communes in China have nothing whatsoever to do with the image that the word "commune" conjures up in most American minds (i.e. ten hippies on an abandoned farm). In rural China the people's communes are geographical, administrative, and political units comprising several thousand households each. China as a whole is comprised of twenty-seven provinces (including Taiwan) and autonomous regions. Autonomous regions, such as Tibet and Inner Mongolia, are areas in which national minorities make up a substantial part of the population. Minority people are included in the governing bodies, and national policies are said to be especially modified to meet local needs. Each province and region is divided into districts which in turn encompass several counties. Counties are divided into many communes. As a result, almost anywhere you set foot in the Chinese countryside you are in a commune. Red Star Commune has 78,000 members and 17,000 households, making it a relatively populous commune, and it occupies an area of 160 square kilometers. Like other Chinese communes it is divided into many production brigades (124 to be exact), and these are further divided into production teams. Unlike many other communes, Red Star Commune puts its production brigades in ten "administrative districts," eight devoted to farming, one to industrial enterprises, and one whose function was not specified. It may be that Red Star Commune's large size makes an extra administrative level necessary.

We spent one day at Red Star Commune, during which our hosts, Mr. Sen and Ms. Liu, a young woman in charge of women's affairs at the commune, guided us through a dairy, a small commissary street, a medical clinic, several peasants' homes, greenhouses, a junior high school, a horse-breeding farm, and a screw factory. Our experiences at the clinic and the school are described in other chapters. Here we will try to convey how the commune members themselves portray the development of agricultural development on the commune.

Grains—rice and wheat—are China's staple foods. Raising the output of grain is fundamental to China's economic development. The Chinese express this in the slogan "taking grain as the key link," and Mr. Sen made it clear that the Red Star people see grain production and standard of living as integrally related: ". . . the living conditions, the cultural and material conditions [at Red Star] are changing with the increase in the output of grain." Before Liberation people in the commune area grew only about 700 kilograms of grain per hectare (about two and a half acres). In 1972 the commune achieved a yield of 4700 kilos per hectare in the face of the worst drought in a hundred years. In 1971 the yield was 5000 kilos per hectare. Most of the grain grown at Red Star now is rice, which is in itself remarkable because, we were told, no rice at all grew in the area before Liberation. Before then the vicinity of Red Star Commune was a waste area of poor alkaline soil and was used mainly for hunting.

Irrigation has been an important factor in transforming the Red Star area into productive land. The commune members have sunk more than 700 electrically powered wells and bring in water from a reservoir 150 kilometers away to irrigate more than 95 percent of the cultivated land. This allows intensive cultivation and 50 percent of the land is double cropped. Along with irrigation has come the use of machines to work the land. The commune has 96 tractors, 100 small "walking tractors,"* and 35 trucks, allowing machine cultivation of 70 percent of the land. Despite these achievements, Mr. Sen told us, the degree of mechanization is still insufficient.

In noting the shortcomings of his commune, Sen referred to the fact that Tachai Brigade in 1972 produced almost 7000 kilos of grain per hectare despite the bad drought. Tachai is a very famous production brigade in Shansi Province in the mountains of north central China. Mao Tse-tung has singled it out for praise and emulation because in the face of very poor physical conditions it has raised production and the standard of living of its people tremendously. In China you often hear Mao's phrase: "In agriculture, learn from Tachai." Sen said that when a poor mountain commune can obtain higher yields than a flatland commune, Red Star still has much to learn. It should be pointed out that the Chinese regard Tachai not as an example of a poor brigade that made good, but as a model of indefatigable struggle to overcome obstacles to further progress. As one official has put it: "The experi-

---

*"Walking tractors" are the Chinese counterpart to the American Rototiller, a motorized, handguided cultivator.

ence of Tachai is not the experience of a poor brigade but an experience in the revolutionization of man's thinking."

Animal husbandry is an important activity at Red Star. The commune has nine dairy farms with 3200 cows producing 30,000 gallons of milk a day. We visited a small dairy farm with 119 Holsteins ("black and white cows"). This breed was originally imported from Holland and then crossed with local breeds to produce a high-yielding breed adapted to the local climate. The commune, we were casually informed, has stations that specialize in the scientific breeding of farm animals. In the years before Liberation and the formation of large-scale collectives in the rural areas, scientifically bred and improved animals would have been unimaginable. In retrospect we realized that this was our first contact with the practice of science in China.

We also visited a horse-breeding station later in the day. In the long run the Chinese aim to completely mechanize their agriculture, but for the short- and medium-term future draft animals will continue to be of great importance. In respect to the abundance and use of draft animals, stepping into the North China countryside is like stepping back into rural America in the early twentieth century. The horse-breeding station is run as a state-owned enterprise within the commune. Overall the commune now has more than 3,000 horses.

Pigs (in addition to chickens) seem to be the major source of meat in the Chinese diet. In contrast to cows and horses, at Red Star they are raised as part of the private economy, and the commune restricts its role to breeding and selling piglets to individual households. As we walked and drove around Red Star Commune, single pigs in individual brick-and-mud pigpens were a common sight in each village. In 1972 the commune bred 68,000 pigs, but, Mr. Sen told us, "we should try to improve our work breeding pigs because according to government directives we should breed one pig per *mu* [about one-sixth of an acre] of cultivated land. So according to this we should breed 100,000 pigs. This way we can increase our output of grain." He later elaborated that "Chairman Mao puts very great emphasis on the breeding of pigs. One pig equals a little fertilizer factory." The commune also has three farms that produce force-fed ducks for the tables of Peking. Altogether, about a thousand people on the commune devote their time to animal husbandry.

A view of another "sideline" activity took us to the warmest place we visited in North China. We pulled up at the edge of a field that appeared to be lined with row after row of glass-windowed earth bunkers. These turned out to be large greenhouses, fashioned lean-to style, with windows facing south and thick earth walls keeping out the northern winds. They were set into the ground and we had to bend and stoop to walk down narrow dirt aisles, our glasses and camera lenses fogging rapidly in the warm, humid world of hothouse plants. Bed after bed of chives stretched out before us and long, prickly Chinese cucumbers dangled from tendrils climbing twine supports. Such greenhouses supply Peking, a city about the size of Chicago, with fresh winter vegetables. Since 1949 the number of greenhouses around Peking has increased fourteenfold and the year-round per capita consumption of fresh vegetables in Peking (now a little over a pound a day) has increased threefold. The Red Star greenhouses are heated by steam using coal fuel.

Red Star Commune has a number of light industries. They include a powdered-milk plant, a farm equipment repair factory, a paper mill, a plant for milling grain and pressing vegetable oil, and a screw factory. These small plants employ about two thousand commune members. Light industry in the countryside now plays a key role in China's economic and political development, the reasons for which will be clearer if we pause for a moment to consider the history of rural development in most Asian, African, and Latin American countries in recent times.

This sketch will greatly oversimplify the situation to present the ideas in a brief space. Certainly each nation is different, and local history and social structure influence the scenario. But generally, in most underdeveloped countries industry first grows up in the cities, under the control of foreign investors or local businessmen closely allied with them. The importation of foreign-manufactured goods and the distribution of city-manufactured goods in the countryside often ruins traditional handicraft industries. Large numbers of displaced artisans then flee to the cities, where they are absorbed into a growing class of industrial workers. In addition, many peasants are attracted to the cities by the prospect of work and a higher standard of living. The countryside provides a marginal living for many peasants even in the best of times, so people move when the opportunity is presented. In the cities the new urban people are viciously exploited economically, but they are exposed to new influences and over time they adopt a more cosmopolitan world view. At least a segment of the urban workers becomes politically sophisticated and is sympathetic to socialist programs. The urban work force develops programs of its own and becomes a new political force.

The countryside in the meantime is stagnating. Shorn of traditional handicrafts and besieged by a system of cash taxes replacing a system of payment in kind, the old peasant society slowly begins to disintegrate. The old landlord class in the rural areas seeks an alliance with the city industrialists who, along with the foreign investors, now control the country's destiny. Sometimes the landlords are successful in making this alliance, as was the case in China. In other instances they are not. In the first case more and more peasants are driven from the land by expropriation by a newly empowered landlord class. In the latter case expropriation of the landlords themselves by the city rulers leads to a system of rural landholding with no room for small producers. In either case the peasants who remain are forced to abandon food production for cash crops and the condition of the countryside slowly worsens, driving more and more peasants to the cities.

But the cities can provide jobs for only a small number of these peasants. The foreign investors aren't anxious to spawn new industrial competitors in the Third World, so their investments are very selective and unbalanced, concentrated in extractive and labor-intensive industries and laying no groundwork for ongoing economic development.

Finding little or no livelihood, the displaced peasants settle on the margins of the cities, forming rings of squalid slums. There they act as a brake on the radical tendencies of the old industrial labor force, scabbing during strikes, working for minimal wages, and available to join repressive military forces should a real threat arise to the foreigners or the local rulers.

In such situations strong currents work to divide city and country people, workers and peasants. The peasants remaining in the country have an intense suspicion of cities, the source of tax collectors and occupying armies fed by the country and giving nothing in return but financial woe. The workers in turn come to look on the countryside with foreboding. The backwardness of the peasants makes them subject to manipulation by the same conservative forces with which the workers are in conflict, and peasants streaming in from the countryside compete for their jobs and threaten their livelihood. A gulf grows between the people of the countryside and of the cities and is reinforced by the kinds of city slicker–country bumpkin notions apparent in a different context in our own society.

The success of Third World revolutions has lain in being able to bridge this gulf and bring the peasants into the struggle against the foreigners and on the side of the city workers. The Chinese Revolution is a classic example of the success of this strategy. But the differences that have developed between town and countryside don't disappear with the victory of the revolution. In so far as the victory frees city industry for more growth without modifying backward agricultural practices in the rural areas, the differences will continue to grow, even with land reform. And without a developing rural economy to feed local industry and consume its products, the door to dependence on foreign investors slips open again and, caught in a vicious circle, the economy stagnates. Witness the history of Mexico in the twentieth century.

The Chinese are determined to unite the countryside and the cities in joint parallel development. To do this they must work hard to counter the spontaneous tendency for industry and wealth to concentrate in the large cities.

This, to get back to the main thread of our story, is where rural light industry comes in. By encouraging communes and counties to set up small factories, the Chinese are providing the industrial base for the mechanization of agriculture and at the same time countering the countryside's dependence on the cities. The cities can concentrate on heavy industry requiring large capital investment and the country people meanwhile begin to experience and master the machinery and techniques of modern industry. The Chinese believe that through large-scale mechanization the peasants will become agricultural workers in the same sense that steel workers are workers. As Liu Hsi-yao put it during our Great Hall interview: "In terms of technology there is no line of demarcation between agriculture and industry." In China there are still large differences between worker and peasant and countryside and city, but the long-term aim is to eliminate these differences completely.

Historically, Chinese rural industry got its first big boost during the Great Leap Forward period in 1958, when agricultural producers' cooperatives across the country merged to form the communes. During the Cultural Revolution one of the major charges against Liu Shao-ch'i and his followers was that they had taken an ax to rural light industry in the early sixties. By doing this, it is claimed, they stifled the technological initiative of the communes and stymied the progress of the countryside, forcing rural people to depend on the cities for all manufactured goods.

We saw our first example of rural light industry in the Red Star commune. The commune's screw factory is not picturesque. We arrived in late afternoon to find several long one-story buildings lining a wide dirt lane at right angles; different parts of the screw-making process were distributed among the buildings. Bits and pieces of rusting metal parts lay strewn over the area between some of the buildings. In the first shop we visited, workers fed heavy coils of steel wire into a machine that straightened it and corrected its thickness. In another shop batteries of separate machines, each with an individual operator, cut the wire into standard lengths and milled these pieces into basic screw shapes. The machines were all old and had all been made in China; the equipment was probably acquired when it became obsolete in a larger, city factory. The noise in the room was deafening, the lighting a bit dim.

The scene at the factory was reminiscent of photographs of nascent heavy industry in the United States, of carriage workers turning out the first automobiles in small Midwest cities. But China's industrial revolution is taking place in a very different social context, and even in the unsophisticated Red Star screw factory the differences were telling. In each shop men and women worked side by side, dressed similarly, and apparently performed similar tasks. Men outnumbered women, but the women were there as equals. The building walls were covered with remnants of old and recent political slogans. The supervisors dressed like other workers, and we couldn't tell them apart by sight, either by their clothes or by their bearing. Finally, the peasant workers were there as a result of commune decisions, not because they fled the land in hunger or went to work for individual profit. These differences are fundamental.

Now we have an overview of Red Star Commune's agricultural effort, an effort in which light industrialization is an important and growing element. At Red Star, as it turned out, we didn't directly discuss efforts at scientific research. Mr. Sen did mention in passing that the commune and each administrative division have scientific and technical stations, but we never had time to discuss their function. To investigate these aspects we would have to wait until our stay at Hsikou.

Hsikou Commune—People's Science in Action. Hsikou People's Commune lies about three hundred miles southwest of Peking, high up in the T'aihang Mountains in southeastern Shansi Province. Four members of our group lived at Hsikou for four days, and our entire group spent one day there together. We wanted to go to Hsikou because in discussions with American friends we had heard that it was an interesting and exciting commune and had had very few foreign visitors. Our hosts readily agreed to our request and when we arrived in Peking our visit had already been arranged. As it turned out, getting to Hsikou was an adventure in itself.

Our journey to Hsikou began early one morning at Peking Railway Station. The station itself looked more like an airport terminal than an American train station. It was clean, very busy, and had no vagrants sleeping on benches or wandering aimlessly down the aisles. It was also the only place in China we saw escalators. All our hosts from the Foreign Affairs Bureau of the Scientific and Technical Association turned out to see us off and chat with us in our car until the train was ready to pull out of the station. In fact they stayed to chat a bit too long and had to leap from our car as it began moving. For a moment it looked as if we might have an extra interpreter on our trip, but at the last minute Chu Yung-hang gathered his courage and leaped to the platform. We were off on our ride across the North China plain.

We rode all morning and into the afternoon through the winter landscape, counting our progress south by the gradual greening and growth of the passing rows of winter wheat. In some small-town squares we were amazed to see two-humped camels used as beasts of burden. Once, when the train stopped briefly in a small city, we could see English and German manufacturers' names clearly stamped on the steel beams of an old railway pedestrian walk. Most of the way we talked and rubbernecked from our European-style railway coach compartment, our conversation shifting for lunch to a dining car toward the head of the train. In midafternoon we arrived at Anyang, an ancient provincial city and capital of the Shang Dynasty three thousand years ago. There we transferred to Mercedes-Benz microbuses for a two-hour drive west to the county town of Lin County.

The countryside between Anyang and Lin County is very different from the countryside around Peking. In contrast to the flat-roofed houses of gray fired brick typical of the capital area, the peasants around Anyang live in peaked-roof houses of brown adobe brick. The horse carts around Peking have flat, solid-wood beds and the drivers usually perch with their whips on one front corner. Outside Anyang, the horse and ox carts along the crowded road are smaller and are built half of wickerwork, rather like baskets on wheels, and people sit inside them to drive. There are also innumerable hand-drawn wicker carts, and as we passed by we saw that many of these were set with billowing sails between two poles, to catch any rear wind that might help speed the load on its way. They resembled miniature prairie schooners.

We spent the night in Lin County at the county reception center. There at the hotel desk we discovered a delicious local product that we thought was dates, looked a little like figs, and turned out to be dried persimmons. In the morning we boarded a caravan of jeeps to ride to Hsikou, a four-hour journey to the west. The excellent four-wheel-drive jeeps were made in China; the Chinese called them "jee-pu."

The final leg of the journey to Hsikou began on flat land but soon we were riding up a river valley into the T'aihang Mountains, through landscapes of great beauty and variety. Around us were jagged gray eroded peaks. Below us and sometimes next to us a slow, shallow river flowed down a wide, sandy, steep-sided valley, with dusty white-and-yellow villages perched on narrow little plateaus between the stream bed and the mountains. Small terraced fields of winter wheat clung to the hillsides. Along the valley bottom in some places stretches of flat field had been wrested from the stream bed by stone dams and walls. In areas of water seepage along the river bank small rice paddies has been carved from the rock and mud. Everywhere small and large canals wound along the hillsides, carrying water to the lower slopes for irrigation. At intervals we passed places where great cascades of water poured from one of these canals into the river below, sometimes powering a mill. With the exception of these waterworks and the small fields and scattered but substantial villages, the area looked for all the world like the Dakota Badlands or parts of Utah or Nevada. This was our introduction to a "poor" area of China.

The last part of our trip took us along a very rocky road up a dry river bed. When at last we left the river bed and climbed a road cut in the earth of the hillside, we were in Hsikou Commune, in Ping Hsün County. Soon we reached the main village of Hsikou Production Brigade, where local "responsible persons" greeted us and made us welcome. Making one welcome at Hsikou includes, in addition to tea and cigarettes, plates of delicious caramelized walnuts. Our rooms for the stay were in a large building constructed with the help of county funds and serving as a county reception center. On our arrival each room was supplied with plates of walnut meats and apples. The rooms were heated by coal stoves with the flue out the window and were furnished simply—two red-orange wooden writing tables and chairs, two beds, and two washstands in each. The beds had no mattresses (in contrast to those of city hotels) and consisted of a flat hard board covered by a blanket and a course cloth with a color design. For covers there were two heavy wool blankets and a thick quilt with a beautifully patterned red-silk cover. The rooms had no wastebaskets; we were to discover very few in rural China.

To set the context for our investigation of the Hsikou scientific and technical effort in agriculture, a few initial social and physical facts follow. Hsikou People's Commune has 15,000 members divided into ten production brigades. Hsikou Production Brigade, the scene of our visit and the subject of the story that follows, is part of Hsikou People's Commune and has 1600 members (380 households) divided into twelve production teams and scattered among forty-four small villages. The brigade occupies several small and large valleys, lies about 1500 meters above sea level, and has about 150 frost-free days a year.

In several ways Hsikou is not a "typical" production brigade. Since the early 1950s it has been a model social unit, noted by Mao Tse-tung himself for special attention. Each year many people from all over China visit Hsikou to study its agricultural and political successes. In the short time we spent there at least two large groups of people visited—one a group of peasants from nearby areas, the other a group of People's Liberation Army officers. And though Hsikou is not a "rich" brigade, it is unusually "advanced" in some political respects. Private plots are a case in point. In most places in China households are allotted a certain amount of land for private use. The size of these plots and the emphasis put on them has been a subject of controversy within the Communist Party, but everyone seems to agree that they are necessary in most places during the period of socialist transition (that is, until the entire economy is collectivized at the state level) and therefore will be around for a long time to come. Hsikou, we were surprised to discover, has no private plots. The people there, we were told, find it more profitable as individuals to till all the land collectively.

With this background in mind, we can move forward to discuss our interview with the Hsikou Production Brigade Scientific and Technical Group. We interviewed this group late in our stay at Hsikou, but its members gave us information that was crucial in many respects to our understanding of science as applied to agriculture both in Hsikou and in the rest of China. Accordingly, we will present the Hsikou agricultural effort in terms of the categories used in their discussion with us—that is, as the Hsikou people see it themselves.

We met with the scientific and technical group in the second-floor meeting room of the reception center, a room dominated by a single long table. Around the edge of the room bright yellow-painted wooden chairs with cloth cushions lined the walls, but the chairs around the table were more spartan. A single coal stove burned feebly to heat the room to about 50 degrees Fahrenheit. Our hosts poured (premade) tea from large thermoses and we drank from plain water glasses. Five people had come to participate in the discussion: 1) Kuo Kang-chu—vice-chairman of the brigade revolutionary committee and person responsible for agriculture production, a young man, probably in his late thirties, with an authoritative and competent air about him. 2) Ch'ui Fu-hsing—experienced peasant-techni-

cian, probably in his sixties. 3) Wang Ju-shen—member of
the brigade forestry team, a middle-aged man. 4) Chang
Ming-chao—technician for the tenth production brigade, a
young man. 5) Hsia Shan-yün—technician from the P'ing
Hsün County Agricultural Experiment Station, a young-
to-middle-aged woman.

Kuo led off the discussion by saying simply, "We've
done some scientific research work." And then he defined
the principles that guide the group's approach: "Science
and technology must serve production and serve the people under the leadership of the Communist Party and
Chairman Mao." By "serve production" he meant that at
Hsikou the fundamental role of science is to boost agricultural output. To illustrate this idea Kuo ran down the history of grain production at Hsikou.

Before Liberation (1937 in Hsikou, which was on the
border of the Communist-held territories during the war
against Japan), people grew only about 100 *chin* (a *chin* is
about a pound) of grain per *mu*. In 1943 some peasants
established mutual-aid teams in which they helped each
other in the fields on a coordinated basis. Grain production rose to about 200 *chin* per *mu*. In 1951 mutual-aid
team members pooled their land and farming implements
to form producers' cooperatives. The cooperatives' yearly
incomes were distributed on the basis of a household's
original contributions of land and implements as well as
on amounts of work performed. These cooperatives raised
production to 300 *chin* of grain per *mu* per year. In 1955
the Hsikou cooperatives adopted the principle of distribut-
ing yearly income entirely on the basis of work performed. The resulting "advanced cooperatives" achieved a
grain output of 400 *chin* per *mu* per year. In 1958 the
advanced cooperatives around the Hsikou area merged to
form a people's commune, making possible larger-scale
water conservancy efforts, and production rose to more
than 600 *chin* per *mu* per year. By 1969, after the Cultural
Revolution, yield had increased to more than 800 *chin* per
mu and in the years 1970–72 it averaged more than 1000
chin per *mu* a tenfold increase over prerevolutionary production. Between the period of the cooperatives and the

present, yearly per capita grain production increased from 300 to 500 *chin*.

In each of these periods of increase in production, advances in social organization permitted application of more advanced techniques and rational planning to agriculture. Social change has preceded and fostered technical advance. This is an important principle in understanding China, and Kuo made it clear that it applies to future scientific achievements at Hsikou. The job of the scientific and technical group, he said, is to determine "how to improve our scientific research work and how to make scientific research work serve production. The only way for us to do this is to mobilize and encourage all members of our brigade to take part in scientific research work. It is the only way we can learn about nature in a better and faster way."

Kuo went on to outline the agricultural effort at Hsikou in terms of the "Eight Point Charter," or "Eight Character Constitution," of agriculture put forward by Mao Tsetung in 1958. He didn't mention the origin of the eight points and probably just assumed we knew about their authorship, a small but telling demonstration of Mao's tremendous influence in the Chinese countryside. In the sections that follow we present Hsikou in terms of these eight points (in the order they were given to us), combining information we received directly from Kuo with things we learned in the course of the rest of our stay.

1. Soil Improvement (*T'u*). Hsikou Brigade occupies an area about 7½ kilometers long and 4 kilometers wide. It is all exceedingly hilly. In fact the brigade has counted and there are 233 hills in all. The total area of the brigade is about 30,000 *mu* but only 1500 are cultivated. Most of the crops are grown in small terraced fields held in place by rock walls cut into the hillsides or extending up ravines. In North China the yearly rainfall is concentrated in July, August, and September. Hsikou gets only 50 centimeters of rain a year—about the same as the arid western part of Nebraska—half of which falls in July and August. There is a prolonged drought from midwinter through spring. In

the past, when the summer rains finally hit the parched hills the water ran off quickly, rushing in torrents down the mountain ravines to carry away the soil and crops in the terraced fields along the way.

In this circumstance, Kuo said, "The major task is to hold the water in the soil." The Hsikou people have accordingly developed several farsighted projects that mesh together for one purpose—hold on to the water, hold on to the soil. On the slopes high above the brigade they have planted great numbers of trees to strengthen the soil and hold rain water near its source. Farther down the slopes they have built stone dams across the ravines at intervals to slow down the torrents and turn each ravine into a series of mini-reservoirs. In the lower parts of the ravines they have hauled in soil to create new fields behind these dams.

Tung Yü-kou Valley, longest of the seven major valleys encompassed by the brigade, an example of this effort. The valley is 4½ kilometers long and is worked by 32 households scattered in fourteen small villages. Since Liberation the people of the valley have built 130 dams and terraces and created 30 *mu* of cropland where no soil at all existed before. On the hillsides above the valley they have forested 300 *mu* of land. As a result of their efforts they harvested 1000 *chin* of grain per *mu* in 1971.

We drove up Tung Yü-Kou Valley one afternoon to look at the terracing work. In the part of the valley we examined closely a rather narrow gulch that had obviously at one time been a deeply eroded and worthless gully had been transformed into a neatly laid-out staircase of small fields. A narrow rock terrace wall separated each level from the next, and at every third or fourth field this wall was about a yard thick and strongly built, to withstand the worst of the summer floods. These fields had all been created by hauling in soil from nearby excavations. Hsikou has an abundance of loess soil, a yellowish, wind-deposited, very fine-grained soil that occurs in thick deposits in the hills of northern China. Traditionally the Hsikou peasants lived in caves carved in cliffs of this soil, and many of them still live in these earth-cave homes. It is abundant loess soil, easily dug and useful for agriculture, that makes Hsikou's tremendous land fill efforts possible.

These land fills are most impressive on the floor of the main Hsikou Brigade valley, which lies below the village where we stayed. In the past this valley contained only a rock- and boulder-strewn river bed and a road of poor quality. Come the summer rains, the river flooded. By spring it ran dry, and nothing useful grew in the valley bottom. In 1958 the Hsikou people built a large reservoir and cordoned off the river course between closely set strong rock walls. On either side of these walls they have now terraced and filled in 500,000 cubic meters of earth, turning most of the valley floor into fields and orchards. We were told that before reforestation and other water control efforts, it was impossible here for one strong man to turn even two *mu* of riverside land into cultivated fields. It still takes one person three months to terrace and fill one *mu* of land one meter deep with soil. From this figure we got an idea of the immense human effort involved in terracing. The 500,000 cubic meters of earth filled in, if laid side by side, would stretch 300 miles. Hsikou has now begun to mechanize its land fill operations. While we were there the brigade had three small bulldozers leveling loess hills into a large field on a little plateau above the valley floor. One of these machines belonged to the brigade, the other two were on loan from the county.

2. Rational Application of Fertilizer (*Fei*). Walking around at Hsikou we noticed piles of blackish earthlike material set at intervals in the bare plowed fields. These turned out to be piles of fertilizer, vital for replenishing and boosting the nitrogen content of the soil. Most of Hsikou's fertilizer comes from humans and animals in the form of night soil and manure. Night soil is China's traditional fertilizer and has maintained the fertility of Chinese fields through hundreds of years of continuous cultivation. Since the Revolution the role of manure has increased dramatically with the rapid growth of animal husbandry. In 1952, at the beginning of the cooperative period, there were only 300 sheep and goats at Hsikou; now the brigade's flock has grown to 1300. In the same period pigs

have increased nine times and now number 300. The brigade also has more than 150 head of cattle and more than 190 donkeys. The Hsikou people carefully conserve the manure of all these animals. On one hillside we saw a shepherd's hut and a cornstalk enclosure where the flocks are gathered together to defecate in one place. Altogether, we were told, the animals produce 15,000,000 *chin* of manure a year for the fields, and the increase in fertilizer is the single most important factor in the increase in yields over the years.

Americans, particularly urban Americans, are usually squeamish about handling manure, fresh or composted. For Chinese peasants the trek to the fields each year with shoulder-pole buckets of accumulated manure is as much a part of life as plowing and seeding. It has to be done, and on schedule. But there is nothing indigenously Chinese about the uninhibited handling of manure. We spoke to a young woman, a former student from the port city of Tientsin, who had come to Hsikou in answer to Mao's call for youth to go to the countryside. Confronted with the task of carrying goat manure, she balked at first because she thought it was just too dirty to handle. But, she told us, she went through a mental struggle and finally "realized that this was a petty-bourgeois idea." For the peasants manure application was one of life's necessities, not an optional activity subject to choice, and she felt that her own disgust stemmed from her middle-class city background.

In addition to night soil and manure, Hsikou Brigade uses some "vegetable fertilizer" like sorghum straw and buys a little manufactured fertilizer from the government. It also maintains a very remarkable "local fertilizer" factory as an annex to the local school. We visited this factory during our tour of the school, where it occupies part of a low building set behind the classroom buildings. A young woman greeted us and led us to a stick-and-mud-roofed room where she tried to explain to us how the brigade makes bacterial fertilizer using simple techniques and local materials. We say tried because some of the technical words were beyond us, our interpreter, and any available dictionary. Despite this difficulty we did manage to get the broad outline of the technique.

The story goes something like this. The factory makes "5406 powder," a bacterial product that is mixed with soil and applied to fields as fertilizer. In addition to its function as fertilizer the mixture is reported to help crops absorb nitrogen, to protect them against more than thirty-two bacterial diseases, and to promote speedier seed germination and a shorter growing period. The brigade applies it to corn, millet, and all their wheat fields. To make the powder the factory technicians (it appeared that there were three) steam-peel potatoes, mash them, and mix them with sugar, bran, agar (a gelatin-like material), water, and small amounts of the chemicals magnesium sulfate and potassium phosphate. Then they heat the mixture to boiling to sterilize it and dissolve the ingredients, after which they pour it into glass tubes to cool and form a stiff medium (or food surface) for growing the bacteria. Live bacteria are smeared on this medium and then grown for several days while the tubes are kept in a warm room. At the end of this period the bacteria are somehow collected, dried, and mixed with earth (8 *chin* of bacteria to 100 *chin* of earth) to make the final product.

When we walked down the hall to visit the little factory, two young men in lab coats were in the process of inoculating tubes of medium with bacteria. They worked in another small room, remarkable by Hsikou winter standards for its warmth. An ultraviolet lamp swung suspended from the ceiling above their workbench, apparently to help insure the culture against contamination by the wrong microorganisms. In a side room with an electric heater stood racks of simple low wooden boxes full of medium tubes with growing (incubating) bacteria cultures. The culture room was maintained between 15 and 30 degrees Centigrade and both rooms were sealed off from the cold outside by heavy carpets hanging in the doorways.

Such small factories producing microbial products seem now to be common in the Chinese countryside. In a later section we'll discuss the similar production of bacterial insecticides. We asked a little about the history of the project

at Hsikou and found that the school originally took on the
project as part of a larger effort to make scientific education serve production. They first heard of the process
when the Southeast Shansi District had a meeting at which
someone from the Ch'angchih school spoke about making
bacterial fertilizer. To learn the process they sent two people to Ch'angchih (the largest city in southeast Shansi) to
attend lectures and practice techniques for four or five
days. Since mastering the art, Hsikou has in turn taught
bacterial fertilizer making to people from about twenty
other communes. Similar processes of face-to-face contact
and exchange appear to be exceedingly important in the
transmission and popularization of science in China. Because such exchange generates little or no printed material, western observers, who tend to believe that all scientific communication of any note eventually reaches print,
are likely to overlook what appears to be a vast network
of informal scientific exchange in the Chinese countryside.

3. Building Water Conservancy Works (*Shui*). Irrigation
at Hsikou necessarily encompasses broad efforts at water
conservancy and such efforts, as we have seen, are closely
linked with efforts to conserve soil. Two large dams and
reservoirs are the keys to Hsikou's water conservation and
flood control program. The first of these reservoirs lies
above the reclaimed valley bottom land we mentioned earlier and was built in 1958 during the Great Leap Forward
period of commune formation. During this time the commune "paid great attention to the local militia" as a collective force for socialist construction. The militia members themselves designed and built the dam, which is earth
covered with stone and is 100 meters wide at the base.
They completed it in less than a year by day and night
work. Carved in stone on the face of the dam is the inscription "Militia Fighting Reservoir." The reservoir itself
has a capacity of 1,700,000 cubic meters of water.

The second reservoir stands farther up the main valley
and represents an even greater human effort. It was begun
in August 1968 and finished at the end of September
1971. Inspiration for its construction came from the
county after serious water shortages and a bad drought in

the 1960s forced the area to import water. After the county decided the project should be undertaken, the work of building fell to Hsikou Brigade itself, apparently because it would be the main beneficiary. The brigade had help with the design from the county department of hydraulics, and the commune militia pitched in to help with part of the work, but the brigade did most of the work and footed the bill.

The dam is solid stone (33,136 cubic meters' worth) and measures 178 meters long by 25 meters high. At the base it is 25 meters wide and at the top it slims to a 2-meter-wide walkway festooned with red flags. The entire dam was built without heavy machinery. A gravity-powered cable operation brought stone down from mountainside quarries. The reservoir has a 615,000-cubic-meter capacity and receives most of its water from the rainy season run-off, with about 90,000 cubic meters a year coming from a small spring at the bottom.

The name of the reservoir, "Hsikou Prepare for War," is emblazoned in red characters on the dam. It has solved the problem of year-round drinking water for 10,000 people and 5000 animals. In addition to Hsikou it serves three other communes, eight production brigades, and a few small factories. It is also the focus of Hsikou's irrigation program. Below the dam three canals (with a total length of 12.5 kilometers) branch out to deliver water along the hillsides of the valleys below. In about a year, when side canals from the three trunk lines are completed, Hsikou expects to be able to irrigate 1000 *mu* of land, two-thirds of its cultivated area. In concert with other improvements, this is projected to lead to yields of 1500 *chin* of grain per *mu* by 1975, an increase of almost 50 percent over present levels. The reservoir itself now contributes fish to the brigade food supply. It was stocked by the district fish hatchery in Ch'angchih and people fish with nets to haul in four- and five-pound carp in an area that never had fish before.

The Hsikou people depend to some extent on wells and ground water, a source of water that has also increased in capacity as the reservoirs raise the local water table. Finally, they see each and every field as a small reservoir during the rainy season. Following the slogan "keep the water in the dish" they build the edges of each terraced field a little higher than the center so that it slows down and retains the water passing through. This slogan, incidentally, came up in a more general conversation with peasants about how Hsikou people view the world. Just before quoting it the speaker had noted that, "Although we are in Hsikou, with our eyes we look all over the world. We take all revolutions as our own." He went on to tie the Hsikou struggle to keep soil and water in place directly to the world revolution, a feat of integration that provides a good example of the level of political consciousness in China's countryside.

4. Popularization of Good Varieties (*Chung*). The introduction and development of new crop varieties has formed a major part of Hsikou Brigade's scientific agricultural effort. Traditionally Hsikou relied for its corn on two local varieties that yielded poorly. Since the mid-sixties the brigade has experimented with producing hybrid corn adapted to give high yields under Hsikou conditions. This technique involves crossing two "pure line" corn varieties to produce seeds which grow into plants bearing genes from each parental variety. These plants often give much higher yields than either parental line. Each year the same cross must be repeated to get seeds for the next year, and the parent "pure lines" must be bred and maintained for this purpose. Such a complex breeding system requires effort and planning that would be impossible in a peasant economy without the collective system of the communes, brigades, and work teams.

Since 1958 Hsikou Brigade has planted self-produced hybrid corn and now achieves 1300–1500 *chin* per *mu* on many fields, a yield equal to that reached in the more temperate climate and fertile soil of the lower Yangtze River area. The brigade is also experimenting with four-way hybrid crosses, an even more complex system that requires four sets of parental pure lines and two years of breeding to get seed. Hybridization techniques are also being applied to produce new sorghum (*kaoliang*) varieties.

Whereas the old local variety yielded only about 100 *chin* per *mu*, locally produced hybrids now yield up to 1500 *chin* per *mu*.

The brigade itself has not produced new wheat varieties, but it has widely introduced and tested improved strains developed elsewhere. Currently the science and technical group of popularizing strains called Nongba 311, Peking 8, and Ch'angchih 515, named after the experiment stations that originally developed them. Ch'angchih 515 seems to give the best yield under Hsikou conditions.

Finally, the traditional Hsikou millet suffered from the twin disadvantages of low yield and a long growth period. Now four or five newly introduced varieties have helped boost yields from 300 or 400 *chin* to 600 *chin* per *mu*. In all these cases, increased water and fertilizer and improved farming techniques have also greatly influenced yields, but there is no doubt that improved varieties have played a very important role.

5. Rational Close Planting (*Mi*). Close planting, the practice of sowing seeds densely, seems to have been a subject of debate in China over the years since Liberation. The original rationale for it must have been something like this: As the cooperatives and communes began to transform miserably poor farm land into productive land, the peasants still tended to sow the low densities of seed appropriate to sparse growth under the old conditions. The new fields, with more water, more fertilizer, and higher yielding varieties, could support much denser stands of plants, and it became important to adopt new seeding densities to achieve the highest possible yields. At Hsikou in the past, for example, it took only 1600–1700 corn grains to plant one *mu* of land. Now, using the new hybrid varieties, farmers plant 2500 grains per *mu*. And while the old local sorghum variety was planted at only 300–400 seeds to a *mu*, they now plant the new hybrid varieties at the rate of 6000–8000 seeds to a *mu*.

Even under the old conditions, denser seeding could often have increased production, but extra seed was unavailable since the people had to eat most of the grain to live. As conditions improved during the 1950s more and more surplus grain became available each year to serve as potential seed for next year's crops. So close planting was never simply an adjunct to other techniques.

There are obvious limits to close planting as a technique for increasing yield. As conditions improved and individual plants grew larger and stronger and needed more space in the fields, a counter tendency set in. In some cases seeding too densely began to reduce total yields, and there is evidence that in some places in China the enthusiasm for close planting got out of hand. This passage from a December 1972 issue of *Peking Review* discusses the resolution of a small conflict over close planting at Tachai Brigade and is an interesting example of the respect scientific experiments have gained in the eyes of China's peasants.

Last year the question arose as to whether maize [corn] should be planted close together or more spaced out. A few years ago, the answer would have been the former. But now opinions differed. Some people said: "Close planting was certainly necessary when our land was poor. Now that it's more fertile, the plants would grow much too big and dense for the air and light to get through. Yields will surely suffer then." Comrade Ch'en Yung-kuei, secretary of the brigade Party branch, was of this opinion.

However, another Party branch committee member who disagreed challenged the others to a contest. In spring he planted maize the way he thought best in a plot next to Ch'en Yung-kuei's experimental one. The ears of maize on his plot came out small, and the stalks thin and the leaves sparse. People predicted failure but he refused to admit defeat. "The ears may be smaller," he thought, "but there are more of them. Who knows who'll win in the end?" Autumn harvest came, and his plot, the same size as Ch'en Yung-kuei's, produced 100 *chin* less. He was finally convinced.

6. Plant Protection (*Pao*). The Hsikou people approach health care for crops the same way they approach health

care for people: they stress prevention. They put their emphasis on early detection of diseases and insect pests so that infestations can be nipped in the bud. Light traps set in the fields at night serve as a major weapon against insects. The insects are attracted to them by a burning lamp and fall into a pan of water and drown. Insecticides also find some use, although people said that DDT hadn't been too effective and they now use other compounds.

7. Innovations in Farm Implements (*Kung*). The necessity of introducing modern tools and machines into Chinese agriculture is the basis of one of Mao Tse-tung's most famous pronouncements: "The fundamental way out for agriculture lies in mechanization." By this Mao means that the ultimate goals of raising peasant living standards to equal those of city workers and constructing an agricultural base for large-scale heavy industry can be reached only when farming is carried out using machines.

The relationship between the growth of collective farming and the mechanization of farm work was a point of critical difference between Mao's supporters and those of Liu Shao-ch'i in the early 1950s. Liu argued, "Only with nationalization of industry can large quantities of machinery be supplied the peasants and only then will it be possible to nationalize the land and collective agriculture." This idea has been christened the theory of "mechanization before cooperation." Liu held that not until the machines were available should peasants be encouraged or even allowed to collectivize. Rather, the peasant economy should be left in the realm of private enterprise.

Mao took strong exception to Liu's stand:

In agriculture, with conditions as they are in our country cooperation must precede the use of big machinery . . . therefore we must on no account regard industry and agriculture, socialist industrialization and socialist transformation of agriculture, as two separate and isolated things, and on no account must we emphasize one and play down the other.

Otherwise, he argued, the natural inclination of the peasants toward petty entrepreneurism would redivide the countryside into exploiting and exploited classes. This would slow down the development of agricultural production and cripple efforts in large industry by choking off its supply of raw materials, thereby completely undermining the basis of the socialist state and making the long-term mechanization of agriculture impossible.

After a hard struggle Mao's viewpoint won the support of the Party, and the money needed to purchase machinery for farming was amassed through the formation of cooperatives and communes. In this way collectivization has preceded mechanization and the people in rural China have become "increasingly well off together." The behind-the-scenes conflict between Mao and Liu did not become public knowledge until the Cultural Revolution. The Chinese version of the story, including the quotations above, has been published as a pamphlet, "The Struggle Between the Two Roads in China's Countryside" (Foreign Languages Press, Peking, 1968).

At Hsikou Brigade mechanization now means six tractors (one 60 horsepower, one 40 horsepower, and four 10 horsepower) and two trucks. Before Liberation and cooperation people had to carry all burdens on shoulder poles along narrow paths. Now their trucks run on hillside roads built during the Great Leap Forward. In the past, using oxen, it was difficult to cultivate more than the first few inches of soil; their tractors now plow to a depth of 0.8 to 1.0 *ch'ih* (one *ch'ih* is about one foot). They have also introduced machine threshing and set up a small factory to process their crops. One small group of workers has picked up the skills needed to repair farm tools and machinery and the brigade can even build its own electric motors. Summing up their achievements, Kuo said, "So up to now we can say we have done semimechanization."

8. Field Management (*Kuan*). Back at Red Star Commune our host, Mr. Sen, had told us that good management had been an important factor in successfully staving off the worst effects of last year's drought. As he put it:

. . . through the superiority of the people's commune

and the leadership of the Communist Party we have paid great attention to administrative work [in capital construction and water conservancy]. Otherwise we would have suffered from the drought and many of us, had we been in the old society, would have become beggars. It was not that way last year. Some brigades actually increased their output of grain because of hard work and good planning. Some, as I said, reduced their output of grain. It showed us that organizational work is very important.

At Hsikou the peasants brought out even more clearly their grasp of the importance of long-term planning combined with close day-to-day attention to detail. All fields are planted, even the tiniest and most distant. Each field is planted with crops that best utilize its special features, sun or shade, wet or dry, etc. Seedlings especially are closely watched for signs of trouble and distant fields are monitored for problems as closely as those nearby. Long-term planning means just that. The brigade people speak of a "hundred-year plan" that encompasses their efforts in reforestation, water conservancy, animal husbandry, and other areas. The scale of this plan will become clear when we examine the foresty project. Hsikou people take pride in noting that the well-being of the entire nation is the principle guiding their work. They say: "We stand on the T'aihang Mountains but we take a view of the whole world."

This ends our overview of the Hsikou scientific-agricultural effort as it can be conveniently encompassed by the categories of the Eight Point Charter. Following Kuo's rundown of the eight points, our discussion with the Hsikou scientific and technical people moved on to the question of the group's structure. All the while as we talked and listened our hosts would dash the cold tea in the bottoms of our glasses over the concrete floor and pour us hot tea anew.

Again Kuo took the lead:

Now in order to meet the need of research work we formed a section of science and technology in the brigade, and a small group for each [production] team. We in the brigade section carry out experimental scientific work. The groups in the teams serve as advanced models for the peasants and show them how to do all kinds of new techniques in science.

[Our section is organized according to the principles of] what we call a three-in-one combination. That is [it includes] leading members of the brigade, aged experienced peasants, and the young, as well as technicians from the county who give us help.

In each team there is also a three-in-one combination: the wise leader, the experienced peasant, and what we call the local technician. Some fields [we plant] for experimental work, some fields just for a model, and in this way the majority of our members, the majority of our peasants, can take part in this kind of activity.

And in this way we can use scientific results to serve the people and the whole people can control the scientific work.

We asked who exactly makes up the brigade science section and the whole group pitched in to help fill out the picture. The section has seven members. They are chosen by the revolutionary committee of the brigade. One vice-chairman of the revolutionary committee, Kuo, has special responsibility for overseeing the brigade's scientific effort and is a member of the section. Two other section members (who weren't present at our meeting) are deputy leaders from the brigade Communist Party branch. These three people constitute the leading members in the three-in-one combination and are chosen for their administrative experience and responsibility for production.

The fourth section member is an old peasant-technician, Ch'ui Fu-hsing, chosen for his years of experience in past production. The fifth member, Chang Ming-chao, is a young "local technician" attached to the tenth production team and chosen in part for academic scientific knowledge. Local technicians are responsible for summing up the teams' experience testing varieties, etc., and bringing these experiences to the attention of the brigade section. They also bring the work and experience of the section to the teams, in turn. This is an example in science of what the Chinese call the mass line, which is summarized in the slogan "from the masses, to the masses." The other two members of the section are a young woman and a young man (neither of them present) whom we met earlier at the school bacterial fertilizer factory.

The conversation then turned to Hsia Shan-yün, the women technician from the county experiment station. We asked if she could describe the station and its activities and her relationship with the people at Hsikou. This is the story she told:

There are nine workers at our scientific and technical station, which is responsible for popularizing science and technology in our county. Four of us are agricultural college graduates and four of us are graduates of agricultural technical schools. Another one [of us] is an old man who has been working many years in agriculture.

We spend the greater part of our time in the countryside among the poor and lower-middle peasants, and we carry out scientific research and experiments with them and popularize science and technology in agriculture.

We settle down in four places [in the countryside] according to different weather conditions. The first place we regard as a warmer place, that is, along the river bank. And another place is the coldest in our county. The third station is in the small hill region with yellow soil. And the fourth one is here in Hsikou Brigade.

We spend one-third of our time in the countryside and one-third outside of our county to learn from other stations and countryside [areas]. Also we spend one third of [our time] to sum up our experiences within our county. Now we spend from April to

December . . . in the countryside. After December
we return to our station. From April to December
some time is [also] spent going to meetings as well
as learning in other counties. While visiting and
meeting we learn the advanced results gained by
the whole county and when we return to the brigades
in these four sections we combine with local people
and make some scientific experiments.

Visiting and taking part in meetings is not the only
way to learn from other places. Sometimes technicians
in the brigade groups are also with us. So when we
return we can make some scientific experiments together. And each year we have a meeting in the
county, either in winter or spring. Technicians, members of scientific and technical groups, take part in
these kinds of meetings.

For instance, my duty is to introduce improved,
better seeds of corn. These are bred by the scientific
institutes, and we introduce these better, improved
seeds of corn by just making some experiments according to our local situation. Then we popularize
better seeds. At the first stage we introduce [them] and
then together with the whole brigade and the people
of the scientific and technical group here we'll breed,
select, and popularize these better seeds.

For instance, I myself will make scientific experiments with the groups here and also take part in
physical labor and production and in this way also
try to increase my knowledge in agriculture. And
gradually I combine the theory, which I gained in
school, with practice.

The people here in Hsikou work hard and transform these regions into cultivated land . . . And I
learn from them and I can use my knowledge I gained
in my school and make my contribution to my
motherland at the same time.

I should say that I have done only a little work and
I try my best to improve myself, so that is why this
year I am determined to stay here and to learn to

carry out experiments with the poor and lower-middle peasants here.

Hsia Shan-yun's statement gives us a glimpse of how the county experiment stations serve to unite local agriculture with the national scientific research effort. It's also worth noting that having a female "county agent"—the nearest equivalent American social role—was taken for granted at Hsikou.

We went on to discuss the brigade reforestation effort with Kuo and Wang Ju-shen, the forester, the story of which we'll postpone to a later section of its own. At the end of the meeting we said we would be glad to try, in our turn, to answer questions and the group eagerly asked about new improved seed varieties in the United States. Embarrassed by our total lack of relevant knowledge, we fumbled the question and muttered something about problems arising out of extreme genetic uniformity in some crops combined with a variety of specific crop diseases. Then we remembered that one person in our group had brought along a couple of recent Burpee seed catalogs to give to people in China. We asked if they'd be interested in seeing them and, receiving nods and smiles of assent, we brought them out for presentation to the group. It was one of our great moments in China. The old peasant, the county agent, the forester, and the others stood close in a circle paging through the catalog and exclaiming over the pictures of familiar and unfamiliar vegetables and flowers.

At that point, even though it had gotten quite late in the day, the group quickly asked us to come see the brigade experiment station.

This caused a minor crisis because the invitation was apparently issued on the spur of the moment and caught our jeep drivers napping. Five minutes of horn honking and a little turmoil among our hosts eventually got us down the road to the station, which turned out to be housed in a small single-story building running along the back wall of a brick-walled enclosure that appeared to be the local granary. To get in our hosts had to unpadlock a large gate. Then we walked back through a yard filled with large cylindrical open-air corncribs to get to the station. The station itself, set up in 1964, consisted of a single long narrow room with a table down the center and laboratory benches lining one long wall and both ends.

On one bench sat displays of ears of corn, there to demonstrate the results of the brigade's work in hybridization. Two or three microscopes occupied the workbench at the far end of the room, and a conventional laboratory drying oven sat in one corner. They used it in determining the moisture content of soil samples. The station also had a setup for measuring the pH (acidity or alkalinity) of soil samples. On the center table in plastic bags lay samples of green powder said to be a plant hormone that increases corn production by 35 *chin* per *mu*. There were also samples of a white herbicide powder used to kill weeds in cornfields. We couldn't find out whether these samples were either 2,4-D or 2,4,5-T. Neither name was familiar to anyone there. The walls of the room were covered all over with insect pest life-cycle charts. In the midst of these hung a portrait of Chairman Mao, looking to us quite at home among the agricultural paraphernalia. On either side of Mao hung his words: "The core leading our cause forward is the Chinese Communist Party" and "The theory guiding our practice is Marxism-Leninism."

The Hsikou Brigade Science and Technology Section was very proud to show us their small station, and the old peasant Ch'ui seemed to be proudest of all. He beamed as we walked around the station and bade us an especially warm good-by as we got back in the jeeps to return to our rooms. We had all read enough history to know that in the old rural society in China the landlord families produced almost all the scholars; that systematic knowledge was a possession of the wealthy and powerful and the mass of peasants lived in ignorance as well as poverty. The achievements of the scholars were based on the experiences of the common people, but the common people gained little from them. Now before us as we said good-by and boarded the jeeps stood an old peasant, in worn black homemade clothes, who in his own lifetime had won from former masters the right to know the rules of nature and to make use of his knowledge for the betterment of the people. It was a good ending to our meeting with the people who oversee science at Hsikou.

•

Perhaps the most impressive single program at Hsikou is the brigade reforestation program. We visited parts of this program on our first afternoon in Hsikou, just after visiting the original home of the brigade's towering political figure, Li Shun-ta. Crossing a dry stream bed on the narrow valley bottom, our hosts led us up into the hills overlooking the brigade, starting from Li's old house. As it turned out, at one point in history Li Shun-ta's leadership of the brigade had been tied closely to the reforestation project. So before we proceed, let us introduce Li Shun-ta, a leading person of Hsikou, vice-chairman of the Shansi Province Revolutionary Committee, and member of the Central Committee of the Chinese Communist Party.

Li was born into a poor peasant family in Lin County, Honan Province (the area where we had stopped on our way up to Hsikou). His family succumbed to crushing debt and was forced to surrender its meager 1½ *mu* of land to the local landlord, after which his father left to labor as a house builder for the Kuomintang (Chinese Nationalist) Army in Shansi Province. Eventually, in the course of a struggle to receive back wages, Li's father was beaten to death. In the meantime the family had fled to Hsikou, where they eked out a miserable living as goatherds and subsisted on wild plants. They rented 5½ *mu* of land but in 1932 a drought took most of their crops and the landlord took the rest. To survive they had to sell Li's sister.

In 1937 the Red Army came to the Hsikou area. The next year Li and five others met in a remote cave to found the local branch of the Communist Party. In 1942 there was another drought and Li's household united with six other poor peasant households—all without draft animals—to form a mutual-aid team to reclaim land and share the plowing. Their effort resulted in two bumper harvests. In 1944 Li was elected a "labor model first class" and the team was cited as a fine example of mutual aid. This was the period of the Anti-Japanese War. Hsikou people fought the Japanese eighteen times and twice the Japanese invaded Hsikou itself. The first time they killed several people and looted everything. "This taught the people the importance of arms." By the time the Japanese returned, the people, with the aid of the Party, had armed themselves. Led by Li Shun-ta they routed the Japanese and took many casualties.

Between 1949 and 1951 Mao received Li three times and urged him to lead the transformation of the mountain regions into "a new village of socialism." In 1951 Li led in the formation of an agricultural cooperative. The next year his cooperative reaped a bumper harvest and won a gold-star medal from the Ministry of Agriculture. But, we were told, in 1953 local officials, following the views of Liu Shao-ch'i, intervened to try to turn the cooperatives back into mutual-aid groups. Li fought this move and refused to yield, so the Hsikou cooperative held firm. Some nearby cooperatives did slip backward but Li was instrumental in talking with them and putting them back on the right path. Li was vindicated when in 1955 Mao wrote: ". . . about the cooperative on T'aihang Mountain led by Li Shun-ta. In three years great changes have taken place. If this can be done in a poor mountain area, why can't other places do it?"

The reforestation project began in 1953, in the midst of the struggle over the cooperatives. Li Shun-ta and Hsun Ta-lai (labor heroine and assistant secretary of the brigade party branch) led some cooperative members in seeding 300 *mu* of barren mountainside with pine and cypress. A good deal of controversy preceded this action. Many older people argued that it would be better to plant willows and poplars, which would grow quickly and yield benefits in their lifetimes. Pines, they said, would take a hundred years to grow and cypress a thousand. If it was to be pines or cypress, they concluded, they'd "like to rest and not to plant at this time." But they were countered by people who pointed out that willows and poplars, water-loving plants, would not grow at all on the dry hillsides and that pines and cypress yield more useful wood. Another line of opposition came from people who thought that no trees at all would grow on the Hsikou hills. If it could be done, they argued, our forebears would have reforested the land. After all, the hills had been bare throughout recorded history and at the time of Liberation they barely even supported grass.

The results of the first year's seeding seemed to support the dissident viewpoints. Only about 10 percent of the expected seedlings grew, and a man from the county, apparently a representative of the anti-cooperative forces, came to Hsikou and ridiculed Li Shun-ta, saying that Li had such high capabilities that he "planted 300 *mu* and only one tree came up." Li countered that 10 percent wasn't a dismal failure and that at least it showed positively that trees could grow on the slopes. He encouraged the people to learn from their mistakes, analyze the reasons for the setback, and move forward.

To this end the brigade sent a member to study the experience of other cooperatives with more experience planting trees. Among other things, they learned that successful reforestation requires that the area to be seeded be blockaded to animals because grazing animals eat young trees. At Hsikou itself the peasants went to the planted area to investigate reasons for the poor results. They decided that most seeds had been planted too deeply to germinate or so shallowly that they had been killed by the sun. It also appeared that many had been devoured by birds and insects. So the problem, they decided, wasn't intractable physical conditions, but poor management of the seeding operation due to lack of experience.

Armed with this information the Hsikou people tried again in 1954, this time working on rainy days and carefully placing the seeds at medium depth among sticks and stones to protect them from insects, birds, and sun. This time the planting succeeded, and since 1954 the Hsikou people have taken part in the reforestation of 12,000 *mu* of land on four mountain slopes. One of the twelve brigade production teams now devotes all its time to forestry. Years after 1953, with the forests well established, many people admitted that during the first effort they had no expectation of success and simply tossed seeds around at random, contributing to the poor showing. The area sown in 1953 was never reseeded. Its sparsely scattered pines stand as a monument to an important episode in the brigade's history.

The pines planted in the following seasons have now grown into ten- to twenty-foot trees. Needles cover the ground beneath them and wild flowers and other small plants have begun to take hold on the forest floor. As we walked with our hosts that first day down narrow forest paths we could look out through the pines to see the slopes of the other side of the valley still barren and brown, in sharp contrast to the green pine forest. This, we discovered, is intentional, an integral part of the brigade's "hundred-year plan." Goats and sheep are an important source of income and manure for the brigade and they can't graze on land in the process of reforestation. Accordingly, the brigade has reforested only its north-facing slopes, leaving the south slopes, which have more sun and thicker grass, open for grazing. In a couple of years the trees in the old reforested areas will have grown tall and thick enough to resist the nibbling of goats and sheep. Then the herds will be allowed in to graze among the trees, gradually freeing the south slopes for reforestation themselves. Over thirty- or forty-year periods grazing and forestry will shift back and forth between slopes.

There are now about 30 *mu* of pine and cypress for each household in the brigade (more than 2000 timber trees each). This represents a cash value of some 10,000 *yüan* (about $5000). In five years the value of the timber will have grown to 10,000 *yüan* per person. In China, where 1000 *yüan* a year is good pay for factory work, this represents a tremendous capital accumulation, and a very great collective economic achievement. It is also an important gain for the national economy in a country which inherited severely limited forestry resources at the time of Liberation. In the early 1950s only 8 percent of China's land area was forested, as compared to 34 percent of the land in the Soviet Union and 33 percent in the United States.

In addition to their pine and cypress plantations, the

Hsikou people have planted about 1,000,000 trees as small saplings. These include willows, poplars, and locusts along the river banks and in ravines, and a great number of apples and walnuts. Now each household is represented by an average of 200 "dry" fruit trees (e.g. walnuts and dates) and more than 20 apple trees. Apples were not grown in Hsikou traditionally. Li brought the first saplings, which came from northeastern China, back from Peking. During the mid-fifties experiments showed that apples grow best at Hsikou when they are grafted onto the root stock of a native tree species. On this basis the brigade did mass planting of apple trees and now grows 300 *mu* of orchards in the valley and 200 *mu* on the mountainsides. Each year they harvest 170,000 *chin* of apples of five different varieties.

We left Hsikou with a feeling of exhilaration. There, in the face of very inauspicious physical conditions and an ancient tradition of local poverty and cultural deprivation, the people had built their "socialist village." They had achieved modest prosperity where before the Revolution crops failed in nine out of ten years, planted forests where none grew before, and turned a stony river bottom into good fields.

The people of Hsikou are still peasants. They work the soil, mostly by hand, and live in simple houses and caves. But these people, who before the Revolution were reduced to marginal farming and begging, have in a deep and genuine sense seized the constructive powers of science in their own hands. They have put science and technology to work with an optimism and confidence in the future securely grounded in their own experience and abilities.

It's important to emphasize that the Hsikou people did not seem alone or even unusual in their accomplishments. We spent altogether more than fifteen hours riding in jeeps and microbuses down back roads through parts of Shansi and Honan provinces between Anyang, Lin County, Hsikou, and Ch'engchou, the capital of Honan. Everywhere we drove we saw accomplishments comparable to those at Hsikou: irrigation projects; new buildings; well-kept, prosperous-looking villages; and small factories scattered about the countryside. And everywhere the people seemed to walk with the same confidence that marked the Hsikou peasants. Hsikou is a model brigade, but it is a model that reflects great achievements in rural China.

3 ASPECTS OF INDUSTRY

Our introduction to science as applied to industry in China came at the Shanghai Industrial Exhibition, a trade show open year-round where the accomplishments and advances of Chinese industrial technology are displayed. On our tour we were shown working models and products ranging from a 12,000-ton hydraulic press designed and built by workers at the Shanghai Heavy Machinery Plant to a portable 16-mm. sound projector that can be run by a bicycle-powered generator in rural areas lacking electricity. New models of cars, trucks, tractors, and construction equipment stood next to precision electronic equipment, electron microscopes, and medical apparatus. Textile and consumer goods including synthetic fibers, toys, handicrafts, and musical instruments were also shown. It was an impressive lesson for us, graphically demonstrating the extent to which China has advanced from a semifeudal state of underdevelopment in less than twenty-five years.

Our guide reminded us that before Liberation in 1949, what little industrial plant the Chinese had was designed and built by European or Japanese interests and had been in the hands of the Japanese for most of World War II. Following Liberation, the Chinese had depended heavily on Soviet planning and technical assistance until July 1960, when the Soviets abruptly terminated all aid. Almost overnight it had been necessary not only to take over the physical plant but also to train a technical staff and an industrial work force. The exhibition we were witnessing was testimony to their success in meeting this challenge.

But the exhibition was more than an exercise in pride for foreign visitors, it was also a means of displaying models for the Chinese people to learn from in concrete and specific ways. Workers, administrators, and technicians from all over China came to study new developments in technology for application in their production units at home. The exhibits themselves are staffed by workers from the factories where the equipment was produced or used who demonstrate the machinery and explain its operations. In this way the exhibition serves as a conduit through which technological advances flow to the population at large as quickly as possible.

Our visits to other factories brought out different aspects of industry in China. At the Peking Number 3 Textile Mill we visited the residential community and saw how the workers and their families live. We also learned something about industrial health and safety problems. At the Shanghai Electrochemical Works the emphasis was on the multipurpose use of waste materials in production. Our visit to the Scientific and Technological Exchange Station in Shanghai gave us another chance to see how the knowledge and uses of technology are spread among the Chinese people. [The Number 2 Low-Tension Electrical Factory in Shanghai employs a majority of blind and deaf-mute workers. The workers there told us about their role as handicapped people in industry and in Chinese society in general.]

Shanghai Machine Tool Works. The Shanghai Machine Tool Works has been proposed as a model institution because of its success in education and its ability to mobilize worker initiative in technical innovation. On July 21,

1968, Chairman Mao issued an important directive on the reform of education in the *People's Daily*:

Take the road of the Shanghai Machine Tools Plant in training technicians from among the workers. Students should be selected from among workers and peasants with practical experience, and they should return to production after a few years' study.

We visited the factory, in the outskirts of the central part of the city, on a Sunday afternoon. Shanghai looks more like a western city than any of the others we saw in China. There were no draft animals in the streets, as in Peking; cars and trucks shared the way with a multitude of bicycles. We drove through the section of the city built by the Europeans, with its large stone buildings, into more residential areas with two- and three-story houses, shopping streets with store fronts and painted signs (many in familiar roman letters), and occasional large apartment houses. There is a promenade, the Bund, by the Whangpoo River, busy with the commercial traffic of large freighters, small ferries, and sailboats. As we left the center of the city the streets became wider and the buildings smaller. From time to time there would be open spaces planted with crops and small bridges over creeks. Finally the cars drove past a large billboard, through a gate, into the center of the Machine Tool Works.

We were in the midst of a sprawling industrial complex that extended over many acres. It consisted of large shed-like buildings that housed rows of machine tools and metal working machines, as well as office blocks, warehouses, smokestacks, and a water tower, all spread out amid greenery, roads, and walkways.

The Shanghai Machine Tool Works specializes in producing precision grinding machines. The plant grew out of a small agricultural equipment factory that was established with United Nations relief funds after the Anti-Japanese War and started by turning out simple types of farm implements. Now there are 6000 workers in ten shops, both men and women, turning out the most advanced types of machine tools. Chinese workers have an eight-hour day and a six-day week. More people have Sunday as their day off than any other, but the parks and recreation areas have many visitors on weekdays.

We visited one area that was completely enclosed and temperature controlled for the manufacture of high precision parts. Large, polished shafts and worm gears were being worked on under fluorescent lights. In other areas within the low buildings we saw all sorts of equipment in use: overhead cranes, large flat-bed grinding machines, and lathes of various types. These factory buildings are separated from each other by paved storage areas and plantings. Other buildings on the site contain meeting rooms and offices, an Institute for Grinding Machinery, a nursery for workers' children, and a sanatorium for sick and injured workers.

On our tour we talked with Chou Ch'ing-tzu, a member of the plant's revolutionary committee, the central administrative body, who described the kind of work done in the factory. "We emphasize initiative, independence, and self-reliance," he told us. More than 250 kinds of grinding machines have been designed and manufactured on a trial basis at the plant. "The Cultural Revolution," Chou said, "was a big impetus for production. Since three-in-one teams for designing were instituted, over 100 varieties of grinding machines have been formulated."

The three-in-one concept has become more important in China since the Cultural Revolution and is used in many contexts. It embodies the idea of bringing together the diverse components of any situation into one body. Different combinations that we heard about or saw were old, middle-aged, young; masses, cadres, People's Liberation Army; and research, production, education. Whenever a problem is confronted, the three-in-one concept is applied to its solution. The machine tools factory focuses its human resources in teams consisting of workers, technicians, and cadres. The term cadre is used in China to denote someone in authority, either a political organizer or a manager. It refers to people we would call administrators as well as to Communist Party members whose duties are mainly political.

The Shanghai Machine Tool Works has been singled out as an industrial model because of its training programs for engineers and technicians. Originally that training was done on the job within the context of a three-in-one team, but since the time of Chairman Mao's directive, new methods for training have been developed at the plant. One is through the Institute of Machine Grinding, which is responsible for the development and design of new machinery at the factory. It was explained to us that for each research problem undertaken at the institute, a new three-in-one team of workers, technicians, and cadres is set up. Usually the workers who take part in these teams have applied to the institute and have been evaluated by their fellow workers and leaders. Most of them have more than seven years' experience. After several more years of working on the team they become technicians, their training supervised by the experienced technician on the team. The cadre member serves an organizing function and contributes administrative experience to the design process. When the group has solved the particular problem it was working on it is dissolved and a new three-in-one team is set up to work on another problem.

Technicians are also trained in the "July 21 Workers College," which was set up at the plant two months after Chairman Mao's directive. It is a three-year full-time technical school on the site that trains worker-technicians who are roughly equivalent to our engineers. During our tour we looked in on two classes at the Workers College, one in hydraulics and another in grinding machine mechanics. Both blackboards were covered with complicated mathematical equations in familiar roman numerals and mathematical symbols, interspersed with diagrams and Chinese characters. The subject matter being studied seemed to us to be on the later college or early graduate school level. About one quarter of the classes was composed of women, which seemed to be about the same percentage as in the shop. Fifty-two students had just graduated at the time of our visit and another group of ninety-eight were in their second year of study. Forty of them came from other machinery plants in Shanghai.

Like selection for work at the institute, admission to the Workers College is decided by the applicant's fellow workers and leaders. More workers apply than can be admitted, for the class size is limited by the number of teachers and the amount of space in classrooms and living quarters. To be eligible, a worker must have a lower middle school education and at least three years of practical experience, and be under thirty-five years of age. At present, we were told, the average student age is twenty-six years, with eight years of work experience.

One of the people we spoke to in the factory, Ting Lu-chu, a woman who seemed to be in her thirties, had been a lathe worker before becoming a student in the college. She had applied to the Research Institute for Grinding Machines and was being considered by her fellow workers and the leadership before being admitted. She told us:

> Before the Cultural Revolution I could not have gone to the Research Institute, because I was a worker. Then, only intellectuals were in the institute. I had difficulty with research work, especially theory. In order to learn more and to meet the needs of the Party, I applied to the college.

Like the other students, Ting Lu-chu lives in the school dormitory. Her children live with her husband and retired mother-in-law. While in school she receives her regular pay. After finishing her course of study, she will return to design work in the shop, earning about the same wage she got before studying. One of the younger student-workers at the Workers College told us he had applied so that he could "work better for socialism, not for higher pay." The salary range is 42–80 yüan a month for students in the college (1 yüan is equal to about 50 American cents) and 42–124 yüan for workers in the shop, with the average about 68 yüan a month. Technicians get more than 70 yüan and a few even earn more than 100. A small number of technician-engineers earn more than 200 yüan a month.

Pay differentials in China are said to be based on work experience. The highest salaries, such as those for the engineers at the Machine Tool Works, seem to be left over from at least before the Cultural Revolution. Older, highly paid professional workers probably continue to receive their original salaries, but younger professionals seem to earn roughly the same salary as regular workers. Among production workers salaries also vary according to experience and productivity.

The curriculum of the Workers College includes mechanics and mechanical theory, mathematics, electricity, hydraulics, grinding machine design, and English. Our hosts described the program as beginning with the basic theories and a general background in machine technology, and then proceeding to the production of typical grinding machines, theoretical study at a higher level, and finally to the individual design and production of a complete machine tool. Throughout their studies the students continue to maintain contact with the shop by doing productive work. This was described as a way of combining theory with practice to raise the level of both.

The daily schedule at the school consists of six hours of classes, one hour of recreation, and one and a half hours of evening study. The staff includes twenty teachers from universities and more than thirty worker-technicians. We were told that the quality of work at the college is the same as at the universities, where, since the Cultural Revolution, students are now admitted from factories and communes, and not directly out of middle school. Some workers from the machine tool plant have gone to universities to be trained as technicians.

In addition to the July 21 Workers College there is educational activity at the Machine Tool Works that is not related to training technicians. There is a "July 21" spare-time school attended by 1000 of the 6000 workers. They meet twice a week after work for classes in politics, technology, and culture, where they study Marxism-Leninism and current events. Another part-time political institute is mainly for group leaders. All the workers in the factory were described as engaged in some form of political study.

Middle school students from the neighboring schools visit the plant with their teachers, sometimes for periods of more than a month, to do productive work and attend classes taught by workers in the factory. University students come to the Machine Tool Works on a similar basis. A technical middle school on the grounds of the factory stopped running during the Cultural Revolution but has since been reopened at the request of the municipal government. For two of the school's three years the students spend alternate weeks in classroom study and at practical work; the last year consists entirely of practice. The school has its own small plant, in which it produces parts for lathes, that will soon be upgraded so that it can produce complete grinding machines.

One way to evaluate the Shanghai Machine Tool Works would be to assess the quantity and quality of its products relative to the investment of capital and personnel. Another would be to test the skills of the technician force, over half of which has been trained by the methods we were told about. Specialists in the machine tool field will have to provide these evaluations. We can only report what one of our hosts, Chou Ch'ing-tzu of the plant revolutionary committee, told us:

> There are still shortcomings which are not included in the pamphlet you have read (about the factory), but we will mention them to give a true point of view. Automation in our works is not so high, so our efficiency is not so high. We can produce over 600 varieties of machine, but we are short of experience in running our plant. Therefore at the start of the month things are sometimes disorganized and the quality of the product is lowered. Our educational methods are still experimental.

But the efficiency of a factory should be judged not just by its success as a production unit, but also by its impact on the society as a whole. This would include taking into account such matters as the involvement of rank-and-file production workers in decision making, both inside and outside the factory.

At the Shanghai Machine Tool Works we sensed that the factory was an educational facility in addition to being a source of production. The training of technicians and engineers was an important correlative to the production of machine tools, and the workers themselves, rather than managers or publicists, told us about the technical aspects of running the factory. The Chinese we talked with considered factories not only important for producing society's needs but equally important as schools for learning to run the society.

Taking the suggestions and criticisms of the workers is not an idea the Chinese invented, but it seems to stand close to the center of their ideology and is exemplified in such often-heard phrases as "The people alone are the motive force in history," and "Science is the summation of the experience of the laboring people." The program of the Machine Tool Works is a serious attempt to put these ideas into practice, to promote the initiative of ordinary workers and to create a force of technicians who do not regard themselves as being different from the workers. Time and again during our stay in China our hosts would refer to Pre-Cultural Revolution problems related to this subject: cadres who didn't listen to suggestions—perhaps to enhance their own authority; technicians who felt very self-important—often to hide their incompetence; and rank-and-file workers who acquiesced to these circumstances. When we heard the Chinese speak of this situation, we remarked that it sounded very much like our experiences at home; this suggested a partial explanation for the widespread use of another phrase: "the capitalist road."

We got an idea of how the Chinese criticize their own new educational programs by reading the pamphlet "Strive to Build a Socialist University of Science and Engineering" (Foreign Languages Press, Peking, 1972). The pamphlet includes the transcript of a panel discussion held in Shanghai in 1970. One of the participants was Wang Shao-tung, a worker-technician and the Party branch secretary of the July 21 Workers College at the Machine Tool Works. During the discussion Wang described some of the bad attitudes of the students at the Workers College. There were those who said that they had been sent to the college to study and that their task was to learn designing. Often their attitudes were influenced by the so-called revisionist line in education, which makes a sharp division between book learning and practical experience, with the emphasis on book learning. There were also students whose attitudes were excessive in the other direction. "Some students," Wang said, "first thought that if they were to learn through practice, they should go back to the workshop rather than attend college." Discussions were organized to help them understand "for whom" (the Chinese answer is "for the people") they had come to study. Gradually they came around to the basic job of learning to design machine tools.

Another problem, according to Wang, was that "some workshops in our plant think only of their own departments and will not send their best workers to school." Someone at the conference suggested putting up "big-character posters criticizing people who indulge in departmentalism, for they don't understand the workers' genuine desire to study and are short-sighted, closing their eyes to long-term interests." Workers who did not want to continue studying should be encouraged to go on and learn to continue the Revolution.

The panel discussed the problems of setting up new educational programs, including the need for basic education among the workers, and administrative ways of fitting these programs into the existing educational systems. But most of the time was spent on the reshaping of attitudes among both workers and educators.

Two points in the discussion are worth mentioning here. The emphasis on the initiative and abilities of workers in the technical field, and on their dominant role in the political field, creates special morale problems among intellectuals. One participant in the symposium, representing a chemical engineering institute involved in pesticide production, said:

At one point, some of our comrades were in low spirits. They thought they were unlucky to have had a few years of college education; otherwise they could be members of a Workers' Mao Tse-tung Thought Propaganda Team. After being re-educated by the poor and lower middle peasants, they are no longer disheartened because the poor and lower middle peasants are so eager to conduct scientific experiments.

This sense of being cut off from the rest of the people because of scientific education and concerns was familiar to us from our experiences at home.

The Chinese don't believe that simply training workers to become technicians and engineers will solve problems of technical elitism automatically. After all, America is full of "self-made" men who now run businesses or work at professions just like their colleagues, and many workers aspire to open their own businesses or get professional jobs. Our Chinese hosts would often repeat that a working-class background does not insure a socialist perspective. In this respect, intellectuals and professionals have to speak up as well. The problem was stated by a leader of the Hutung Shipyard Workers University:

Among the students were some who thought that they were "born red" and that their main task in the university was to acquire professional knowledge. When they were told to study politics, they said they might better learn it in the workshops. The teachers dared not criticize these things, thinking that they themselves had come merely to receive re-education; also many of the worker-students were leading members and veteran workers. So some teachers would accept whatever the students said, right or wrong.

The pamphlet made it clear that the current experimental efforts in education have not been completely worked out. It is important to remember that the new programs were at most four years old at the time of our visit. From our limited vantage point, we came to share the Chinese optimism about the future of these efforts.

Peking Number 3 Cotton Textile Mill. As we drove east from the center of Peking, large smokestacks began to replace trees as the dominant feature of the landscape. The Number 3 Cotton Textile Mill is in this section of the city, across the street from its large residential community. Our visit to the mill gave us a chance to see how industry relates to the way people live in China and the conditions in which they work.

Our guides at the mill told us that it was designed in 1954 and went into production in 1957, that its 3200 automatic looms and 87,000 spindles were all designed and installed without foreign aid, and that the level of production is now 100 million square meters of cotton cloth a year. Sixty-four hundred workers are employed at the plant, of whom 70 percent are women. The workers were dressed only in light clothing because of the warm temperature in the work area, a shock to us coming in from the cold Peking winter. Cotton production can take place only in special temperature- and humidity-controlled conditions. Many of the workers were also wearing surgical masks to keep out the cotton dust in the air. They moved from machine to machine at a regular pace, checking the process in which cotton is taken from bales and transformed into finished cloth.

We saw a number of technological innovations that were comparable to those we were familiar with in western cotton mills. In the early days of the plant, cotton had to be torn up by hand before it could be used in production. An automatic cotton-mixing machine was developed to speed the process—a giant vacuum cleaner that glides back and forth over the bales of cotton, sucking material into its innards where it is agitated and mixed. Another machine developed in the plant automatically connects the yarn of different spools so that it can be spun continuously, a process previously done by hand. Small labor-saving devices like carts that enable operators to move back and forth between machines without walking have also been the products of local ingenuity. The use of this automated machinery requires a certain amount of training in an apprentice program, but the length of the training period for an operator was shortened from over a year to several months after the Cultural Revolution.

We had heard that in 1971 and 1972 the factories were filled with *ta-tzu-pao*, big-character posters on political matters. But on our tour we saw only a few bulletin boards with messages related to production and one large blackboard with the theme "Learn from Lei Feng," decorated with a hand-drawn picture. Lei Feng was a model People's Liberation Army soldier whose life is considered exemplary because, in addition to fulfilling his military duties, he studied politics diligently and worked hard at production without claiming any credit for his accomplishments. Our trip took place around the tenth anniversary of his death, and we saw posters and displays commemorating his life in many places we visited.

Across the street from the mill is its residential community, a self-contained village of 10,000 people under the administration of the mill's revolutionary committee. Like all factories we visited or read about, the textile mill has a medical clinic where workers get free medical care. Pregnant women workers get prenatal care and, after seven months of pregnancy, are given lighter work, shorter hours, and one less day of work per week. After childbirth they have fifty-six days of maternity leave, and when they return to work they get two extra work breaks per day for 14 months for nursing.

The residential area has a day-care center for the workers' children. When we looked in on one of the rooms a group of six-year-olds were seated at tables with their toys or playing on the floor with bright-colored toy animals and trucks. They applauded when they saw us and chanted in Chinese, "Warmly welcome American friends." Another group of children sang and danced for us. Both were pleasant surprises. The residential community also has primary schools and a middle school for the workers' older children.

At the workers' canteen, a large dining hall directly across the street from the factory, we were treated to a tour of the kitchen. Large trays of vegetables and meats had been set out in preparation for the evening meal, which was served late in the afternoon for workers getting off shift. The general menu at this canteen contained a variety of choices: vegetable meals cost 8 *fen* and meat meals cost 15. Here as elsewhere there was no visible shortage of food during our visit—eating places for the average Chinese seemed well stocked, and food stores displayed a large variety of meats, fruits, vegetables and canned goods. The dining hall was empty when we stopped by, except for some canteen workers who were seated at a few tables having a political study meeting. In winter the room is used once a week for movies, which are shown outside in the summer.

In the center of the residential area was a large soccer field, where a game was in progress on the afternoon we visited. There were no bleachers around the field, but a fairly large crowd of spectators was enjoying the action. The textile mill's soccer team together with its basketball and table tennis teams, provides the community with athletic entertainment. There is also a theatrical troupe, called a "propaganda team," for cultural entertainment.

The housing complex itself consists of four-story redbrick buildings spread out over a large area. We visited one apartment that consisted of one large and one small room plus kitchen and bath, occupied by a maintenance worker and his wife, who both work at the textile mill, and their three children. The husband and wife work on different shifts so that one of them can be at home to take care of the children. Like many workers in China they work rotating shifts, changing from night to day to swing shift after a week on each. The workers are organized into squads of ten to twenty that move from shift to shift as a group and also serve as political study units. Rent for the apartment, including gas, electricity, water, and furniture, is 9 *yüan*, 20 *fen* a month (about $4.60). The husband's monthly wage is 75 *yüan* and the wife's is 70 *yüan* (about $72 altogether). The husband told us that he had been a textile worker for thirty-three years and that, after coming to Peking from northeastern China sixteen years ago, he had helped to open the Number 3 Textile Mill and worked in setting up the machinery and building the housing complex.

Some retired workers also live in the residential area, we were told. Retirement, although not mandatory, is usually at age sixty for men and fifty for women, except for women cadres, who retire at fifty-five. If we add it all together—work in the factory, children attending community schools from nursery to higher middle school, medical care, canteen, sports and cultural events—it sounds like an insulated company town. But we think that view would be incorrect. The Chinese say that the control of factories is in the hands of the workers who run it. This is how they explained it to us: The everyday operations of the textile mill are controlled by its revolutionary committee. Set up during the Cultural Revolution these committees were established to involve ordinary workers, especially those who were not Party activists, in the running of factories and other institutions. Members of the People's Liberation Army were also sent in to provide political leadership. At Number 3 Textile Mill the revolutionary committee uses two three-in-one combinations: cadres, People's Liberation Army, and masses; and old, middle-aged, and young. It has twenty-one members, seven of whom are standing members and the rest representatives of the workers.

Revolutionary committees are officially under the leadership of the Communist Party organization. The 800 Party members in the textile mill are for the most part regular workers whose Party function is in addition to their regular jobs. They are divided into four branches that meet once a month, although members have some Party activity every week. From our observations there was no way of telling who was a Party member and who wasn't, but from conversations with our hosts, other visitors, and Americans who have worked in China, we formed some idea about the role of rank-and-file Party members. The kind of person likely to be a Party member is similar to the kind who would be a union activist in an American factory. Party membership is considered an honor, and members would be expected to be exemplary workers, which means coming earlier, working harder, and staying later, as well as leading political study groups and attending Party meetings. In the factories we visited, Party members comprised about 10 percent of the work force. Each work group would probably have one or two Party members in it, and when they meet once or twice a week for political study the Party members would be likely to lead the discussions.

One of the questions we were particularly interested in was what had happened to the trade unions as a result of the Cultural Revolution. One of the factory representatives answered:

Before the Cultural Revolution we had actual unions [national unions were reestablished in the summer of 1973]. But their task was interfered with by the Liu Shao-ch'i line so that during the Cultural Revolution the broad masses of the workers rose in criticism of their revisionist line. For instance, the former trade unions didn't organize workers to solve their problems directly; they used money to provide incentives for the workers and thus misled them.

We know that China's industrial work force has taken an important role in national affairs and education. During the Cultural Revolution workers were organized into propaganda teams to go into many nonindustrial institutions and oversee the implementation of proletarian politics. One of the members of the revolutionary committee told us:

In the past I knew nothing about the superstructure;* what I knew was to work in my cotton mill. During the Cultural Revolution, Chairman Mao said that the working class should exercise leadership over everything, and so we workers went to the units of

---

* In marxist analysis the superstructure is the pattern of institutions, organizations, chains of authority, traditions, culture and habits of thought which characterize a society.

the superstructure. The visits first took place at Tsinghua University.

This woman was later part of a team of workers who visited the Academy of Sciences. The role of these teams is discussed further in the chapters on research and education. Briefly, workers from factories in Peking went into the university during the Cultural Revolution to help resolve political disputes between different factions of students and teachers. Now teachers and students come to the mill to work, to learn from the workers, and to receive reeducation from them.

Shanghai Electrochemical Works. The Electrochemical Works in Shanghai is a leader in experimentation with multipurpose use of industrial wastes, a policy of striving to convert all parts of a raw material into useful products. It produces chlorine, caustic soda, and other chemical materials by electrolysis of purified sea water. With 2300 workers and staff, the plant is considered a medium-sized complex. It was established in 1959 and its early annual output included 15,000 tons of caustic soda, as well as three or four other products. In 1972 it produced 75,000 tons of caustic soda and more than twenty other main products. But as production has increased, so has the quantities of liquid, gaseous, and solid waste.

A representative of the factory told us that before the Cultural Revolution the complex was a big polluter but it was "following the Liu Shao-ch'i line," and little effort was made to convert the wastes:

Peasants made complaints and suggestions, but cadres ignored them and made excuses. Sometimes peasants even came to the factory, and they would quarrel. At that time the leaders just considered production. Workers also made reasonable suggestions, but the leading cadres relied only on engineers and technicians, and ignored the suggestions.

The speaker himself was evidence of the change. Ts'ao Ch'ing-ta, who looked to be less than thirty, was a worker representative on the revolutionary committee of the factory. He had been elected to the committee some four years previously (around 1968), and spoke with authority and understanding, sometimes looking in a notebook for statistics. The other spokesman for the factory was Wu Hsing-tu, an older man whose glasses, cap, and scarf made him look like a university professor. Wu was the technician in charge of "multipurpose use." He led us on our tour of the factory, excitedly and proudly describing his work, alternating between English and Chinese.

The factory stands in the midst of a farming area about five miles from Shanghai proper. Driving out we saw a mixture of factories, blocks of houses, open fields, and stockpiles of industrial goods as our car dodged trucks, buses, and bicycles. The location of newer industry away from the center of the city, and the establishment of housing in the new areas, was part of the early planning for the reconstruction of Shanghai. The factory complex, with its maze of building and equipment, tanks and pipes, was a great scene for photography on the rainy, gloomy day of our visit. As elsewhere we traveled in China, there was no restriction on our taking photographs.

Ts'ao continued his outline of the history of the factory and its pollution problems. Some of the liquid waste and solid residue, such as sulfuric acid and calcium sulfate, which polluted rivers and damaged crops, were neutralized with alkali, but the alkali itself further polluted the waterways. For some of the waste gases like the chlorine that leaked from electrolysis cells, the cadres tried containment, improving the seals around the cells; but the leakage continued. Often workers had to wear masks for protection, and the peasants received compensation for their damaged crops. Not until the attitude that productivity alone is the overriding goal was challenged during the Cultural Revolution were the pollution problems dealt with.

As a result of the Cultural Revolution, the "Liu Shao-ch'i line" was overcome. Wilfred Burchett, the Australian journalist, visited the plant in 1972 and described his visit in the April 19, 1972, issue of the *Guardian*. The workers told him about their cleanup efforts:

> As a first step, we sent workers to check up in the fields. They were horrified at the harm being done, and the effect it would eventually have on the worker-peasant alliance. We set to work, relying mainly on the knowledge and initiative of the veteran workers. Within three months, and with an investment of 10,000 *yüan*, we discovered how to turn a bad thing into a good thing.

How good a thing they discovered was described to us as follows: of the 92,000 cubic meters of waste gases now produced per month, 85 percent is treated; 75 percent of the 28,000 tons a month of liquid wastes is treated; and 95 percent of the 500 tons of solid residue produced each month is treated. All in all, during 1972 the factory recovered 3000 tons of new chemical raw materials with a value of 600,000 *yüan* in thirty multipurpose-use projects.

One section of the electrochemical plant produces 99 percent hydrofluoric acid and its associated waste liquids, gases, and solid residues. It was these toxic fumes, largely hydrogen fluoride, that forced workers to wear masks when they approached the factory. Fluorides ruin fruit and cause plant leaves to "burn" at the tips and eventually drop off, so these fumes were a disaster to the crops in the vicinity of the factory. Research showed that the waste gas could be converted into cryolite, a sodium-aluminum fluoride (Na_3AlF_6) which is used as a flux in the electrolytic production of aluminum, at an average cost of 4000 *yüan* a ton. As the market value of cryolite is only 1400 *yüan* a ton, each ton ends up costing the factory 2600 *yüan* to produce.

During the Cultural Revolution debate raged over the question "for whom" the Shanghai Electrochemical works existed. Should it serve itself and the production of chemical raw materials, or the people as a whole? The workers learned that the first road meant "putting profit in command" and was the line advocated by Liu Shao-ch'i. Instead, they agreed that although the recycling of wastes cost the factory money, the cryolite project should be carried out to benefit the health and livelihood of the workers and peasants. In 1972, 38 tons of cryolite were produced at a loss of almost 100,000 *yüan*, ten times the annual compensation that used to be paid to the peasants for the destruction of their crops.

For the most part, however, the Electrochemical Works pays attention to the policy of "making revolution more economically." By the end of 1972 further research had found another function for the waste gases; they are now used in the production of a type of liquid hydrofluoric acid used in metallurgical extraction. Thirteen tons were produced last year at an average cost of 700 *yüan* and a market value of 1200 *yüan* a ton. This discovery helped resolve the contradiction between beneficial and harmful products of industry and helped the plant economically. Workers had also devised methods to recover carbon disulfide from noxious waste waters. Several large tanks made entirely of old, discarded equipment, now supply raw materials for carbon tetrachloride and rayon at practically no operating cost.

The utilization of waste, whether or not it is profitable to do so, helps to solve China's pollution problem. At the same time it increases productivity and economy in industry by the development of new spin-off factories, by the further use of existing factories, and by a more comprehensive deployment of raw materials. Broadening workers' skills and widening the operations of machines and workshops also increases productivity, as does the development of integrated complexes that include small production units to process the wastes of the larger units.

The hydrofluoric acid workshop of the Shanghai Electrochemical Works demonstrates these practices. At the entrance to the shop there is a large multicolored display entitled "The Three Wastes Are Transformed into the Three Treasures." It describes the gas, liquid, and solid or residue waste products of the shop, their hazards, and the processes by which they are utilized. Polytetrafluoroethylene (known to most Americans by the trade name Teflon) is no longer the only useful product of the shop, as can be seen from this diagram:

Main Production	CaF^2 ——	H_2SO_4 ——	HF ——	$\rightarrow C_2F_4 \rightarrow$ Teflon
Main composition of wastes	waste gas (HF)	waste liquid (H_2SO_4)	waste residue ($CaSo_4$)	waste gas (C_2F_4)
Utilization	liquid HF acid (formerly cryolite)	fertilizer	cement	$C_2F_4Br_2$ for fire extinguishers

Multipurpose use of waste products has paralleled in some respects the shift toward decentralization in Chinese industry. In its recent history China has had traditions of both centralism and decentralism. Along with their manufactured products, the imperial powers of Europe, Japan, and America exported capital to China in the latter half of the nineteenth century for the development of industries that would exploit the cheap labor and take advantage of unprotected natural resources. The factories were built exclusively in the large coastal cities, where the labor potential could be concentrated and from which it would be easier to transport products to foreign markets.

Decentralization, on the other hand, has been a characteristic of the revolutionary movement in China. Beginning with the base areas of the 1930s—mountainous areas liberated by the Red Army—Mao Tse-tung's embattled guerrillas found that their meager industrial production as well as government administration functioned best when decentralized. Since Liberation, experiments along these lines have increased. One of the policies that emerged from the Cultural Revolution was to encourage each county to become self-sufficient in the "five small industries": chemical fertilizers, iron and steel, cement, machinery, and energy.

Several reasons were explained to us for the development of small, decentralized industries. One is that they provide for a more complete utilization of widely scattered resources. Big industries often need to concentrate at the site of large resource deposits. Small industries can also meet China's wide variety of special local needs, such as subtropical clothes and tools for farming mountainous land. Perhaps the key reason is that decentralization unifies industrial development and agriculture. This unity provides industry with an increasing variety of raw materials and provides agriculture with mechanical and chemical devices to increase productivity. One of the goals of China's socialist revolution is the abolition of what the Chinese call "the big differences": differences between industrial and agricultural development, between country and city life, and between mental and manual labor. Until these differences are eliminated, the Chinese say, people will not be able to enjoy the benefits of society equally or develop their full potential for contributing to it. Both the trend toward decentralization and the practice of multipurpose use help to overcome the differences.

One of the most common products of waste utilization is fertile irrigation water. In the area around Shihchiachuang, in Hopei Province, northern China, cadres, peasants, workers, and technicians experimented for ten years with utilizing industrial waste waters. Now the city's daily 400,000 tons of sewage is processed to fertilize and irrigate 12,930 hectares of farmland. Communes that previously lacked the necessary water and fertilizer can grow rice, and the productivity of some fields has more than doubled. The city's industries, which also recover chemicals, acids, and dyes, save nearly a millian *yüan* a year in disposal costs through the new sewage treatment scheme. Reciprocally, agricultural wastes such as cottonseed shells, corncobs, sugar-cane residue, and animal viscera become raw materials for developing commune-owned industries. So industrial wastes are transformed to increase agricultural development and the utilization of agricultural wastes extends industrialization.

Decentralization and multipurpose use of wastes have,

besides integrating industry and agriculture, been used to control industrial pollution. Like the relocation of factories, pollution control is generally coordinated on the local level. Under the Shanghai Municipal Revolutionary Committee special city and district groups for multipurpose use planning are composed of administrative cadres, technicians, factory workers, and peasants who farm near the factories. These groups coordinate waste use programs, match one factory's waste with another's use capabilities, and supervise compliance with pollution regulations.

Another aspect of Chinese industry that promotes the comprehensive use of wastes is the emphasis on integrated complexes. Large factories are encouraged to diversify their facilities or to initiate different processes using new equipment. Frank Kehl, an anthropologist who visited China in 1971, told us what happened at the Medium Rolling Mill of the massive Anshan Iron and Steel Complex. During the Cultural Revolution the workers apparently rejected the "Liu Shao-ch'i line" that exhaust heat losses from reheating furnaces were reasonable and decided to utilize the waste heat to generate electricity. With assistance from neighboring factories, they built a 3000-kilowatt power station in two months, saving 36,000 tons of coal a year for the mill.

Behind the successful implementation of multipurpose use lies the central role of politics in industry, specifically of what the Chinese refer to as the dominance of the mass line. In "Surplus Labour Has Found a Way Out" (1955) Chairman Mao wrote:

> The masses have boundless creative power. They can organize themselves and concentrate on places and branches of work where they can give full play to their energy; they can concentrate on production in breadth and depth and create more and more welfare undertakings for themselves.

Three-in-one groups are set up to insure that the wisdom, initiative, and creativity of ordinary people are taken into account, and that leadership no longer suffers from "expertise in command"—which occurs when experts have no practical experience and are the product of elitist training.

The phrase "walking on two legs," as applied to industry, is another aspect of utilizing industrial wastes through the mass line. Developed widely during the Great Leap Forward in 1958, it means production on a small-scale basis using whatever equipment is available, to complement large-scale production in modern factories. As a result of this movement, small production and processing groups have sprung up all over China.

The Chinese seem to enjoy illustrating their political ideals with model stories. From northern China comes the example of the old "waste man" of Hsiyang County, Shansi Province. Although crippled since infancy and a beggar before Liberation, he was determined to contribute to production and help China walk on two legs. He gathered scraps of metal around the village and made them into turnip graters in the cave where he lived. The thousands of graters he made were sold to the state by his production brigade, and he has became a model of initiative and self-reliance.

Farmyard, street, and schoolyard industries have become more sophisticated since the 1950s. Our hosts told us that they now carry a significant share of China's productivity, freeing larger factories for more complex operations and giving millions of Chinese an intimate acquaintance with industrial planning and production. For example, young women of the Taku Fishery Commune, near Tientsin, began a multipurpose use factory in a mat shed they set up on a barren beach. After many experiments they devised methods of extracting medicinal sodium chloride from the waste residue of a nearby chemical plant. Production has expanded and the one shed has grown to twenty rooms. Walking on two legs, even if unevenly, instead of waiting for the magic wand of heavy industrialization, has been the method adopted by the Chinese to fully utilize their country's resources and "turn wastes into treasures."

Another frequently mentioned example was the Lifei

Chemical Plant in Tsingtao, Shantung, which used to buy household scrap metal and broken glass for recycling. Fifty of its older workers decided to try and extract silver from broken thermos bottles and mirrors. They got an earthen pot and a broken bottle for crucible and funnel, and started with a dollar's worth of reagents. After some two hundred experiments they developed sufficient techniques to recover silver from industrial waste water as well as from discarded film and mirrors. In four years since the Cultural Revolution they have extracted 1250 kilograms of silver and recovered seven other materials, including gold, alum, and magnesium sulfate, from waste water using methods they developed themselves.

One final method of promoting the comprehensive use of wastes is the diversification of skills and functions in industry. This practice further extends the attack on extreme specialization of factory production and sharp separation between industries, as described by Chi Wei in "Multi-Purpose Use: Turning the Harmful into the Beneficial," an article which appeared in the *Peking Review*, January 28, 1972:

A factory is divided into several parts; one raw material is used in many ways; a piece of machinery is used for many purposes; one worker is capable of many kinds of work apart from his specialty; and a factory can produce many things while engaging mainly in one product.

Chi Wei cited the Kiangmen Sugar-Cane Chemical Plant, in Kwangtung Province, which used to be a sugar-producing factory in operation for only half of each year. Its sugar-cane wastes are now transformed into chemicals, fiberboard, and several kinds of paper. The half-year that once saw the factory idle is now filled with the production of more chemicals, building materials, and medicines, using the same equipment.

Appreciation of the vigor and depth of the waste utilization movement calls for an understanding of its philosophical and ideological basis. The key phrase, "one divides

into two," often used in Chinese discussions of multipurpose use, refers to the fact that we often view an object or
process superficially, without realizing that there are positive and negative qualities to everything. Waste has not
only obvious negative characteristics but also, necessarily,
some beneficial aspects that a thorough dialectical analysis
will reveal. Another article on multipurpose use, in the
February 5, 1971, *Peking Review*, stated:

> In making one product, resources are partially
> transformed into this product and the rest becomes
> "waste." The question is how to look at this
> "waste"—from which point of view, and with
> what attitude. From the metaphysical point of view,
> waste cannot be used and should be gotten rid of. On
> the contrary, the materialist dialectical view holds
> that what is waste and what is not waste are relative
> terms. There is nothing in the world which is abso-
> lutely waste. "Waste" under one condition may be
> valuable under different ones ... After being trans-
> formed and utilized, "waste material" can become ...
> useful material.

What at first looks like a completely bad situation, industrial waste and its pollution, really has two possibilities,
one beneficial and the other harmful. Left to themselves,
industrial by-products poison and pollute, but when the
composition of the wastes is studied and manipulated, useful raw materials and products can be gleaned. Waste disposal problems can then become "use" problems. At a cotton mill that once burned its cottonseed shells to get rid of
them, the workers began to analyze the particular properties of the shells. Now they are processed to produce furfural, an organic compound; acetone is made from the
waste gas and glucose is made from the waste residue of
the furfural production. Residues left from the glucose become glycerine, alcohols, and an artifical flavoring.

There are some materials in which the waste characteristics are still dominant, either because their beneficial aspects have not yet been understood or because suitable

techniques have not been developed to utilize them. It is believed in China that all waste "contradictions" can eventually be resolved favorably, and the reason it is considered so important to resolve them is that they are part of the crucial contradiction between the beneficial and harmful effects of industry. Wastes damage crops, pollute the air, poison rivers, and are hazardous to the health of people and animals. Although they are generally the lesser part of industrial production, the harmful effects of waste may be far from negligible and are in direct contradiction to the fundamental purpose of industry: to produce goods that improve the lives of the people.

Mao Tse-tung's view, in "Tactics Against Japanese Imperialism" (1935), is that

In approaching a problem a Marxist should see the whole as well as the parts. A frog in a well says, "The sky is no bigger than the mouth of the well." That is untrue, for the sky is not just the size of the mouth of the well. If it said, "A part of the sky is the size of the mouth of a well," that would be true, for it tallies with the facts.

The multipurpose use of industrial wastes is an example of approaching a problem as a whole. Individual shops and factories may suffer a loss in waste utilization, but when all the costs and benefits are tallied, the people come out ahead. This idea is clearly expressed in "Industrial Development and Pollution," in the February 1973 issue of *China Reconstructs*:

In our country, what benefits the people, the country and the whole is given first consideration in everything that is done. Therefore some areas and enterprises allocate a certain portion of their funds for treatment of sewage and other wastes. This may yield them little or no profit, but from the point of view of the whole, of preventing pollution of the air, rivers and water sources, protecting aquatic life and supporting agriculture, this means great profit indeed.

As dialectical materialists, the Chinese believe that the interconnections between the objects and phenomena of the real world and the laws governing their relations are knowable. Waste utilization has successfully helped to end pollution problems and has significantly furthered industrial and social development. Within the practice of multipurpose use are joined the means raising China's level of industrialization, a way of "making revolution more economically," fully utilizing resources, and guaranteeing the health of the Chinese people and their environment. It is the means by which people, resources, machinery, and the physical plant can work together in the most rational manner, to the fullest benefit of the entire society.

Shanghai Scientific and Technological Exchange Station. Traveling around in Shanghai we would often pass long sidewalk displays that were being looked at by hundreds of people. These, we were told, were exhibitions of working models of the latest developments in science, medicine, and industry, presented for the people of Shanghai to study, discuss, and comment upon. They were part of the work of the Scientific and Technological Exchange Station.

The exchange station is a branch of the Scientific Exchange Institute, a national organization whose job is to spread the knowledge and experience of science and technology among the masses of the Chinese people. There are branches of the institute in the cities and the countryside throughout China; each one adapts itself to local needs for technological problem solving and exchanging scientific information. Shanghai has several of these branches and we visited one of them toward the end of our stay in the city.

The exchange station we saw was housed in a former social club, the recreational center of the French Settlement before Liberation. The rooms had high ceilings and wood paneling and were lavishly carved and molded. But they were no longer the scene of the imperialists' entertainment; now they provided a center for ordinary people to participate in the scientific and technological development of their country.

The work of the exchange station is carried out in several different ways: there are development teams of specialists who publicize their work; there are classes, conferences, and publications mostly geared for people in scientific fields; and there are the large exhibits and the work done at youth palaces, both aimed at the general public. In the exchange stations of Shanghai there are sixty-three development teams altogether, in fields that include electroplating and laser technology, with more than four thousand members. Part of their job is to popularize new techniques and processes among workers and technicians. The station we visited was emphasizing the use of statistical and systems analysis for selecting the best production methods. The teams also set up large exhibitions in their own buildings where the results of particular three-in-one combinations are displayed, with the participants usually available to discuss their work. An exhibit of the local uses of microbiology was on at the time of our visit, it had been seen by 300,000 people in five months. When specific problem solving is required, factory workers and technicians come to the exchange station for consultations with development teams or specialists with experience in related areas.

Most of the work we saw was going on in classes and conferences. Each year the station arranges at least ten conferences with two or three thousand participants on particular questions of science and technology. It also offered sixty-nine courses during 1972, many taught by experienced workers and technicians. In general the classes run from two to five months; last year they were attended by 40,000 people.

We visited a group that was discussing the use of the laser in retinal attachment operations and watched the laser in operation. The group has thirty-five members, meets once a week, and is made up of equal numbers of workers, technicians, and political cadres. Then, in a big lecture room, we sat in on part of a lecture on computer memories. The course covers the use of computers in industrial control systems and runs for six months. Students learn some basic computer theory, study the hardware and the software, and investigate examples of industrial application. Half of the two hundred students in the class were factory workers and half were technicians.

One of the ornately decorated dining rooms of the former social club had been turned into a theater, and a film on multipurpose use of industrial wastes was being shown to a class. The film showed different experiences that factories have had in utilizing their wastes and concentrated specifically on the recovery of solid particles from smoke for use in making bricks and fertilizers. It showed how people can become involved in controlling industrial pollution by raising the problem with factory workers. In the film, factory workers and technicians in three-in-one teams were working on the problems and debating the politics of pollution control. Animated sequences explained the action and mechanism of various control methods. It was clear that motivation was considered as important as technique in tackling a technical problem, and that even in technical education the "experts only" approach was scorned.

Written communication also spreads science and technology. At this station a group from Shanghai hospitals and different departments at Futan University was writing a book on current medical uses of radioisotopes. It is being written both for mobile medical teams in rural areas and to provide basic theory and practical applications for barefoot doctors. To understand the situation in the countryside, members of the writing group often leave their city jobs to do investigatory work in rural areas.

Through these various methods the exchange station spreads the knowledge and application of technology among the Chinese people. "Exchange" is absolutely essential if the fruits of science are to be enjoyed by everyone in society.

Factory Health and Safety. After our tour of the Peking Number 3 Textile Mill one of our hosts said to us:

> Though we have achieved some of our purposes in the past years, we still have some shortcomings in our work. For instance, in the work of cleaning and tidying our shop; there are pieces of cotton flying in the air and the sounds are too noisy. So we are organizing the workers to make improvements on these shortcomings.

The noise level in the loom room and also in one of the spinning rooms was in fact quite high. Excessive noise is uncomfortable and tiring, but it is more than a nuisance: it can cause a form of deafness that cannot be corrected by a hearing aid. Occupational noise exposure causes the ear to lose sensitivity to high-pitched sounds but not to low ones, and the sensitivity can't be restored by the amplification of a hearing aid because it amplifies all tones equally. Therefore either the high tones will be too soft to be heard, or the low tones will be too loud. Because speech is made up of a full range of different tones, victims of occupational hearing loss are unable to understand speech.

Cotton dust is also a health hazard. Many people are sensitive to some part of the dust and suffer a type of asthmatic reaction to it. Continued exposure can result in damage to the lungs, a disease called byssinosis, or "brown lung." These hazards are common in industry in the United States as well as the rest of the world. In particular, the cotton dust problem exists in the most modern textile plants in the West.

The Chinese attitude toward these problems was of course a matter of interest to us. As a part of the factory medical program, hearing tests are given to the workers: most were all right, said our hosts, but a few had shown hearing problems. We were disturbed to learn, however, that the latter had not been routinely rotated from noisier to quieter jobs; it was said that this would hurt the quality of production. We also noticed that workers did not wear

ear plugs in the textile mill or other factories. The leadership said that the workers did not like ear plugs and that the effort needed to have them worn has not been made. One of our hosts presented the attitude of the factory leadership toward the noise problem:

> The noise from the looms is mainly coming from the shuttles banging against the machine. So now we are experimenting on a new machine that has a shuttleless loom. In some countries, such as western ones and Japan, they have already put these machines into practice. We are trying to learn from that practice so as to reduce the noise.

In other words, engineering changes will be relied on to solve the noise problem.

Both excessive noise and cotton dust pose threats of a peculiar kind. Their irreversible ill effects appear slowly and are often not apparent to the victim or those around him or her until the problem is fairly far along. A long exposure is needed before the threshold of obvious appearance is reached, until hearing has become sufficiently impaired, or lung function sufficiently deficient, for the victim to become conscious of it. And, although a large number of workers may be subjected to the hazard, only a small fraction of them will show sufficient ill effects for it to be noticed.

In this sense, experience is very important: sufficient industrial experience so that the work force is exposed to conditions over a period of time, and sufficient medical experience to observe the effects. China has had a very limited amount of both types of experience, especially a medical system concerned with the masses of workers. Or course there is a considerable amount of material on this subject in the international medical literature, and the Chinese indicated that they were making use of it. We encouraged them to do so, for this was one instance where it seemed to us that pure self-reliance could have ill effects on Chinese workers.

Occupational health consciousness in the United States

has recently received a big push from the environmental movement. People started worrying about the toxic properties of the relatively low amounts of dangerous chemicals in the environment, like pesticides and air pollutants. Once the public began to worry about health problems that were not immediately visible, the dangers in the industrial environment received widespread publicity. In America the aggressive attitude that many people have toward such threats is probably tied to a distrust of the motives and methods of industry. We have no doubt, on the basis of what we saw in China, that the workers there will not be kept uninformed of these hazards or forced to acquiesce to their existence. Instead, because they control the system, they will be able to evaluate the problems and set priorities for solving them.

The factory medical system and the workers' organizations in China seem to do an excellent job in dealing with acute medical problems and accidents. One of the workers at the Shanghai Machine Tool Works gave us some information about the program there:

There is a professional safety section in this factory to prevent accidents. It frequently gives education on safety and insurance, and tells workers that they must work according to production regulations. It tries to mobilize workers to spend their spare time preventing accidents. If an accident happens, it organizes workers in the area to discuss it and to use it in educating others, in connection with Chairman Mao's teachings to turn bad things into good things.

Injured workers get full pay for as long as they need to recover and return to work. If a hospital stay is required it is paid for, along with a special food allowance. Of course accidents are a much more immediate and recognizable problem in the shop than hidden health threats. But the involvement of rank-and-file workers in the investigation of these problems and the suggestion of new work rules indicates that the factory leadership is not trying to hush up or minimize these matters.

Medical workers at the Shanghai plant told us that workers exposed to nickel and other metals were given regular blood tests and were rotated to other jobs if such material turned up in their blood. They also told us about an aspect of production that uses benzene as a lacquer solvent: "It gives workers a headache and makes them feel weak. We took some measures, improved ventilation and cooled down the operation to reduce the spread in the air." Benzene is an especially toxic material that is implicated in causing leukemia and other blood diseases. We suggested that other, less toxic solvents be substituted for it whenever possible. The solution resorted to in this case was another example of engineering controls—modifying some aspect of the process to make it safer and to solve the immediate problem.

At the Machine Tool Works the three-in-one team concerned with industrial health and safety has made a thorough investigation of working conditions. Machine tool manufacturing happens to be the kind of industry that has fewer health than safety problems.

One observation that came out of our visits to various factories is that concern for the health of workers is now a political issue in China. Comrade Ts'ao, a worker representative to the Revolutionary Committee of the Shanghai Electrochemical Works, gave us some background:

Before the Cultural Revolution, when new workers enrolled, the leaders were afraid to tell them what kind of chemicals were harmful to people. They were not willing to tell the truth because they were afraid that the workers would not work in the factory. When workers were poisoned, they were afraid to tell them about the diseases they had.

The cost of this attitude of the leadership was measured in terms of fourteen workers who were found to have been poisoned between the time the plant was opened and the start of the Cultural Revolution in 1966. Ts'ao said that these workers had recovered sufficiently to return to work, although not at the same jobs.

Now a week-to-ten-day course is given to all newcomers to the Electrochemical Works. The introduction to the plant includes information about the job, medical information, a study of the work rules, and a discussion about the hazardous properties of the chemicals used. The course also includes political study. The factory medical program is oriented toward the health hazards involved in chemical work. Three of the doctors at the clinic are mainly concerned with occupational disease. They oversee a series of periodic examinations of workers, including liver tests, lung function tests, and special nerve tests for those who work with carbon disulfide. If signs of trouble arise during these examinations, more comprehensive examinations and treatment follow. Job rotation usually comes after the discovery of ill effects; the factory also shares a rest house if bed rest is required. Ts'ao told us that since the Cultural Revolution three-in-one groups have been set up for the treatment of environmental contaminants and have greatly improved the health situation. "Since then," he said "not a single worker has suffered from occupational disease."

Handicapped workers (The Number 2 Low-Tension Electrical Factory, Shanghai)

In 1959 I came to this factory to take part in production. Before Liberation I was a fortuneteller for seven or eight years, but I never had enough to eat. Now I work in this factory; I got married and have two children who are studying in the third and fourth grade at primary school. In the old society I couldn't read or write, but after Liberation I went to school to learn Braille, and now I too can study. The thing I feel most deeply is that in the old society we blind people were looked down upon by others, while now we are politically and economically equal with all other people. With the help of the Communist Party and Chairman Mao, I was able to attend the national conference of blind and deaf-mute people. Premier Chou En-lai was very busy, but he took the time to confer with us. We blind people owe our great happiness today to the wise leadership of Chairman Mao and the Communist Party. In the old society we could never have even dreamed of this. The old society's bitterness made many normal people blind, deaf, or disabled; now we are disabled only physically, but are healthy in hand and mind. We not only take part in productive labor, we have cultural events and join the normal soldiers, peasants, and workers in meetings to write poems in praise of the leadership of our Party.

The speaker was one of the older factory workers, a tall man who had been blind since childhood. We met him when we visited the Number 2 Low-Tension Electrical Factory in Shanghai. This factory showed us a different side of Chinese industry; its main task is to organize blind and deaf-mute people to take part in production. Of the 409 workers and staff at the plant, 117 are blind, 85 are deaf-mute, 40 are disabled, and 167 are normal. The factory was built in 1958 and, with eleven workers, started producing rulers. Now its main products are electrical plugs and sockets and all its machines have special characteristics to suit deaf and blind workers. The blind workers mainly produce copper parts and the deaf-mute workers concentrate on the plastic parts. In addition, they study the works of Marx, Engels, Lenin, Stalin, and Chairman Mao to help them deal with their physical problems. In the electrical factory there are handicapped members of the Communist Party and the Communist Youth League. Since the Cultural Revolution, we were told, the blind and deaf workers have started to take part in the management of the factory and are now in all levels of its leadership.

The old blind worker continued his story, describing the oppression of the handicapped before Liberation.

When I think of the bitterness of the old society, when our country was semifeudal and semicolonial, I recall that the broad masses of working people had no jobs. At that time we blind people especially were looked down upon by other people. . . . Because I had no job I was forced to earn a living by telling people that they were either lucky and would have good fortune or that they were unlucky and would have a miserable life. Even when it was cold and snowing I had to go out with my stick. Sometimes I could get a little money and eat, but very often I went hungry. We not only suffered from cold and hunger, but also from the hooligans who oppressed us. Whether we had gotten a little money or not, we had to pay off the hooligans. If we didn't pay them, they would not allow us in the street. We had a saying among the blind people about the greatest terror being cold. When it snowed there were not many people in the street to give us money, so many of the blind people died of cold and hunger.

I would like to tell you how I came to realize that fortunetelling was not the truth. At the beginning, I did not see this clearly. We blind people had been fortunetellers for years, but we could not tell where our own fortunes lay—why we were oppressed by the others. I only knew that we were unfortunate in not having what others had; while I thought that capitalists were just very lucky people. I knew nothing about class struggle. After Liberation we carried out many political movements, especially in 1952 and '53 when we criticized fetishes and the reactionary rulers who had used them to oppress people. Through this education I raised my own consciousness.

Before I was fourteen my eyes were normal. In 1938 I got some disease in my eye. It was not serious, but we had no money for a doctor, so it became more and more serious, Eventually my right eye went blind, but my left eye could still see. My mother was very poor and believed in fetishes. She asked a fetish man to come and see me. He said that the cover [sclera] of my eye should be taken off and put on a chicken so that I could see again. She let him do that, and then my left eye also became blind. From my own experience I learned how wrong it was to use fetishes on other people. . . .

We began to study politics and the works of Chairman Mao. He said in his "Report on an Investigation of the Peasant Movement in Hunan" that the peasants were raising their fortunes through their own struggles; I began to realize that "fortune" was not due to luck. I learned why we laboring people suffered in the old society; how the state was run by one class to oppress the other. . . . Chairman Mao said that if oppressed people want to win their liberation, they must first wage their own struggle and then they must win the support of people in other countries. Many people in the world are still oppressed, and we must fight for them as well as for ourselves.

There is a clinic in the factory in which health workers treat common diseases, do health teaching and propaganda work among the workers, and immunize the babies in the factory nursery. Because there are eighty-five deaf-mutes in the factory, part of the clinic's job is different from that of similar industrial clinics. A health worker "trained from the workers" administers acupuncture treatment to the deaf-mutes. This new use for acupuncture originated in 1968 with an army medical team in Northeast China. After repeated experiments on themselves, they located the nerve points that affect hearing. Teams were then sent all over China to set up schools and introduce the new method to existing institutions.

During our visit to the clinic one of the deaf-mute workers was receiving an acupuncture treatment. A point near the ear was being stimulated by the needle. This point, we were told, gives faster but more temporary results than points farther away in the hands and arms, which give slower but more permanent effects. Some patients respond after a few treatments while others take longer. Some don't respond at all. The health worker told us that results are better with young people, although all the deaf-mutes are treated regardless of age. Reports indicate that there has been some success in treatment in 90 percent of the cases where the affliction is a result of childhood disease. Of 168 students at the deaf-mute school in Liaoyüan that were treated by the army team in 1968, 157 regained their hearing and 149 were able to speak, according to a study described in *Sealing the Peaks in Medical Science* (published in Peking by the Foreign Languages Press, 1972).

After receiving the acupuncture treatment the worker, a young man in his late twenties, stood up and began singing "The East Is Red." He pronounced the words clearly and sang in a steady voice. After the song he clenched his fist, smiled broadly at us, and said, "Long live the friendship between the Chinese and American people."

Deaf-mute people, who were also looked down upon in the old society, have been emancipated and given a sense of self-reliance and pride. Their daily lives are normal: they work eight hours a day like other workers, and play ping-pong and watch movies in their spare time. There are translators for them at meetings, but other than that they can do most things for themselves. They do their own shopping and cooking; they marry and lead family lives.

The last personal testament we heard in the Low-Tension Electrical Factory was that of a blind worker who had to overcome the additional oppression of being a woman:

Today is March 11, and International Women's Day was three days ago. We blind women also have reason to celebrate this festival. We learned ... that in 1909 the laboring women in Chicago held a demonstration for equal rights, and today I was told that among the American friends here half of them are women, so the feeling is closer. I learned that the laboring masses in the United States of America have a rich revolutionary tradition. Today is a good chance for me to learn from you; you have learned a lot.

More than half of the workers in this factory are women. Just now, my comrades have told you of the bitterness in the old society when compared with the new society. This difference in the two societies we blind women have deep feeling about. Chairman Mao has said that in the old society the men were oppressed by three powers or mountains: politics, the feudal system, and feudal ideas. But women also suffered from the power of their husbands. So before Liberation women couldn't enjoy equal rights with men, politically, economically, or intellectually. But today we enjoy equal rights in every aspect with men. I'd like to take myself as an example.

In working time and in the operation of machines we women are equal to men. In our spare time we attend political and cultural classes. Of course there are many difficulties with this. The first is that there is much noise in the workshops with the machines running, and at first we blind people were afraid. After studying Chairman Mao's works, especially "The Foolish Old Man Who Removed the Mountains," and the quotation, "Be resolute, fear no sacrifice, and surmount every difficulty to win victories," we built correct ideas to overcome these difficulties. The experienced normal workers taught us hand in hand, and we just listened to them with our ears and remembered things with our minds. We touched the machines with our own hands and, after one or two weeks' training, we were operating the machines ourselves. Now we not only operate the machines, we can also take care of minor repairs.

In learning how to read and write we also experienced difficulties. We have to touch the words with our hands and feel them; words are written in fifty-two letters with six points each. At the beginning, after only a few minutes of touching the words, we would develop headaches. In winter, when it was cold, it was difficult to tell the difference in the points, and in summer sweat would distort our feeling of them. But after studying Chairman Mao's works

we learned that everything in the world is dialectical
and that we could understand our difficulties, seeing
everything from two different aspects. Among our
difficulties we then found some favorable aspects. The
first one was that Braille is different from characters
in that every word touched can be read, and that if
we were cold at night in the winter, we could take
our books under the quilts where it was warm and
read. Since we were reading with our hands, it was
unnecessary to turn on a light. We could study whenever we had time. After recognizing these favorable
conditions we were full of confidence to overcome
the difficulties.

Now all the blind people are reading the works of
Chairman Mao, Marx and Engels, and Stalin. We
also use Braille to write articles criticizing reactionary
lines and to praise today's happiness. We are very
glad to be in this factory and we are also very happy
to be in families. When blind people grow up now
they can get married and do some of the housework.
In the old society we were looked down on by others,
but in the new society all the people take care of us.
When I walk, many people whom I don't even know
lead me across the street or take me to a bus stop, or
even home. And the comrades from social service often come to our factory; even the vegetable markets
and banks send people to the factory to make things
easier. We know deeply that only in the new society
. . . can we blind people have such happiness.

Premier Chou En-lai has said that the American nation is a great nation and that the American people
are a great people. There is a tradition of friendship
between the Chinese and American peoples, and we
hope that many more American friends will come to
visit our factory.

It wasn't until we returned through Hong Kong, where
blind and crippled people sit in rows begging for a living,
that the full impact of the liberation of handicapped people in China really struck us. The phrase we heard so of-

ten, "People do not look down on those with problems," was in accordance with what we saw in China: bicycles driven by legless people using hand-cranked wheels, wheel chairs even in remote parts of the countryside, and blind people constantly being helped. The thorough integration of the handicapped into this vast and still poor society is another impressive indication that present-day China is a country in which the concept of refuse, human or material, is being overcome: everyone and everything is considered useful.

4 RESEARCH INSTITUTES

Scientific research in the United States is symbolized by white coats, air-conditioned buildings, fluorescent lights, and impressive electronic equipment in the hands of experts. There is a door between the laboratory and the world outside, and the door is usually kept closed to keep the air-conditioning in and non-scientists out. The Chinese are trying to create a different type of scientific research, a system in which the research worker and the production worker are united in serving the people, in which each understands the skills and contributions of the other, and in which eventually the distinctions between professionals and workers will be eliminated and their work will be fully integrated.

Chinese research workers are preeminently concerned with solving practical problems, making improvements, and serving immediate needs in agriculture, industrial production, and medical care. Fundamental research problems are expected to grow out of practical questions and to be tied to some demonstrated need, not merely devised by the scientist.

But emphasis on applied research is not the distinguishing feature of Chinese science. More important are the motivation and manner of research work. Every institution we saw emphasized the importance of working with and learning from the masses. It is this political outlook that determines the way researchers work on practical problems.

Scientists spend time at the farms and factories where their work will be applied, living with the peasants and workers and participating in the normal routine of work and study, as well as carrying out their technical role. During these visits they teach the local people about the theoretical basis of the various practical problems they face. The local people, in turn, take part in the research work and help the scientists. Mass mobilization, such as insect-control work in Peking or cancer screening in Shanghai, has advantages for scientific work. Likewise, working with the masses serves to reeducate the professional workers politically and give their research direction. In every research institute we saw evidence of this strong bond between science and the people. It is the open door to the outside.

Institute of Computer Technology, Shanghai. In Shanghai we visited one of China's centers of computer research. The Shanghai Computer Center began work in 1969, and in 1972 formed the basis for what is now the Shanghai Institute of Computer Technology. The Institute has a staff of 277 who work with its two digital computers, one a second-generation or transistor type, the other a third-generation or integrated-circuit type. The Institute's task, we were told, is to discover ways in which computers can both serve industry and further scientific research. Computer science must also serve "proletarian politics and socialist production," which means that the technology must be controlled by the working people and used to improve the workplace and the quality of life in general.

Theory and practice are linked in the Institute's work. Scientists researching theoretical problems of computer science are involved in practicalities as well. Working in the factories where the computers are built and tested, the scientists gain a better understanding of the machines and how they are constructed. By contrast, most computer programmers in the United States have very little idea how computers are built or how they function. The computer programmer in our delegation, who had five years' experience in programming, said he often felt quite ignorant when shown various computer hardware.

First on our tour of the Institute was the second-generation computer, which has a core memory of 8000 forty-two bit words and whose primary input device is a photoelectric paper tape reader handling 800 words a minute. Tapes are punched by the programmers themselves and most programs are written in ALGOL 60, a standard international programming language. Two small drums with an average access time of eighty milliseconds are used for auxiliary storage. The computer is operational for twenty-two hours a day, with the remaining two hours used for maintenance. A spark printer that works on special heat-sensitive paper is used for output. It prints dots in a five-by-seven matrix and has a set of sixty-four characters that includes numerals, the Roman alphabet, and arithmetic symbols. It can print 1500 characters a second.

Members of the Institute described the kind of work the computers are used for. Most of it is what we would call scientific programming: mathematical problems of engineering, statistical analysis, crystalline structure analysis, etc., as opposed to commercial programming or information systems. Among other large projects is the application of linear programming methods to such problems as scheduling of shipbuilding operations.

Chinese computer applications are primarily scientific rather than commercial. Commercial life in China is quite different from that of the United States. Charge accounts, credit cards, and many other things to which we apply computers in the United States do not exist in the Chinese economic system.

A particular problem in the use of computers for information processing in China is written Chinese. The 4000-plus characters of basic Chinese are too many to be used easily with computers. Some information is stored in a phonetic transcription of the common language, but this is not suitable for names of people, places, and so on because it is not uncommon for two names with exactly the same pronunciation to be written in Chinese with entirely different characters. A straight phonetic representation of names can cause ambiguities and confusion. This is not an insurmountable problem, but is nevertheless troublesome.

At the third-generation computer we watched a mathematician running his own program which was used to forecast ocean tides. This computer is larger and faster than the first one, with a core memory of 32,000 forty-eight bit words and handling 110,000 instructions a second. It has an 800-words-a-minute photoelectric paper tape reader, two spark printers, and four 1500-rpm drums with an average access time of forty milliseconds and a capacity of 14,000 words each. The central processing unit has forty-five instructions and is expandable to seventy.

Not long after our return from China, *Peking Review* reported the completion of China's first 1,000,000-instructions-per-second computer. Clearly the ones we saw were not the most advanced of Chinese computers.

We saw other computers during our visits to Tsinghua and Futan universities. The second-generation computer at Tsinghua, in Peking, was built by the students and is used for teaching computer science. This university was the scene of intense struggle during the Cultural Revolution, when rival factions of the student movement fought over how the university was to be run and who was to run it. We asked at the computer center whether the computer had been an object of battle on campus. They told us not at all, and were interested to hear that at American universities during the student movements of the 1960s the computer centers were on many occasions the location of protests by students opposed to university policies. At Tsinghua, however, the computers were simply used for teaching and research, and were not instruments of administrative policy or power. As in many other unexpected places, the words "Serve the People" were written in large characters on the top of the computer.

After our tour of the Shanghai Computer Institute,

several of our hosts took us over to the Shanghai Door Handle Street Factory. Street factories, small enterprises in urban neighborhoods of China, are collectively owned by the people who work in them. The workers are predominantly former housewives and other people who were previously outside the workforce. Depending upon the skills and materials available in the area, the products of such factories vary from handicrafts to integrated circuits.

This street factory had 437 workers, 80 percent of them former housewives with almost no education. Its main products were door handles and arm rests for automobiles. In 1970, our hosts explained, the street factory established a computer section; 74 of its workers began to meet with members of the Shanghai Institute of Computer Technology and the Computer Science Department of Shanghai's Futan University, to see if they could make computers at the factory. This three-in-one team set out to build advanced third-generation computers. Many obstacles had to be overcome, especially the lack of education among the workers in the street factory. Some of them had no idea what a computer was. Yet within a year and a half they finished their first computer. The second was finished a year later: the machine that we had seen at the computer institute. The third computer was being finished after three months' work and they hoped to finish four more this year.

The workers in the street factory spend a great deal of time learning about computers as they build them. Many of them visit the Institute and the University, as well as other computer factories, to increase their knowledge, and a full quarter of the time at work is spent studying the fundamentals of electricity, electronics, and computer architecture. We were told that workers learn quickly because they are involved in the processes they are studying, and that their work improves as a result of their increased understanding.

People from the University and the Institute do more than just contribute the plans and designs for the factory's computers. They spend one day a week working alongside the factory workers. The computer workers said that the scientists and the workers learned from each other. Both considered the three-in-one combination of factory, institute, and university an important step toward the goal of eventually eliminating the distinction between mental and manual work.

At the street factory we traced some of the steps involved in the construction of a computer. In one room we saw iron cores being tested on oscilloscopes. These tiny doughnut-shaped rings of iron, less than a millimeter in diameter, are the basic component of the memory of most modern computers. When magnetized they have a north and a south magnetic pole which the computer uses as a binary digit: the north'pole being up would correspond to 1, and the south pole up would be 0. Wires running through the cores can detect and reverse the direction of magnetization, thus making it possible to store information and later retrieve it from the memory of the computer.

These cores must therefore be perfectly uniform in their magnetic properties; they will not work reliably if they contain impurities or are chipped. Oscilloscopes are used to test the tiny cores thoroughly. Each one in is put on a steel platform and a metal-pointed stylus is placed in the hole in its center. The oscilloscope then shows a wave pattern on the screen, from which the worker can tell if the core is electronically suitable. Each core is tested three times before it is sent to the weaving room. By that time almost all the defective cores have been eliminated.

We visited the core weaving room where the cores are strung onto wires and then woven into sheets of about nine by fourteen inches. Each sheet contains over 40,000 cores. Every core has both a vertical and a horizontal wire running through it so that the computer can "select" a single core out of the 40,000 by referencing one of the horizontal wires and one of the vertical wires. A separate wire, known as the sense wire, is woven through every core on the panel to detect any change in magnetization of the cores. When the computer references the core storage, it excites one of the horizontal wires and one of the vertical ones with half the required current to cause a core to change polarity of magnetization. Only in the single core passed through by both wires is there enough current to force the polarity of magnetization in the specified core to be in the same direction as the current. If the core is already magnetized in that direction, no change of polarity occurs and the sense wire is never excited; if the core was previously polarized in the opposite direction, a change of polarity occurs, causing current to flow in the sense wire. This is the way the memory of a computer is altered or referenced. Because there are no mechanical parts, the computer memory can store information which can then be accessed at incredibly high speeds.

After the cores are woven into panels, each panel must be thoroughly tested. If any cores are found to be defective—and some do get chipped during the weaving process—the wires passing through them must be removed and the cores replaced. Other rooms in the factory are devoted to testing the core panels electronically against ones which are known to be good.

The scene had a larger significance than merely one factory building in Shanghai. American computers are built in much the same way and by a comparable work force: most of the world's core weaving is done in Hong Kong, South Korea, and Taiwan, in addition to Mexico, Puerto Rico, and other parts of South America. The low cost of labor in these areas makes it profitable for computer companies to make the iron cores in the United States, ship them away to be strung and woven, and then return them to the United States to be assembled. These areas of cheap labor are vital to the profits of American computer companies. National liberation struggles in Indochina and elsewhere threaten the United States' economic and political control of East Asia. Consequently, the American computer companies have been active supporters of the war in Vietnam, as well as suppliers of material and technology.

Institute for Chemistry, Peking. Throughout our tour we found Chinese scientists eager to make contact with their

American counterparts and share common experiences. We received this kind of warm welcome at the Institute for Chemistry in Peking, where we were greeted by a group that included members of its revolutionary committee. Most of the initial talking was done by Liu Ta-kang, who was the acting director of the Institute and seemed to be its senior scientist. He was a member of the revolutionary committee, but he was addressed as "professor," which suggested that an older system of administration along academic lines still existed beside the newer revolutionary committee. Liu told us that the Institute was established in 1957 and now has a staff of some 600, half of them college graduates or experienced researchers. A hundred members of the staff have had some graduate training, and thirty or forty have studied abroad. About 40 percent of the researchers are women.

"Our work is mostly connected with industrial production," Liu told us, "and the concept of three-in-one is applied [research, education, and production as an integrated team]. Those who go to the factories face practical problems and learn from the workers. From these practical problems we will uncover fundamental ones for basic or exploratory research."

Most of the research at the Institute is in polymer chemistry. A polymer is a large molecule made up of many repeated chemical units. The properties of the material depend on the nature of the units. Fabrics such as rayon and nylon, adhesives such as epoxy, and all plastics are different types of synthetic polymers. Many natural materials are also polymers.

The institute is housed in a large, low building with the bare appearance one sees so often in northern China. The gray-painted hallways are dim, with light spilling in from the laboratories on either side. No effort has been expended on decoration; everything is functional. There is almost a frontier quality about these buildings. The rooms are cold, like the rest of Peking in winter. One image sticks: a chemist wearing a cap, weighing something on a laboratory scale, his white lab coat covering a padded jacket.

Comparison of laboratory equipment with that of the United States inevitably arose during our tour of the Institute. The clearest difference is the smaller number of major analytical instruments, which have been the main development in chemistry over the past two decades. Most were available in a central location, rather than in every laboratory as in America. Much of the work we saw at the Institute did not require such equipment, but of course research is usually tailored to the equipment available. During our discussions Liu Ta-kang and another senior scientist, Ch'ien Hen-yuan, who had been to the United States, mentioned the lack of these instruments as a shortcoming. Much of the other equipment in the laboratories appeared to be homemade but serviceable.

In most of the laboratories we visited the researcher had a card with a chemical structure or process displayed and often a sample of the product to illustrate the practical applications of the process. It was somewhat like a display of "Better Living through Chemistry."

One of the laboratories specialized in the alkaline polymerization of caprolactam. Su P'ing-lo, the researcher in charge, explained that here the task was to apply a knowledge of the mechanism of the chemical reaction to get a more quality-controlled product. Nylon, a synthetic polymer, is a long chain of smaller molecules made by condensing carboxylic acid and amine groups into amide linkages. These bonds resemble the ones that hold together proteins such as silk and wool, which is why nylon can mimic the properties of natural materials. Caprolactam, which reacts rapidly when treated with alkali to form nylon, is also called polyamide. The strength of the material formed depends on the length of the chain produced, and that is in turn the result of the rate of reaction and the way the materials are mixed together. Some aspects of the problem can be investigated in the laboratory, but ultimately it has to be worked out in the factory equipment. Su spends time in the factory with workers, and together they carry out experiments in which different conditions for the reaction are tried and the quality of the resultant material tested. Veteran workers understand the process quite well, according to Su, and he contributes any understanding they lack. The work in the factory also suggests ideas for laboratory studies on the nature of the reaction.

Another example of process development work that we saw concerned reinforced polyamide laminates, layers of glass filler stuck together by polymer polyamide into a solid block. This material is useful for various applications in electronics. Wo Yao, a woman in her thirties, explained the problem with the process to us. Small molecules are linked together to form medium-sized ones, creating a material called resin. To form the finished product, the reaction has to be completed, in this case by heat. The problem was that a solvent was needed and the only suitable one, dimethylformamide, was difficult to work with because of its high boiling point and its high toxicity to workers. By modifying the chemical composition of the resin, Wo Yao had been able to produce a resin which was soluble in alcohol and water, solving the toxicity problem and also producing a stronger material.

The finished product of another laboratory was on display: various articles of clothing held together by "glue," in this case a polyurethane adhesive. The idea for this work came from a factory that had problems with the shrinkage of thread. The workers hoped that the new adhesives would increase quality and production.

In a laboratory concerned with photosensitive polymers, a printing plate made with these materials was shown, along with the colored picture that had been made from the plate. Other researchers displayed acrylic adhesives for medical use, such as false teeth. Another group was developing applications for silicone polymers.

By contrast the research of another laboratory was without immediate application. Organic photoconductors, materials whose electrical properties change when they are struck by a particular wave length of light, were being tested in a rather elaborate but homemade apparatus involving light sources, timing devices, and an oscilloscope. The woman researcher told us that this project had been started after the Cultural Revolution and was simply exploratory, having been taken up because they thought it would be interesting, and because organic photoconductors might prove more practical than inorganic alternatives.

When we were in China the practices of Chinese institutions were always related to the Cultural Revolution and a major topic of discussion was change since that period. But the changes are not always simple to understand. One preconception we had about the effect of the Cultural Revolution on science was that it had channeled all efforts into applied fields, making scientific work justifiable only in terms of direct usefulness. Yet this photoconductive effect had been taken up as a subject for investigation after the Cultural Revolution, specifically because it was an interesting effect and not for immediate practical value. We were told that the Institute was also doing exploratory work on analytical chemistry techniques, the physical chemistry of polymer solutions, and other physical chemistry problems. The work of these laboratories seemed less directly related to specific production processes or products than the ones we visited.

Unlike the universities, the Research Institute for Chemistry remained in operation during the Cultural Revolution like other productive facilities such as factories. A few laboratories shut down for a while but, according to Liu Ta-kang, "work continued, mostly in the normal condition. Our [political] work was mainly to struggle against bourgeois ideology. Most of the leading members of the institute are still here." He added that most of the members had gone to work in factories or in the countryside at some point, except for those who were aged or infirm.

Research institutes, rather than universities, do most of the experimental laboratory science in China. In the past, university graduate students did research at the institute, and will probably do so again as graduate schools reopen. Institute members thought that some would return when the requirements of graduate education had been worked out. They doubted that graduate degrees would be granted, however, because such titles enhance the division of researchers from the masses. Although undergraduate university education had been revised and reinstituted through the Cultural Revolution, graduate studies were still under discussion for revision, and graduate schools, as known in the United States, remained closed at the time of our visit. Plans discussed with us indicated that some would reopen shortly. In other areas, such as medicine, curriculum revisions had shortened medical training so that it was not viewed as including "graduate work," but doctors were fully trained. Law schools, on the other hand, were not expected to reopen, because of a revision of the criminal justice system which abandoned adversary hearings in favor of an investigatory process not requiring attorneys. In general, Western distinctions between undergraduate and graduate work may disappear, although courses in different fields will differ in length.

We learned at the Chemistry Institute that international politics are involved even in the arcane subject of chemical nomenclature, which is crucial for any kind of international communication about the science. The Chinese have their own system which they try to adapt to the international usage. They told us that they have no contact with the International Union of Pure and Applied Chemistry, the official international body in the area, because Taiwan is included among its members.

Several points of comparison between research science in China and the United States came out of our visit to this institute. One of the first is the motivation for the application of chemistry to new industrial products. New products for which needs have to be created artificially, and production improvements that put people out of work, are symbols of American technological development for us. Not so in China. There the application of technology is motivated by the needs of the people. "Plastic" has come to be used as a prime pejorative term in America. When we were shown the polyurethane adhesive for clothing (originally suggested by factory workers), one of our group said, "We have this in the United States as well, but it doesn't work." The origin of our negative attitude toward technical innovation is clear; it arises out of the fact that in the United States innovation's first use is for profit, and then perhaps incidentally to improve the quality of people's lives.

Another observation was that some aspects of an older form of research still seemed to exist. This laboratory had operated right through the Cultural Revolution and the decision-making structure in the Institute maintained at least some aspects of the professional hierarchy. Yet other practices in the laboratories—political study groups, criticism/self-criticism meetings, manual labor in factories, and the like—were aimed at breaking down the distinctions between professional and nonprofessional workers. The transformation of the forms of scientific research is a process that is still evolving, and it is not something that the Institute set out on its own to accomplish. It is a part of the revolutionary change of all institutions that was begun by the Communist Party and is intended to occur throughout the entire society. At home many of our group had discussed and pushed for democratizing practices in our workplaces, but we realized that it was in some ways like trying to create an island of good social practice, without the necessary change in the society as a whole— and an insular but good social practice is a "contradiction."

The transformation of the research institute in China is stimulated by its connection with industry. Researchers visit the factories in which their results are applied, where they discuss problems with factory workers and spend time at manual labor and political study with them. This process involves ideological remolding, but it also gives the researcher a better idea of what production is really like and a first-hand observation of the experiment. Workers from industry, also members of the basic three-in-one team, visit the institute in return. They discuss problems under study and take part in the general life of the institute, such as political study groups. In addition, the Institute for Chemistry has an "open house" every week at which representatives from any factory may come to discuss technical issues. Once more the research door is opened to the outside.

This kind of daily contact in the course of work is probably very important in determining the attitudes of Chinese intellectuals. Involvement of the masses in the normal routine of scientists makes it much harder to forget the lessons of the May Seventh Cadre Schools (so called from Mao Tse-tung's directive of that date, in 1968). These schools were established in the countryside during the Cultural Revolution, and many urban intellectuals and cadres spend a time of manual labor and ideological study in them. Factory work, or work in a people's commune, is often used for the same purpose.

Another important aspect of Chinese research is that there is obvious cooperation in the dissemination of scientific discoveries, rather than competition aimed at maintaining the dominant position of one researcher, laboratory, or business. The adhesives, synthetic fabrics, and plastic factories in Peking don't compete against each other for markets or higher profits. Consequently they share the results of scientific innovation rather than concealing them. The laboratories are open for sharing experiences, either during their "open houses" or through institutions like the Scientific and Technological Exchange Station in Shanghai. They are not trying to gain the lead in a race to the patent office.

Genetics Institute, Peking. The Institute of Genetics of the Chinese Academy of Sciences in Peking, like its counterparts in zoology, biochemistry, and entomology, is one of the important institutions backing up Chinese agriculture. Its large building is on the far outskirts of the capital city, appropriately surrounded by fields. We spent a morning there, visiting laboratories and talking to scientists and administrators. As was often the case at scientific institutions, an older staff member who had trained abroad served as an additional translator. At this institute Hu Han, a short, friendly, middle-aged woman who had studied physiological genetics at Ohio State University, interpreted for us and was particularly helpful in clarifying obscure technical words.

Before 1949 there was no genetics institute in China. In 1951 an office of genetics was created with a staff of only twenty. In 1959, when the Academy of Sciences created the Genetics Institute, the staff had grown to seventy. Now 350 people work there, including more than 200 scientists and technicians. The Institute was conducting experiments in three main areas: 1) studies on the transmission and variation of genetic characteristics—an area that includes work on rearing wheat and rice from pollen grains and work on potato and sweet potato genetics; 2) studies on heterosis and male sterility, including work on corn and sorghum genetics; and 3) studies on the structure and function of the principle genetic material deoxyribonucleic acid, or DNA, including work on bacterial genetics.

The first laboratory we visited was concerned with potato genetics. We talked there with Chiang Hsing-ts'un, a researcher who had graduated from Peking Agricultural University in 1959 and had worked with potatoes ever since. He told us that white potatoes are grown by planting pieces of old tubers left over from the preceding year's crop. This requires the winter storage of some potatoes each year to serve as "seed potatoes" for the next generation. In Central and South China problems with the degeneration of stored potatoes have seriously hindered their development as a major food source. In the past, large quantities of potatoes had to be shipped south each year.

Researchers at the Institute have worked on the problem for a number of years, but now they are very critical of the way they approached it before the Cultural Revolution. They relied too heavily, Chiang told us, on book knowledge, both foreign and Chinese. During the Cultural Revolution they began to put more emphasis on studying the problem in the field with the peasants, and since then their work has improved. They now believe that while potato degeneration does depend strongly on the hereditary characteristics of the varieties grown, methods of cultivation and storage are of great importance. For scientists to conclude that the problem they are considering is not primarily governed by factors from their own area of study, genetics in this case, is no small thing. In every Western country without exception any number of scientists are beating their heads against the walls of their own limited specialties, trying to solve in a narrow technical way problems that require a broad approach and knowledge from many fields.

Chiang noted that before Liberation some rich peasants of Anhwei Province, in East Central China, had mastered a potato preservation process but had kept it a secret to drive up the price of seed potatoes. Since Liberation the method had been popularized. From this experience he concluded, "If we work under the correct line, science can serve the people. If science is in the hands of the landlords and capitalists, it can't serve the people."

The laboratory works with sweet potatoes as well as white ones. These can be grown by vine cuttings taken from sprouting tubers. The peasants complained that one popular variety, Victory 100, had deteriorated greatly in the quantity of yield. Tests showed that yields had decreased in average length by 30 percent. Working closely with peasants growing sweet potatoes, the researchers found that they tended to choose long stems for vine cuttings because they are easier to cut than short ones. It happens that within and among single tubers there is genetic variation for vine length. By selecting long stems for cutting, people were choosing plants with an inherited tendency to have long stems and low yields. The researchers looked at other sweet potato varieties and found the same phenomenon, a tendency toward longer stems and lower yields. To counter this trend, the institute workers have selected shorter stems for many generations, and, in the process, created twenty new varieties, one of which, Peking Red, has increased yields by 20 to 30 percent.

During our visit to the potato lab we raised the question of what Chinese geneticists currently think of T. D. Lysenko, the controversial agronomist who once dominated Soviet genetics. Lysenko opposed classical Western genetics on the ground that it was "idealistic and metaphysical," and denounced such historical figures as Mendel and Morgan for hypothesizing imaginary genes and denying the influence of environment on the heredity of organisms (the inheritance of acquired characteristics). To their ideas he opposed the theories of Michurin, a retired Russian railway worker who had achieved great success breeding fruit trees. For a period of time, roughly from 1948 to 1956, Lysenko used his leverage within the Russian Communist Party to suppress debate between the two schools of thought, and enforced a virtual ban on experiments guided by the principles of classical genetics. We had heard that during the same period in China, Lysenko's ideas had strong support, especially in the agricultural research institutes, and that the Chinese scientists who pursued classical genetics were on the defensive intellectually.

In 1956 Lysenko lost some of his power in the Soviet Union and the clash between genetic schools of thought in China became much less one-sided. In 1957 Mao gave a very famous talk, "On the Correct Handling of Contradictions Among the People," in which he put forward ideas on how scientific disputes should be handled in a socialist country:

> We think that it is harmful to the growth of art and science if administrative measures are used to impose one particular style of art or school of thought and to ban another. Questions of right and wrong in the arts and sciences should be settled through free discussion in artistic and scientific circles and in the course of practical work in the arts and sciences. They should not be settled in summary fashion. A period of trial is often needed to determine whether something is right or wrong.

Whatever particular events Mao may have had in mind when he spoke these words, they are an effective critique of the handling of the genetics dispute, both in China and in the Soviet Union. From about 1956 onward it appears that the Michurinist and classical schools of genetics have coexisted in China. In the light of all this we posed our question about Lysenko.

A pause ensued; we pronounced the name again to make sure we had gotten our question across, and then all our hosts broke into a lively group discussion which never got translated. Finally the answer came back: "Lysenko thinks potato degeneration is induced by high temperatures. We think his theory isn't correct." We persisted with a question about Lysenko's more general genetic theories and they replied that it may be that in some cases external or environmental conditions can influence internal or genetic characters, but when and if this is the case, the external conditions are not the main influence. In conclusion, they offered the opinion that the controversy is in fact a theoretical problem that has not yet been studied in much detail. Perhaps Lysenko's period of trial is still going on in China.

We next visited a laboratory specializing in the genetics of bacteria and talked to researcher T'ung Ko-jung. His lab began working with the bacterium *Bacillus subtilis* around 1960. They use it to study a process called "transformation," in which pieces of DNA, the basic genetic material in almost all organisms, are extracted from one strain of bacteria and "fed" to a second. If the first strain of bacteria has hereditary characteristics that the second lacks, the second may come to possess them by incorporating pieces of DNA from the first strain into its own DNA. In the early 1960s, T'ung said, only the Americans had a transformable strain of *Bacillus subtilis*. But because the American government had forbidden all trade with China, the lab was unable to obtain samples of the transformable strain and the Chinese had to isolate their own. Now, he said, they can get bacteria samples directly from the United States.

The bacterial genetics staff also worked on the induction of mutations (permanent genetic changes), using nitrous acid. They were just beginning work on the processes involved in bacterial sporulation—the formation of tough spores which resist killing by light, heat, or desiccation. Interestingly, neither these projects nor the transformation project were being carried out with particular agricultural or industrial applications in mind.

The lab has conducted one research project with very direct industrial applications. It involves the use of protease enzymes in the manufacture of woolens. Enzymes are one kind of protein molecule found in living organisms. They help promote life-sustaining chemical reactions, like breaking down food into simple chemicals during digestion. Proteases are enzymes which perform the special function of breaking down protein molecules into smaller molecules. They are found in the stomach and can be extracted in industrial quantities from certain bacteria. These are the "enzymes" advertised in America for various brands of washday miracle cleansers. The Chinese use proteases in their woolen industry to improve the quality of the product, and researchers from the bacterial genetics lab go to the factories to help work out the process.

We moved on to a laboratory where new wheat and rice varieties are developed using very sophisticated methods. Researchers Ou-yang Ts'un-wei and Ch'en Ying explained to us that they had set up their project in response to complaints from the peasants that it took too long to develop new crop varieties. Traditional methods for breeding new varieties depend heavily on the development of "pure," or genetically homogeneous, lines which are then crossed in a controlled way to produce desired results. These pure lines are bred for genetic uniformity by crossing close relatives for many generations, usually at the rate of one or two generations a year. Because generation times are long, the production of pure lines is slow, and new varieties take years to develop.

The Genetics Institute researchers are developing a technique that circumvents part of this drawn-out process and produces pure lines in a period of a few months. They do this by growing adult plants from single pollen grains rather than from seed. Pollen grains are free-drifting sex organs that produce male germ cells which are similar in certain ways to sperm cells in human males. In effect, the Institute researchers are growing plants from single sperm cells, and thus from single parents. Pollen grains, like sperm cells, carry only half the normal adult amount of genetic material per cell. In normal mating, or pollination, they combine with an egg cell, also containing half the adult amount of genetic material, to produce a fertilized egg cell that will grow into a new adult with the normal amount of genetic material per cell. Technically speaking, the pollen and egg cells are haploid, with only half the adult amount of genetic material, while the cells of the adult they unite to produce are diploid, with a full dose of genetic material.

When a pollen grain grows into an adult plant without uniting with an egg, the adult plant itself is usually haploid. Such plants are smaller than normal, sterile, and not useful for breeding. But occasionally, in the early stages of growth, a single cell of such a haploid plant will spontaneously double its genetic material, forming a normal diploid cell that can grow into an adult capable of breeding. Such a plant can be bred to itself, since individual grain plants have both male and female reproductive organs, to produce a new line of plants with only one original parent. The line will be perfectly "pure" because the original pollen grain came from just one parent and carried just one representative of each kind of gene.

We were told that the method for growing pollen grains into adult plants was developed by an Indian scientist in 1964 and has now been applied to about twenty species, including tobacco, wheat, rice, cabbage, and millet. The Institute has concentrated its work on rice and wheat, China's two most important grain crops. So far the rate of diploid formation in wheat is very low, while in rice 50 percent of the pollen grains that germinate eventually form diploid adults. Scientists at the Institute think that in the future they will be able to control diploidization rates using a chemical called colchicine. They also hope that the haploid-diploid system will be of use in the future, not only in agriculture but also in more general investigations of the genetics of higher plants.

The group put great stress on their interactions with the peasants, saying that the peasants have welcomed varieties developed using the instant pure line technique. Peasants visit their laboratory often, and they in turn work in the fields to develop the new varieties, some of which have now been tested in Heilungkiang Province, in Northeast China, and on the outskirts of Peking.

We asked them whether they really try to teach the peasants ideas as complex as haploid-diploid genetic systems. They replied:

In general we don't introduce such abstract ideas to farmers. But with haploid-diploid we must introduce the idea because the work is at hand. We try to use simple language and find it easier to introduce such ideas to the local scientific staff. Young intellectuals, the new generation out in the countryside, have some knowledge and are much easier to teach when they come to the lab.

This corroborated what we learned elsewhere about the crucial role played by commune and brigade scientific groups in the dissemination of scientific knowledge in rural areas. It also gave us a small idea of the transformation wrought in the countryside by widespread junior high school education.

In the last laboratory we visited at this Institute four researchers described their experiments with male sterility and hybridization in sorghum and corn. These research workers too were enthusiastic about their collaboration with the peasants and drew connections between national political developments and advances in their research. Their work on male sterility had begun in 1958, during the Great Leap Forward. It accelerated during the Cultural Revolution, when they went out to work more closely with the peasants, and in four years they were able to develop more than ten new male-sterile lines of sorghum and forty new crop varieties of sorghum. Male sterility is a mutant genetic condition in which male flowers are defective and produce no functional pollen. When plants from a male-sterile line are grown in a field with a normal pollen-producing variety, all the seeds of the male-sterile plants must be the result of fertilization from the pollen-producing variety. This hybrid seed, or seed resulting from a cross of two different parent varieties, often produces plants which are more vigorous and productive than plants of either parent variety. Such crossbred plants are said to show "hybrid vigor," the technical term for which is "heterosis." Hybrid seed has great potential for raising production. Virtually all American field corn, for example, is grown from hybrid seed.

Our hosts said, "The mass movement in science is growing up rapidly to promote socialist agricultural development. Together with peasants and workers and other scientific institutions we have found problems to work with." One such problem is the abortion of female flowers in male-sterile lines, resulting in no seeds at all. After doing field tests with the aid of peasants, the researchers found that cultivation techniques, sowing time, fertilization, water supply, light, and ventilation all affected the tendency for female flowers to abort. By changing some of these conditions they were able to solve the problem. In the course of this work they also found that the degree of male sterility in male-sterile lines itself varies with the variety and with climatic factors, being higher in the north and at high altitudes.

Corn blight is another serious problem, and the Chinese have put a lot of work into developing blight-resistant varieties. This work has progressed very quickly, we were told, because it is connected to the mass movement. The peasants themselves judge new crosses on a grand scale, permitting mass planting of new varieties just four years after the first test hybrid cross is made. At present China has 26,000,000 *mu* planted in hybrid corn.

At the end of our visit to the Genetics Institute we asked our hosts about the future of research there. In our visits to the laboratories we had noticed the striking absence of young researchers; the youngest scientists we met had attended college in the early 1960's. The age gap, we knew, reflected the impact of the Cultural Revolution, when for several years the universities had simply turned out no graduates. University people told us that most of the upcoming crop of graduates would return to production in agriculture and industry. Our institute hosts expected some future researchers to come directly from peasant backgrounds, but also thought some university graduates would come directly to work at the Institute rather than returning to production. Our impression was that these questions are still being actively considered and debated.

Institute for Biochemistry, Shanghai. In 1965 China announced that scientists at the Institute for Biochemistry in Shanghai had succeeded in synthesizing biologically active insulin. Insulin is a protein of fifty-one amino acids and the task of assembling them into the authentic material was a major scientific achievement that surprised the West nearly as much as Sputnik had some years before. Between that time and the present, however, the Cultural Revolution had intervened, and we were curious to see how the change in social attitudes had affected laboratories concerned with such very basic research.

K'ung Chiang-Fu, introduced as the leading member of the revolutionary committee of the Institute, summarized some of the changes for us:

> Due to the interference of the revisionist line of Liu Shao-ch'i before the Cultural Revolution, there were many bad aspects to our research work. During the Cultural Revolution we followed the leadership of Chairman Mao and repudiated the revisionist line: the line which severs theory from practical application, the line of expertise, and the line that divides intellectuals from laboring people. At present, we adhere strictly to the revolutionary line of Chairman Mao that science must serve the people and proletarian politics, and that scientific research must be related to productive labor. During the Cultural Revolution, our institute formed a revolutionary committee, including old, middle-aged, and young members ... Our research workers go to the countryside and factories to receive reeducation from the peasants and workers. Now, in addition to problems of

theoretical importance, we also study many problems of practical application.

That sounds like the Party line, and it is. But in China that isn't the pejorative term that is in the United States. In fact, K'ung's introduction seemed to be a succinct, carefully worded statement about the situation at the Institute in the light of its recent history. It resembled what many of the intellectuals we met in China who had gone through similar situations told us.

The Institute for Biochemistry shares a building with the Institute of Physiology. Founded after Liberation as a single Institute, the staff was divided into two bodies after the Great Leap Forward began. The Institute for Biochemistry started with fifty members and has now grown to a total of 380, with four major divisions: protein synthesis, enzyme structure and function, nucleic acids, and metabolism. Production facilities at the Institute include the East Wind Biochemicals Factory, set up to supply materials needed for the insulin synthesis work and now branching out to supply chemicals to other institutions as well. The institute's machine shop, in addition to maintenance, makes automatic amino acid analyzers (for determining protein structure), flash evaporators, and fraction collectors.

The protein synthesis work is the most famous accomplishment of this institute. It's interesting to consider the motivation involved in undertaking this kind of project, which at first glance seems to go beyond the priorities of applied research. Only the most minute amount of such a large protein could be produced, and for medical purposes natural sources would continue to furnish the best supply. One of the justifications given us for the project was purely political. Hu Shih-ch'uan, leader of the number one protein synthesis laboratory, has stated:

Our great leader Engels said that protein is a form of life. By synthesizing it from chemicals we proved the correctness of materialism and discredited idealism, which holds that biological substances can only be obtained from living matter.

Comrade Hu, a member of our host group in Shanghai, had been to the United States in 1972 as part of an official group of scientists. From the personal conversations we had with him during our stay in Shanghai, it was clear to us that the abstract basis of the project, as he described it in that statement, was one of the main reasons the work was undertaken.

Of course there were practical aspects as well. The synthetic work is useful for altering the structure of the protein so as to understand the relationship of the structure to the hormonal function. In addition, the techniques developed in insulin synthesis were being applied to the synthesis of chemicals called peptides, which are smaller molecules of the same type as proteins and are reasonable to synthesize in commercial or experimental quantities. The laboratory was already producing oxytocin, a peptide hormone, in hundred-gram lots. Oxytocin is produced in the pituitary gland; it helps to regulate blood pressure and is used in hypertension research. Since diseases associated with high blood pressure, particularly stroke, are a major cause of death in China, this work clearly has a high priority in terms of health research.

A worker in this laboratory, standing next to a model of the insulin molecule, told us that "after the synthesis, the X-ray crystallographic work was completed in three years. The problem had been considered in the West for many years." This proud statement, one of the few we heard that even suggested competitiveness among Chinese scientists, was followed by apologies for the limited facilities in the laboratory. There were few of the automatic instruments and pieces of advanced equipment that would have been considered essential for such an accomplishment in the West. K'ung said, "We have had some successes. But in comparison to the needs of our people, we have many things yet to be done. Our equipment for biochemicals research is rather old; we try to learn advanced techniques from other countries in order to catch up with higher levels of work."

One of the basic aims of the Institute is to meet immediate needs while continuing its fundamental work. A group of biochemists has attempted this with nucleic acids, such as DNA. Because of their importance in genetics, nucleic acids have been the subject of intensive and refined investigations in Western laboratories. While the knowledge gained from these studies is fundamental in every sense of the word, the social application of the research, with the exception of some areas of medicine, has been small.

During the Cultural Revolution the members of the nucleic acid group at the Institute decided to forge a closer connection between their own work and agriculture. One of them said to us:

> Chairman Mao teaches us to prepare against invasion and bad weather. Science must serve the people, so we started to study the application of nucleic acids to agriculture ... Scientific workers go to the countryside, to receive reeducation from poor and lower-middle peasants, so that they can help to elevate the standard of knowledge among the masses. Throughout this work, scientific workers ... breathe together with the masses.

The researchers had read reports, in both foreign and Chinese scientific literature, of nucleic acid mixtures boosting the yields of some crops. After discussion within the group and consultation with leading members of the Institute, they decided to take up work on this problem. As a result, they have shown that spraying rice fields with nucleotide rich hydrolysates increases the yields consistently. Nucleotides are small pieces of nucleic acids. A hydrolysate is just a chemically digested mixture of molecules. To obtain the hydrolysate for their experiments, they processed large quantities of nucleic acid–rich brewers' waste and bean-curd waste. The mechanism behind the increase in yields is not clear, but preliminary experiments using radioactive phosphorus compounds as tracers suggest that nucleotides increase root absorption of water and minerals.

The nucleic acid group conducts its experiments with members of a commune in a Shanghai suburb. They also help with the work on the commune, and one member of the group has lived there since 1970. Peasants from the commune frequently return their visits and come to the institute to ask questions and discuss problems. The group also practices "socialist cooperation between units" by working in concert with the local agricultural research institutes.

It is virtually inconceivable that nucleic acid biochemists in an American Institute or university would even consider working on the problem this group has tackled, let alone involve nonscientists in its solution. The prejudices among this country's biochemists against working with crude chemical preparations and outside the context of sophisticated lab equipment are just too strong. If an individual scientist were to undertake such a project, he would probably face the disapproval of his colleagues on the ground that such work was professionally irrelevant to the main thrust of nucleic acid research. But in China this application of research work is considered exemplary.

We also discussed the work of the metabolism laboratory in the institute, which is concerned with the biochemistry of the liver. In 1970 the lab started a project to devise methods for early diagnosis and cure of liver cancer. The work began in the laboratory and then moved to the field for further testing. The method settled upon, after several were tried, was the alpha-fetal globulin test. Cancer cells become dedifferentiated—that is, they lose the cell characteristics of the particular tissue they come from—and become like the cells in the early stages of the development of the fetus. Alpha-fetal globulin is a particular protein characteristic of the fetus which is not normally present in adult humans but is found in blood when the cancer is present. Very sensitive and advanced methods exist for detecting the presence of particular proteins, and such methods are relatively easy to carry out in practice. The alpha-fetal globulin test, which reaches an 80-

percent-positive diagnosis in primary cancer of the liver, is now used throughout China. Workers in the laboratory go out to the countryside to educate and mobilize the masses in cooperation with local medical personnel, especially the barefoot doctors. Last year, they told us, they had screened between fifty and sixty thousand people.

Another aspect of prevention work concerns the identification and elimination of chemical agents that cause cancer. Some of the research being carried out is concerned with certain molds that produce cancer-causing materials when they grow on foods. The most important of these chemicals being studied, called afflatoxin, produces liver cancer.

There is a coordinated plan of cancer research for the whole of China. In Shanghai the emphasis is on liver cancer, while in Peking it is on cancer of the gastrointestinal tract. Several national institutes, including the Institutes of Experimental Biology, Cancer Research, and Labor Health, seek out factories where the incidence of cancer is high and investigate the causes. There are annual meetings between the different units to share experiences and discuss the future division of tasks. The national coordinating group is in Shanghai. One of the Institute members there described the changes in cancer research work:

> Before the Cultural Revolution we also did cancer research, but we studied the problem in isolation from the great masses, only in the laboratory. During that time papers were published, but they were not used by the people because of the interference of the revisionist line. Now, however, we serve the people wholeheartedly.

The publishing of scientific papers is the main "product" of fundamental research, so that the knowledge gained can be widely disseminated. Many Chinese scientific journals are now resuming publication after a lapse of several years during the Cultural Revolution. Our hosts told us that throughout those years the interchange of scientific knowledge was maintained by personal contacts, short written communications, verbally delivered papers, and meetings. For example, in the midst of the Cultural Revolution a national conference of Chinese scientists discussed the results of work on the crystal structure of insulin. At the time of our visit a report on the further work on insulin structure was at the press and scheduled to be published in *Scientia Sinica*. Other papers are expected to be published in Chinese journals that are distributed internationally, rather than submitted to foreign publications.

We learned that the form current publishing should take is a major topic of discussion in Chinese scientific circles. For instance, the question of whether articles should be signed by individuals or groups is a difficult matter. A discovery is always the result of teamwork, not only within the laboratory that does the research but also among the larger number of people who support the scientists, provide their livelihood, and manufacture their equipment. The general opinion in China is that "Science is the summation of the experience of the laboring people." Still, there are individuals, some with extraordinary talents, who take the final step of making a discovery and should be known. In Western science, of course, individual authorship is intimately bound up with precisely the kinds of personal striving for status and glory that the Chinese criticized severely during the Cultural Revolution.

The reasons for the current plan to have some articles published by individual authors, with the rest bearing the name of the unit or group, were interesting. When we met P'u Chih-lung one of the older scientists at Canton's Chungshan University, he told us that although there was a fear that this practice would "induce a tendency toward individualism," individual names were important in assigning the responsibility for a specific research project. While great numbers of people contribute directly or indirectly to virtually all research achievements, only a small number of individuals bear responsibility for the execution and accuracy of any given piece of work.

This sense of continuing debate over political issues—and all issues are viewed as political—was also present when we asked the Institute staff about the effects of the

Cultural Revolution. The scientists said that a workers' propaganda team had come to the Institute during the period and had been instrumental in effecting the basic changes that got the institution involved in the life of the masses. A workers' Mao Tse-tung Thought propaganda team, an alternative name for a Party work team, is one instrument for correcting political errors in Chinese society. When a factory, commune, university, or any other institution is having trouble, the Communist Party sends such a team to investigate, make suggestions, lead discussions, and oversee changes. Before the Cultural Revolution the Institute seems to have functioned much as a Western or Soviet research laboratory might. But that style was not considered appropriate to New China, and it was the propaganda team that helped carry through the resolution of political issues. Researchers said that the workers had "educated us through their proletarian example" and told stories of the old society. Meetings which included criticism/self-criticism sessions were held in small groups and in the Institute as a whole. Some members of the propaganda team are still there; they do administrative work and participate in political study groups. The result of their work was summed up for us by one of the researchers:

> Before the Cultural Revolution there were three divorces: between politics, practice, and laboring people. Through the education of the workers in political theory, we changed this tendency. Now we go out of the laboratories to the masses.

Institute for Physiology, Shanghai. The Institute for Physiology, with 280 staff members, had five major laboratories: physiology of nerve and muscle; sense organ physiology (vision and hearing); physiology of low oxygen tension, concerned with the adaption of organisms to high altitudes; reproductive physiology; and brain physiology—at present largely concerned with studying the mechanism of acupuncture. In addition, the institute maintained a factory to manufacture electronic equipment for the study of electrophysiology.

Two members of our group had a special interview on acupuncture research with Professor Chang Hsiang-t'ung in a small room off his laboratory, where he had shown us a simple demonstration experiment in acupuncture using a rabbit. The rabbit was suspended in a canvas sling and a pinpoint heat stimulus was applied to its nose. With a stop watch Professor Chang timed its first struggle, the point at which the stimulus became painful. An acupuncture needle for analgesia, or removal of pain, was then inserted in a hind leg and after a little time the heat stimulus was again applied. The pain response was considerably delayed, though the needle had been inserted for only a short time. After its removal, and a lapse of time, the pain response was the same as before the needling.

The laboratory was just beginning a series of single nerve cell recording experiments to trace the nerve signal interactions in various parts of the brain during the analgesic process. A portion of the midbrain, known as the hypothalamus, is the main focus of current research. Single cell recording is a sophisticated electronic technique which Chinese laboratories have not had available until recently. With it, the scientists expect acupuncture analgesia research to progress rapidly in detailing the nervous system mechanisms underlying the effect. The following discussion with Professor Chang, which we give in direct interview form, since it was conducted entirely in English, offers some insight, not only into the techniques, but into the whole framework in which such research is done.

The Professor began: We had very little experience with this whole acupuncture research business because, you know, we are pure neurophysiologists. Before the Cultural Revolution we were divorced from all practical problems. Since the application of acupuncture "to" surgical operations in 1958 or 1959, we had been, like many others, quite uncertain about this technique. But many, many clinical cases proved that it really works. Although the effect varies, more and more cases were 100 percent successful. There were many cases which seemed to me very convincing. You see, even at those early stages of the development of this technique, it was quite amazing that a simple puncture could have such an effect. There must be some neurophysiological basis for it. We thought it was a real challenge to neurophysiologists and we felt that we ought to be able to explain it. That's why we started working on it in 1965 or 1966. Many of our research group went to the hospital to get some first-hand experience with the technique. We participated in the anesthesia part of operations; we learned acupuncture, we practiced the technique, and after our first-hand experience we came back to the laboratory to do some animal experiments. We also did some with normal human subjects and with patients. We decided the effect could be proven with animal subjects. There are many things one cannot do with human subjects, especially in the analysis of the nervous system. You have to assume transfer of the effect on humans to animals so that you can make a deeper analysis.

From 1966 until now, we have tried various ways to develop our theories. There are, of course, many possibilities which have been proposed: notably the neural theory which interprets this acupuncture business from a neurophysiological point of view. Some others believe there may be some chemical implications; that the effect may be transmitted by humoral factors. We cannot say, even now, that it is purely neural or humoral. We do not have enough evidence to prove our point and rule out other possibilities. Although we are concerned with the nervous system and believe that the mechanism is mainly neural, the process is clearly complicated. The organism responds to the procedure of acupuncture with many systems; it mobilizes all it can muster to meet this situation. You have afferent or sensory impulses pouring into the central nervous system, where they interact with each other, producing some effect. On the other hand, the various internal glands also react to this procedure, we believe, with the adrenocorticotrophic hormone (ACTH) or pituitary hormones, or blood pressure and blood sugar changes, and various other processes. But we, being neurophysiologists, are leaving these other problems for others to solve.

Q: Have they found such hormonal changes with acupuncture?

A: I'm not familiar with this work and don't know the details of it, but I think they are trying it; while I feel the main effect is neural. You see, in paraplegic patients who have no sensation or mobility in the lower part of the body due to spinal lesion, we do not get any analgesic effect with acupuncture when the needle is inserted in the lower part of the body. If there are no afferent impulses going into the central nervous system, there is no analgesic effect. I think that is very strong evidence against the humoral theory. If there is a chemical substance produced, as some claim, at the site of acupuncture which is transmitted to other parts of the body to produce the analgesic effects, then the effect should occur in these paraplegics. But it doesn't. The only difference with these patients is the lack of a nervous system which is intact. The humoral aspect of these patients is quite intact, because the blood supply and other body fluids circulate just the same way as in ordinary people; the only difference is that the nervous system isn't intact. Yet they do not show the analgesic effect. We have done quite a number of studies on these patients, testing the pain threshold before and after the application of acupuncture. There is simply no difference at all.

Q: We have read quite a few reports about acupuncture treatment, which apparently is not the same thing as the analgesic effect. Could you say something about the treatment of deaf people, for instance?

A: There are two main divisions of acupuncture: one is acupuncture anesthesia, or analgesia, and the second is acupuncture treatment. I think the mechanisms involved in these two aspects of acupuncture are different. At present we are mainly concerned with analgesia. We haven't even touched upon the problem of acupuncture treatment. I think it is much more complicated than analgesia.

Q: Are any other laboratories doing experiments on the treatment effect?

A: At the moment the main interest is in analgesia because this is the newest effect, having been applied only since 1958, and presents the most interesting research problem. I know very few people who are interested in the analysis of treatment effects; one of the reasons, at least, being the difficulty of analyzing it.

Q: Have systematic observations of the treatment effects been collected?

A: I believe so. There is quite a lot of experience, especially in clinics. But so far as the experimental analysis is concerned, I think there is very little.

Q: At the hospital we went to, we observed the removal of a cancer of the gum, and the patient was anesthetized by finger pressure from a single point. Could you say something about that?

A: This supports my theory. You see, I have a basic concept of acupuncture. We believe that the effect of acupuncture analgesia is a result of the interaction of two different sets of afferent impulses in the central nervous system. One set is the pain, or nociceptive, impulses arising from the site of lesion or pain. The other is the set of non-pain impulses arising from the site of acupuncture. These two impulses meet each other at various levels of the central nervous system, including the spinal cord, the brain stem, the thalamus, and perhaps the cerebral cortex. In those places the nociceptive impulses are inhibited by the non-pain impulses. We believe that all sensory impulses have some kind of analgesic effect, but the particular kind of sensation produced by acupuncture is the most effective. Let me repeat: Any kind of sensory input may have some analgesic effect, but that produced by acupuncture is the most effective. Pressure, mechanical vibration, rubbing or scratching, sound, visual stimuli, etc., have some analgesic effect. But I believe the kind of heavy, sore, very unpleasant feeling produced by the needle prick is the most effective. If you pinch the muscle between your thumb and forefinger hard, you will feel a very unpleasant, though not painful, sensation, which is similar. This explains the phenomenon you saw this morning, where pinching was used instead of a needle. I think needles give the best effects because they are easier to control, and it is not necessary to put your fingers in the operating field, which is clumsy and inconvenient. Needles can easily be controlled remotely with a low electrical current as stimulus. All the parameters, such as duration, pulse frequency, voltage, etc., can be controlled this way.

Q: Has acupuncture analgesia been used for dentistry?

A: Yes, I believe its use is widespread. Let me review what I have said: First, any kind of sensory input can have some analgesic effect, but acupuncture is the most effective; second, acupuncture of any part of the body may have some analgesic effect, but some particular points are more effective. Now you may ask which points are most effective. According to our experimental analyses, we believe that the points which are innervated by nerves arising from the same spinal segments as the nerves innervating the site of pain are the most effective. The further away segmentally, the less the effect. I think this point is of practical importance, because in clinical application you have to choose the best points for each operation. For instance, if you want to perform a thyroidectomy, you have to choose a point. There are many points you can use, but you want to choose the most effective one. So you want an acupuncture site innervated from the same segment that innervates the thyroid area, according to the principle of spinal segmentation.

Q: Has this been demonstrated in your animal experiments?

A: Yes, we found the pain-inhibiting effect of stimulating different nerves greatest according to this principle.

Q: Are the needle points always located in a muscle?

A: Most of them are in muscle-rich sites—some in skin or fascia, but those are less effective. In the ear the points are around the pinna, the outer shell of the ear. This is another branch of acupuncture. People claim that the acupuncture of ear points can be applied to many kinds of operations, such as those on inner organs. You see, the ear, I believe, is the only peripheral organ on the body

surface which is innervated by the vagus nerve, which innervates, as you know, most of the internal organs. The
innervation of the ear around the external meatus, the inner part of the outer ear, is quite complicated. It is innervated by the vagus nerve, the glossopharyngeal nerve, the
cervical nerve, etc. So if impulses from the acupuncture
site come into the vagal nucleus in the central nervous system, they have the opportunity to interact with impulses
from internal organ sites, according to the segmental principle. There the impulses can act on each other for the in-
hibition of pain. That's why acupuncture of the ear is effective with surgery on internal organs.

Q. I understand now how ear sites are effective in inhibiting pain from internal organs, but what about analgesia
of the skin at incision?

A: I think that can be interpreted this way: even in the
ear they use one, two, or more points. Also, there is a
general principle and a specific principle. The general principle is that any sensory stimulus will have some general
analgesic effect. So even a single ear point may have a
specific effect on the visceral organs and also a general effect, which includes the skin.

Q: How would you compare acupuncture analgesia, according to your theory, with the phenomenon of referred
pain?

A: There are some similarities. I think referred pain
also concerns the segmental principle. Referred pain is a
one-way process: it doesn't have the inhibiting effect, only
the pain. Of course, this is really only speculation. In
referred pain, for example, you may have a problem in a
kidney but feel the pain in your back. I have had this experience myself, and it is very unpleasant. When massage
or other physical therapy is given on the back you feel
some kind of relief. It may not be 100 percent effective,
but you cannot deny the effect: you feel some relief. The
effect from the peripheral areas reflects back to the organ.
I think this is according to the principle of segmentation.
So I believe referred pain has something in common with
the acupuncture analgesia effect.

Q: How do you explain the effectiveness of acupuncture

treatment in stopping headaches, especially serious ones such as migraines? When the needle is removed, the headache does not return.

A: This is a problem I don't think I can answer, because it concerns the question of acupuncture treatment.

Q: Do you think, then, that there is more than an analgesic effect in such cases?

A: I think there is more.

Q: Have blood pressure changes been recorded during acupuncture?

A: Sometimes. Let us try once more with this question of acupuncture for migraine headaches. You see, those points which are effective for relief of headaches are mostly located in parts innervated by the trigeminal nerve. Headache, generally speaking, arises from the irritation of the meninges* of the brain. These meninges are innervated, at least in part, by the trigeminal. So our principle still works for acupuncture treatment of headache. But let me add something else which may be of interest. What kinds of nerves have this effect of analgesia? We believe that is the activity of small-diameter fibers. In fact, this is an established principle in neurophysiology, discovered many years ago and proven in animal experiments. If you stimulate the small-diameter fibers, they will inhibit the activity of the smaller ones. So perhaps acupuncture mainly activates the larger fibers, if not the largest. Another important point for the interpretation of the analgesic effect: if pressure or rubbing can relieve or inhibit pain, it is probably because those stimuli do activate large fibers. The ideal conditions for acupuncture are when the needles only activate the large fibers. For instance, if you use electrical stimulation of the needle instead of manual manipulation, you should not use a strong stimulus because it would activate the small-diameter fibers and produce pain. The analgesic effect would not occur; on the contrary, more pain would be produced. You must selectively activate the large fibers.

---

*Meninges are a series of three membranes that enclose the central nervous system. These are not to be confused with blood vessels.

Q: One last question: Are you convinced by the empirical evidence that some deaf people have had hearing at least partially restored by acupuncture treatment?

A: In all fairness, I must say that there has been some effective treatment. You cannot say that any kind of deafness could be treated. I have no direct experience, but some functional disturbances seem to have been treated effectively. If the basic structures are intact, it can work; but if the basic elements are missing, the nerve fibers atrophied or destroyed, I think it would be impossible. We hope for the best, but we must also be realistic. Many patients with speech or hearing defects do have their basic structures intact, and these cases may well be helped. In fact, it is clear from clinical practices that only patients with residual hearing are helped.

Q: In your opinion, are there safety problems in acupuncture? We have seen a lot of young people practicing acupuncture in schools. Are there, for example, any indications of blood vessel or nerve damage with repeated treatments?

A: That is a very sensible question. I would say that it is common to all techniques that safety depends on who uses them and how experienced they are. In comparison to other methods of anesthesia, acupuncture is safer. In the hands of inexperienced people, it may not be safe. It is an easy technique for most people to master, however. You must have basic anatomical knowledge and you must avoid the large blood vessels, the vital organs, and the central nervous system. In the chest you could cause trouble. Generally, you could do little damage in the legs and arms. I think the school children are carefully instructed on simple points, and could cause no more than some pain or very minor tissue damage. Any technique in inexperienced hands could cause trouble.

At this point the time ran out on another fascinating discussion that we were reluctant to end. As research scientists, the feeling we got in this laboratory, where research was so obviously and directly linked to helping people concretely, was very exciting. Professor Chang had learned English while spending many years in the United States, and could share our concerns over the misuse of science. When we returned home to the United States, expensive acupuncture clinics were being opened by the medical profession. To us, acupuncture is true people's science—available to everyone in China at little or no cost, and relieving untold suffering. Very few people in the United States will have access to it in these first high-priced clinics, but we hope that it will become widely accepted and available.

In Shanghai several members of our group were given a detailed lesson in the acupuncture technique by a doctor and were convinced that nurses, aides, and paramedics could easily be trained to bring relief by acupuncture to great numbers of people. We have no doubt that exciting and useful research on the various effects will be carried out in this country and will promote friendship between Chinese and American research workers.

Institute for Zoology, Peking. The goldfish darted down into the lower reaches of the porcelain crock as one of our group leaned over to take its picture. Within the shed there were dozens of fish swimming around in the series of fifteen or twenty such vessels. Although they were normal looking, they were, microscopically, profoundly different from the pets we had seen in several houses. Each cell of these fish had two nuclei. When the fish were still just fertilized eggs, the nucleus of a rat cancer cell had been transplanted into them, alongside the fish cell nucleus. As the egg grew into a fish, the biochemical mechanisms of cell reproduction had dutifully copied both the original nucleus and the extra one.

The shed is in the courtyard of the Institute for Zoology and is part of the cancer research work done in the cytology, or cell study, laboratory. In a small room off the shed researchers were engaged in transplanting cell nuclei. This technique involves inserting the microscopic tip of a glass pipet into a cell, sucking the nucleus into the pipet, then inserting the pipet into the fish egg and expelling the nucleus into the interior of that egg. It is being attempted with tobacco plant cells, to see the result of inserting a plant cell nucleus into an animal cell. Such serious work seemed a bit incongruous in the makeshift room, where an electric hot plate was the major source of warmth against the Peking winter. In a more usual sort of laboratory, in the main building, women were doing similar work transplanting cancer cell nuclei into salamander eggs. Several other variations on this theme were also being tested in the Institute.

Cancer occurs when the normal process of control over the activities of a cell becomes deranged, and cells multiply themselves without end. Since control over the cell resides in the nucleus, the site of the genetic material, its manipulation may furnish basic information about the cause of cancer. Research like this is going on in other parts of the world as well as in China. The cytology laboratory was also investigating some drugs for the treatment of cancer, but had not yet reached the point of clincial testing.

Touring the laboratories at the Institute for Zoology was really fun for us. Most scientific work is hard to grasp if you're not trained in the particular field, and observers can have a difficult time making suggestions or asking intelligent questions. Here the work was understandable and clearly related to important problems.

The cytology workers had formerly been part of a larger laboratory of endocrinology, the study of hormones. Part of the endocrinology work we saw consisted of preparing a cat for an experiment in the mechanism of acupuncture anesthesia. Two women were working on the cat, which was clamped to a board with a breathing tube inserted in its throat. It had been given a local anesthetic and a muscle relaxant to cause paralysis; a nerve in its leg was to be exposed so that it could be stimulated electrically. The effect of acupuncture and other treatments on the pain threshold would be studied by following blood pressure changes as well as the electrical activity in two regions of the brain, the cortex and the hypothalamus. Information about the effect of acupuncture on this threshold would be used to help explain the mechanism of acupuncture and to develop an acupuncture site map for the cat.

At present there are in China three main lines of explanation of the mechanism of acupuncture. Besides the traditional channel theory, there is the neurophysiological one advanced by Professor Chang in Shanghai, and the hormonal theory, which this experiment was testing. The institute's acupuncture research is done in connection with the Friendship Hospital, also in Peking, a large facility whose staff does research.

Another laboratory that we saw in the endocrinology division was investigating fertility and sterility. The experiments involve the effect of gonadotropins, a class of hormone released by the pituitary gland, and prostaglandins, a newly discovered class of hormones. These hormones influence the maintenance of the corpus luteum, an endocrine structure necessary for the continuation of pregnancy. Crude preparations of these hormones, extracted from sheep, were being used in these experiments. Another laboratory was doing related work, studying the chemical and microscopic change in cellular organelles—structures within cells—under the influence of these hormones. Its work made use of the institute's electron microscope. The main application of this work is to increase the fertility of livestock by manipulating hormones to save pregnancies. The researchers did their field work at communes.

One of the experiments in progress was aimed at understanding the relationship of gonadotropins and prostaglandins to the secretion of progesterone, another hormone. Prostaglandins are a class of hormones only recently discovered and investigated: one of their effects is to increase the mobility of sperm. If the level of prostaglandin in semen is depressed, the sperm become less mobile and fertilization is prevented. The work on prostaglandins is of direct interest in the development of a male contraceptive pill. The workers in the laboratory were aware of this implication, but their main concern was increasing the fertility of livestock.

A third laboratory was doing fundamental research on the mechanism of insulin action. It is thought that the insulin molecule reacts or binds to a specific area on the outside of a cell, and that this interaction sets off the metabolic activity insulin is supposed to influence. In the experiments, radioactively labeled insulin is used in trying to identify this receptor site. Two important pieces of foreign equipment were being used in this lab, a gamma ray counter made in Hungary and a special type of scale made in Switzerland.

When the question of the Cultural Revolution was raised, the researchers told us that most of the Institute had continued to operate, although a few of the laboratories closed for a while. Some scientists went to work in the countryside but, as they said, "Many of us already spent a great deal of time in the countryside, so that was not a major change." More than 150 members of the Institute, nearly a third of the staff, had gone to May Seventh Cadre Schools. When we asked which of them were cadres, the entire host group broke into laughter. A woman comrade, who spoke English and had been very helpful to us during the tour, took the arm of one of the men who had been quiet for the entire visit, shook him a bit, and said, "He is our cadre." The humor of the moment suggested that the title and the distinction between cadre and worker is, at least in this case, not all that important.

There are some 500 staff members at the Institute, of whom three-fourths are research workers. The major portion of the work done there, in at least five of the ten laboratories, is with insects and their control. Besides the endocrinology and cytology laboratories already described, there are laboratories of insect physiology and toxicology, insect and mammalian ecology, and taxonomy, or classification of insects, vertebrates, and invertebrates. In addition, a laboratory of new technology is concerned with the maintenance of large equipment for research.

Some of the history of insect control work was told to us by a woman researcher in the taxonomy laboratory:

Before Liberation we had very little science and little knowledge of insects. In those days locusts were a grave problem. Their swarms darkened the sky and they ruined the crops. After Liberation we placed great emphasis on this problem. Scientific workers were sent to investigate the matter, and found that the locusts laid their eggs in marshy areas. They suggested that the water be dammed up, so that it would rise and flood the marshes, leaving the locusts no place to lay eggs.

We saw many of the important insects on display in glass cases, including several beautiful butterflies and a species of insect used in traditional medicine in northwest China. Some of the specimens were collected by the researchers when they went to the fields, others by technicians at the communes. These agricultural technicians, usually supported by the communes themselves, have pest control as one of their major duties. When the research scientists go to the communes they work with them, and sometimes the technicians come to the Institute for training and discussions.

As in the United States today—recently and belatedly—the Chinese insect control program includes the study of insect hormones, especially juvenile hormones and sex pheromones. These methods are potential substitutes for the use of chemical insecticides. The laboratories were equipped to isolate chemicals from insects with various glassware, chromatography columns, extraction apparatus, and so forth. The benches were covered with the beakers and flasks of solutions that indicate work in progress.

These insect control methods try to take advantage of the natural chemistry of the insect. The juvenile hormone is a chemical used by the insect to control its own growth. Insects pass through several stages before they emerge in the adult form, the most widely known example being the caterpillar that turns into a butterfly. The juvenile hormone is secreted to prevent that transformation from taking place before the proper time; but extra applications will cause it to take place too late, or not at all, resulting in the insect's death. This hormone has the advantage of being fairly specific, so that its application to a field might kill only the pest insect and leave most of the others alone. Preliminary experiments have so far been done on the flour beetle, and a display of the effects on the metamorphosis of the beetle was on view. Similar work is in progress on locusts. So far, no insect control applications have been developed, although a crude preparation is being used in silk production. The juvenile hormone delays the metamorphosis of the silkworm by one day, thereby making the cocoons larger and increasing the yield of silk.

Pheromones are chemicals that insects give off into their environment to communicate with each other. The most powerful of these are sex attractants. The aim of the research project was to isolate the sex attractants of important pests, synthesize them chemically, and then use them to bait insect traps.

Another line of attack on insect pests is the investigation of their diseases. This technique is in fairly common use in China now. It consists of growing disease bacteria, which are then dried and powdered and sprayed on fields like insecticide. The insects become infected and die. Again there is a limit to the species of insect that can become infected, so only the target species and a few others are likely to be killed. The Institute was investigating refinement of the process, which consisted of isolating the exotoxin secreted by the bacteria *Bacillus thuringiensis*. This poison is the agent which actually kills the insect; its isolation and use might make the technique more efficient. Since this type of work is difficult to do in the limited facilities of the communes, it was being carried out in the Institute's better equipped laboratories. Research on viral diseases in insects was also going on.

These three ways of attacking insects take advantage of the specific characteristics of the target species—its living habits, its chemistry, and its disease susceptibility—to control it. The application of these methods to agriculture makes ecological sense. One of the drawbacks of chemical insecticides is that they kill a broad spectrum of insects; predatory insects which may control the pest are often wiped out along with it, and repeated spraying is needed. The Chinese are working on this problem, and believe they are well on the way to reconciling high food production with good ecological practices. The methods of control that we saw being studied also have the prospect of being developed and used locally; peasants on the communes, for instance, can grow their own bacterial insecticide. At present such methods control only a portion of all pests, so that now and for some time to come the Chinese will continue to strive to develop chemical insecticides that are both more potent against insects and less toxic to people and other animals.

Our hosts told us that the cooperation between the Institute and peasants goes back to its earliest history. At the time of Liberation the pest problem was very serious and there was almost no technical base in the countryside. The work of the Institute was mostly in the field, directing farmers and predicting insect population changes in order to prepare against infestations. The laboratories were all directed to the control of specific pests, such as grasshoppers, or the pests that attacked specific areas of production—cotton, rice, livestock, and forests. During this early period the gap between the intellectuals and the peasants was still pretty wide, although both felt the importance of working together to improve production. Later, it was a group of peasants who found that DDVP, an organophosphorus insecticide, could be used to control cotton aphids. During the Cultural Revolution a party of scientists took some DDVP to the countryside, but only for environmental controls in their own quarters. The weather was dry at that time and there was an excessive number of cotton aphids. The insecticides then used to control aphids, parathion and systox, failed to do the job successfully that year. One day the farmers simply took the researchers' own material and sprayed it on the fields, with good results. While DDVP is not often used for agricultural purposes, because it has a small residual effect and is quickly destroyed by the chemical reactions going on in the soil and on plant leaves, it was effective enough in this case to make its use worthwhile. DDVP, a phosphate ester, is different in chemical structure from parathion and systox, which are phosphorothionates. This chemical difference, which was responsible for overcoming resistance to the commonly used compounds, suggested further lines of research in the synthesis of new insecticides and in the investigation of the mechanism of action and resistance. The researchers may not have been fully "integrated with the masses" at the time, but their work clearly benefited from the creative cooperation of the peasants.

The Cultural Revolution changed the way scientists go into the countryside. They now live and work with the peasants, which, as many of them told us, produces a better understanding of their research. Another important reason for the increased understanding is the development of a technical base in the countryside. Each production brigade has a technical group and most communes have special teams for the chemical control of insects. The people in these groups are local: either graduates of middle schools, where the agriculture of their region is taught, or older, knowledgeable peasants. Peasants in the chemical control groups are younger, and probably have more education in chemistry and mathematics than the older farmers. When members of the Institute go to the communes, they conduct classes in the middle school and in the commune as a whole. As a result of this close cooperation in the countryside, the work of the Institute can be tested more quickly and efficiently. A new compound they made, called phoxim, was tested on different insects under different conditions all at the same time, because of the cooperation of many communes and organizations in the field.

The safety of chemical pesticides, which is now a matter of great debate in the United States, is a concern of the Chinese too, although their agriculture is much less developed in its use. They regard using chemicals as the only means of pest control as an unsatisfactory system. When they first started they tried every means of pest control, not just chemicals, although they found that some species of pests could only be controlled chemically. As their resources and capability developed, they began to study the new technology in pest control, particularly microbiological and parasite control. Now their approach is an integrated one, tailored to meet the needs of the different regions of the country.

As part of the evaluation of a new compound, its toxicity to people, livestock, and other animals must be determined. The Institute does small-scale, short-term testing in its vetebrate ecology laboratory, which is also concerned with rat control. It is the staff's opinion that organophosphorus types of pesticide are less suspect in terms of long-term build-up and subtle toxicity than organochlorine pesticides like DDT, Aldrin, and Dieldrin. The long-range feeding studies for toxicity are the responsibility of the Ministry of Sanitation. Policy decisions, such as which pesticides to use, methods of production, and directions for research, are made at yearly national meetings. That conference, which was held in Canton at the time of our visit, serves the function of transmitting research and testing results, and is attended by representatives of the Ministries of Agriculture, Commerce, and Chemical Engineering and Fuel, as well as by researchers from all over the country. The SATP group, however, did not attend that meeting.

Entomological Division of Chungshan Sun Yat-sen University, Canton. We learned more about the integrated insect control work being done in China when we visited the Entomological Division of Chungshan University. During our meetings there we were especially helped by two very kind scientists, Li Li-ying and P'u Chih-lung. Li Li-ying, a thin, friendly woman of about forty, wears short, straight hair and glasses. She is a researcher in Canton's Entomological Institute and works on the physiological aspects of insect pest control. She once studied in the Soviet Union, and in this respect is typical of a generation of Chinese scientists who went to Russia or Eastern Europe during the 1950s for their technical training. Her knowledge of technical English words relating to insects is excellent.

P'u Chih-lung represents an older but also important generation of Chinese scientists. He studied entomology from 1946 to 1949 at the University of Minnesota and returned to China in 1949, the year of Liberation. Before 1949 there was no significant graduate education in science in China. Many Chinese scientists studied abroad, in the United States, Western Europe, or Japan. A substantial proportion of these foreign-educated scientists chose to return to or remain in China after the victory of the Revolution, and they have played a crucial role in the development of Chinese science over the last two decades.

P'u, who is short and stout, and who must be about fifty years old, is professor of entomology. An affable man, he speaks good English, no doubt as a result of his American stay, and evidently keeps up with the English-language work in his own and other fields. In addition, he can read German, French, and Russian. As one might expect, he picked up his Russian in the 1950s, when the Soviet Union's influence on Chinese science was very strong. Both P'u's wife and Li's husband are entomologists. P'u's wife works in the same laboratory with him and they often collaborate on pest control work.

During one of our discussions with these two scientists, Li outlined the pest control program in China under five different categories:

1. Chemical Control. When pests swarm in great numbers, a situation that arises often, farmers must resort to pesticides based on organic or inorganic chemicals. This method has serious shortcomings: namely, that the chemicals may harm humans, animals or even the crops being protected.

2. Biological Control. This method, which has ancient precedents in China, utilizes helpful insects to kill harmful ones. It has been developed intensively because the insects used for biological control pose no threat to humans, animals, or the environment. The methods employed are cheap and can be produced by the peasants themselves. But biological control also has shortcomings. It takes a while to produce the helpful insects in adequate numbers,

so the method can't cope with a pest that appears suddenly in large numbers. Also, certain species of helpful insects are very selective about their diet, and will only attack one or a few closely related species of pest insects. Thus large numbers of pest species require large numbers of controlling species, which require a long time to develop.

3. Agricultural Control. Many insect pests can be controlled by selecting crop varieties that are genetically resistant to pests or by manipulating the system of cultivation (time of planting, time of plowing, burning of old stalks, etc.) to hinder the pests' development. Li emphasized that the peasants have had a good understanding of these sorts of methods for a long time. They have an intimate knowledge of the habits of the insects in the fields and use it to develop suitable control procedures.

4. Artificial (Man-made) Control. This category includes simple but often effective methods such as sending hundreds of people out to squash insects or destroy their eggs by hand. This method was applied at Hsikou Commune against a large caterpillar (a moth larva) that threatened the pine plantations. More sophisticated techniques are also used, like the light traps used at Hsikou. These traps, Li told us, have been widely popularized in China.

5. Integrated (Combined or Comprehensive) Control. Ideally, the Chinese try to combine several methods to control all the major pests in a given crop or area, choosing the methods to suit the pests. Li noted the case of sugar-cane pests. Biological control using a minute parasitic wasp, *Trichogramma evanescens*, has been very successful against the sugar-cane borer, a moth larva. Since sugar-cane fields suffer from many other insect pests for which there are as yet no biological control methods, pesticides must still be used. But because pesticides kill the wasps, the two methods have a built-in incompatibility. In any given case, the methods used depend on conditions in the particular field.

P'u Chih-lung elaborated on the relationship between China's social and productive needs and the development of biological control methods. The idea, he noted, isn't new. In some areas of southern China the use of ants to control insect pests in tangerine orchards dates back at least sixteen hundred years. This practice still continues, though it seems to be dying out, as P'u explained:

> Several years ago, in a district near Canton, I saw a place where they use these kinds of ants to control some kinds of insects in the orchards. But in recent years they don't do much of this kind of control. They have two reasons. One is that they use too much chemical control and they kill the ants there. And secondly, the ants can carry a disease of the citrus trees. Gradually the number of orchards practicing this method has become very, very few. But the method is very ancient; so we say that maybe the biological control method was first used in China.

We had been told at the Institute for Zoology that the Cultural Revolution had spurred Chinese scientists to put great efforts into biological and integrated control. That Institute specializes in developing and testing new chemical pesticides, but when the scientists go to the fields with the peasants they still try to control pests by all means other than chemical control. Intense efforts to avoid using chemicals are based especially on prospective dangers to populated areas. For example, during the wheat season parasitic wasps are used in the suburban areas around Peking to shorten the time that chemicals are used and diminish the danger.

P'u strongly agreed with these ideas. The government, he told us, thinks that current pesticide use is too great and is deeply concerned about the problem of pesticide residues in the soil and in the tissues of animals long after application. He said that for the time being, while chemical pesticides are necessary, researchers should develop pesticides that are less toxic to people and more toxic to insects. He criticized the Chinese insecticide industry for relying too much on imitating the products of foreign countries, saying it should put more effort into synthesizing original compounds.

P'u's own research has been directed at the use of parasitic wasps for pest control. These minute insects lay their own eggs inside the eggs of a host species. The wasp larvae hatch inside the host eggs and devour the developing larvae of the host. In general, a given species of parasitic wasp will attack only one host species in nature. A control method using wasps depends upon finding the right wasp species for the pest one wants to control and then developing ways to raise the wasps in large numbers.

In addition to the use of the wasp *Trichogramma evanescens* against the sugar-cane borer, P'u and his coworkers have scored great success in the use of the wasp *Anastatus* against the litchi stink bug, *Tessardtoma papillosa.* The litchi stink bug sucks the sap of litchi trees, causing the fruit to fall off before ripening. To develop control methods against this pest, P'u's group worked in collaboration with people from the Canton Entomological Institute and peasants from Tungkuan County, a major litchi-producing area in Kwangtung Province. In the course of the work, carried out in 1969, the Canton scientists went out to live with the peasants. Working together they overcame many technical difficulties encountered in raising wasps, like low reproduction rates, shortages of female wasps, and high mortality rates, and were thus able to make the wasp method work. P'u himself lived with the peasants for six months, and by the time he returned to Canton he had trained thirty peasant technicians in the art of raising and deploying *Anastatus* wasps against the stink bug. There are now more than fifty stations in Kwangtung Province raising parasitic wasps for pest control.

In the afternoon we went with Li Li-ying to visit P'u's laboratory at Chungshan, the major university of Kwangtung Province. It is on the outskirts of Canton, and its buildings are spread out in a beautiful setting of luxuriant subtropical vegetation. P'u met us in front of the Entomology Division and guided us inside to show us around his quarters. In one room, kept at a cold temperature for

Canton, he has set up an array of cabinets with controlled light and temperature. The temperatures range in a series from 15 to 23 degrees Centigrade (59 to 71 degrees F.) Inside each cabinet there are separate containers with humidities ranging from 75 to nearly 100 percent. Remote control sensors in each cabinet are connected to an elaborate panel in another room, from which the temperatures are regulated. P'u said that the cabinets had been built in 1958 and that all the parts but one had been made in China. Controlled temperature devices are not easy to build and he was obviously proud of his group's achievement.

P'u's group uses the cabinets to determine the best temperature and humidity conditions for rearing insects used in biological control programs. Right now they are studying another *Trichogramma* wasp, one which parasitizes the rice leaf roller, *Cnaphallocrocis medinalis*. To obtain large numbers of this wasp they are rearing it on the eggs of an alternate host insect, the eerie wild silkworm moth (*Samia cynthia ricina*), which is raised for its silk cocoons in some areas of the countryside. Each egg of the natural host, the rice leaf roller, can produce only one or two parasites. The silkworm eggs are comparatively large, and each can therefore produce twenty of the minute wasps. If the wasps reared by this method succeed against the pest, the peasants will be able to combine parasite production with a local silk industry.

In another room two technicians in white lab coats were working at desks with microscopes and the other simple equipment one would expect to find in any American insect lab; glass bottles, forceps, little containers of alcohol. They were seeking ways to increase the rate of parasitization of alternate host eggs in the laboratory. It seems that several wasps in the same space interfere with one another's parasitic activities. This problem had already been solved in part by dividing the bottom of the box in which host eggs and parasites are mixed into a few hundred small cubbyholes, each containing a few host eggs. In this way each wasp had a private space and could parasitize in peace and plenitude. P'u told us that of the three technicians working in his lab, two were university graduates and one had graduated from technical school.

We walked down the hall and entered a room lined with racks of large, speckled, greenish caterpillars contentedly munching on fresh leaves. These were the larvae of the wild silkworm moths that produce the alternate host eggs for the wasps. In addition to using the moth for eggs, P'u's lab had begun to experiment with a virus disease of the larvae called nuclear polyhedrosis. Eventually the scientists hope to work out viral methods of pest control. In the same room they were growing a fungus for such use, one that in the past couple of years had been grown by communes themselves.

P'u thinks that biological control has been more successful in southern China (Kwangtung, Kwangsi, Fukien) than in the north, probably because the warmer weather means that they can produce parasites all year round. In the United States, where biological control research is underfunded and insignificant as compared with the marketable chemical pesticides, which generate great profits, the few American efforts in biological control have so far been limited mainly to California and the Gulf States, areas that share southern China's year-round mild climate and growing season.

In addition to the methods already mentioned, P'u referred to some other areas of research in biological control. Certain communes use ducks to eat insect pests in the crops, a primitive but often effective method. Other communes have developed the use of an infectious bacterium, *Bacillus thuringiensis*, against caterpillar pests in rice, tea, cotton, various vegetables, and forests. He emphasized that in contrast to microbiological control practices in other societies, the people in the Chinese communes produce the bacteria themselves. Some communes grow it in a simple homemade liquid medium made of fish, meat, or beans, and spray the mixture directly onto the fields. Other communes build small factories for bacteria production. Using bacteria sprays, production teams have been able to cut down their use of chemical pesticides by 75 to 80 percent without any loss in yields. In Shantung Province work has begun on screening for microorganisms that can be used to control weeds.

As the afternoon wore on, our conversation with P'u Chih-lung got around to the current structure of science in China and the reforms brought about by the Cultural Revolution. We began by asking P'u about his personal experience of going to the countryside over the years. He is from a city family, and he told us that when he and other scientists first went to the countryside they were not familiar with the living conditions. This was back in the early fifties, when the countryside was still relatively impoverished. Since that time, however, living standards have risen considerably, and many villages in Kwangtung Province, especially those near Canton, now enjoy living conditions almost equal to the city.

He underlined the fact that the views of the peasants are not fundamentally different from those of city people. They welcome visitors from universities and institutes in the cities, especially since the Cultural Revolution. We asked if the attitude of the peasants had changed as a result of the Cultural Revolution, and P'u said he thought so. Before then, he went on, not very many scientists went to the countryside, and because of the influence of the revisionist Liu Shao-ch'i line, the peasants and scientists were not in close contact and there was a gap between them. Often the peasants didn't understand what the scientists were doing, or even what a university was. But since the Cultural Revolution many teachers as well as scientists go to the countryside. According to P'u, they live and work with the peasants and become friendly with them, and the peasants visit the university in return, where they are made to feel welcome. "At my house there are always peasants who come to visit me; someone almost every week and at least every month."

The change from using chemical pesticides was also begun in earnest during the Cultural Revolution. Before then P'u told us, it was possible to do biological control work, on the sugar-cane borer for instance, but it was not always easily accepted by the peasants. During the Cultural Revolution scientific propaganda teams went to villages to popularize the different pest control methods and to organize the peasants for scientific purposes. P'u was referring to the kind of science and technology groups we had seen at Hsikou Commune. Four grades of scientific teams in the countryside—on the levels of the county, commune, brigade, and production team—were organized during and after the Cultural Revolution.

It was generally the university students who went out to the countryside to do propaganda work during the Cultural Revolution. They worked with the peasants and learned from them at the same time as they expanded scientific research and education in the rural areas. Of course this was not done so easily, or without any struggle. P'u said that there were two main groups of students with different and contradictory opinions, and that sometimes when they went to the countryside they found that the peasants held another kind of opinion. This situation led to quarrels. But, as P'u said, paraphrasing Chairman Mao, "The Cultural Revolution was a ... really revolutionary movement. A revolution is not too polite, perhaps."

Whatever differences there may have been between scientists, students, and peasants at that time, it now appears that the movement to popularize science in the countryside was eminently successful. Besides the solid establishment of the local science teams, P'u described as an example a brigade that subjected its rice and vegetable fields to large parasite releases and low chemical pesticide applications. Over a period of two years the number of pests dropped significantly compared to those in nearby fields, and presumably the yield went up. But, we asked, what would have happened if the experiment hadn't panned out and the yield had gone down? Would the peasants still have risked their livelihood on the outcome? P'u said that, yes, they would, and they do. Sometimes experiments do fail and crops are reduced. Brigades are aware of this and yet they still offer their land for experiments. If pest outbreaks become very bad, pesticides can be brought in to save the remaining crop. But the peasants' income is still on the line. Could there be any stronger statement of the value the peasants have come to attach to scientific experiment?

5 SCHOOLS SINCE THE CULTURAL REVOLUTION

The history of mankind is one of continuous development from the realm of necessity to the realm of freedom. This process is never ending. . . . In the fields of the struggle for production and scientific experiment, mankind makes constant progress and nature undergoes constant change; they never remain at the same level. Therefore, man has constantly to sum up experience and go on discovering, inventing, creating and advancing.

—Mao Tse-tung, as quoted by Chou En-lai, "Report on the Work of the Government to the First Session of the Third National People's Congress" (1964)

On our visits to rural farming communes, to factories, and to research facilities we tried to form a composite view of the current state of scientific development in China, but it was the schools that offered us a periscopic view of China's future. Science, we had seen is inseparable from politics. It extends into every aspect of Chinese life. The continuing revolution is a process entered into by all the people as their life work. How and when do they enter this process? If the revolution is to go on for generations, how is it transmitted from one generation to the next? How are Chinese children first exposed to the practice and the theory of science? And once exposed, how is it determined which children will become scientists?

We approached our tour of Chinese schools with a battery of questions on the way science was taught, the effect the Cultural Revolution had had on the schools, and the current trends in education, in addition to a personal interest, as teachers, to hear from Chinese teachers how they integrated into the overall social and political struggle. We toured several primary and middle schools and four major universities in our quest for answers. Knowing that we could not in one month expect to fully comprehend the totality of what we saw, we searched for the paradigm to shed some light on the basic patterns. Depending on subjective impressions, direct observations, and recorded interviews with scientists, science teachers, and students, this section traces the Chinese student's path from a model primary school through a middle school and on to university. We have included accounts of visits to all four universities because we feel that each visit offered us a unique insight into the educational process and therefore the direction of science and education in the new China.

The Happiness Village School. The Happiness Village School, known as "the Shanghai Slum School" before 1949, is now a primary school serving children between the ages of seven and thirteen in the city of Shanghai. The staff of eighty works with 1,500 children in six grades, not only teaching the traditional subjects of language, mathematics, and science, but also basic agricultural and industrial work and military and cultural affairs. As well, the school offers over twenty spare-time activities for children who wish to explore special interests. Attached to the school is a kindergarten/nursery school resembling a day-care center for the children of working parents. We were told that some parents prefer to send their younger children to this preschool because older brothers and sisters are close by in the primary school. The nursery cares for children between the ages of fifty-six days and two and a half years; the kindergarten for children between two and a half and six. We observed similar facilities for the children of working parents at factories and schools throughout our visit, which convinced us that day-care is a high-priority service in China. Not only does this free the parents to engage in productve work and earn a living, but when these centers are at or near the place of work, mothers can nurse their babies and both parents are able to spend time with their children during the work day, besides being available if any problems arise.

Although we were principally concerned with science education, we found that, to understand how children form their early attitudes toward science and its place in the larger culture, we had to get a general feel for the school itself as a basic institution in Chinese society, to observe the early socialization process that takes place on the elementary school level. It was here that we might be afforded a view of the fundamental patterns of the society as they are taught to its inheritors.

Our first impressions were gleaned from our welcoming committee: an effervescent group of students and staff waiting outside the school to greet us. Noisy and excited, they met us with drums and tambourines, cheers and occasional "hellos" in English as we stepped out of our cars. To our surprise, no attempts were made to silence the students or to curb their enthusiasm—instead, a small delegation stepped forward with broad smiles to introduce themselves, and as they began to speak the others quieted down by themselves. After a short speech we entered the main building behind the children, who calmly returned to their rooms without apparent adult direction and noticeably without forming the single lines—boys first, then girls— that we were accustomed to seeing in American schools.

Inside, walking between whitewashed walls, sparsely adorned with brightly colored murals painted by the children, we were struck by the low-key pulse of activity all around us. We passed classrooms where students were already settled in their seats and engaged in school work. Teachers stepped out of their rooms casually and the noise level in their rooms was unaffected. We knew, of course, that the entire school must be on its best behavior, but it was also clear that the students had achieved a level of self-discipline rare in children of this age, rare at least in the context of our experience with American primary schools.

As we toured the school we noticed many children with red neckerchiefs worn as if a mark of distinction, and we asked our hosts what this meant. These, we were told, were Little Red Soldiers, model students chosen by their classmates and teachers on the basis of their work in school, their intellectual, moral, and physical development, and their attitudes about helping others. Model citizens, in effect. But with this distinction came neither special status nor privilege; instead, it placed upon them the added responsibility of serving their fellow students in such a way as to enlarge their ranks, ideally to include the entire student body. In fact, as we looked around, we saw that nearly half the students were Little Red Soldiers! How is it, we wondered, that rewards could be spread so broadly among the children and still retain their appeal? What of the naughty students, and the slow students? Where were their classrooms? Observing the model sections was one thing, but to get a balanced picture of the school we asked to see the lower-tracked classes.

Our hosts' responses to this request was one of both amusement and pride, and their answer proved to be especially enlightening with regard to the effect the Cultural Revolution had had on all levels of Chinese society. After Liberation in 1949 the Chinese had experienced a great surge in education, much like the one we experienced in America after *Sputnik* in 1957. Classrooms were constructed, enrollment increased, the better students were sifted out and encouraged to move forward as quickly as they could. In short, the schools dramatically increased their productivity, turning out educated students as rapidly as possible to fill the needs of the new society. But, we were told, with the advent of the Cultural Revolution and the intense reexamination of the long-term goals of the society, it became obvious that such methods would result in a retrenchment, the formation of new class divisions like the ones that had developed in the Soviet Union. Instead of a hereditary elite, they were creating an educated elite, a management elite (much like the meritocracy concept set forth in the United States as a model of a fluid class structure) more open than the earlier feudal aristocracy but in sharp contrast to the goals of a classless socialistic society. Tracking students into homogeneous ability groups or even achievement groups could only be the precursor of substantial class divisions in adult society.

So the schools were reorganized. Short-term gains were sacrificed for long-term goals, and the results more than vindicated this turnabout, for it was discovered that when the naughty children were paired up with the slow learners, the former were toned down and learned patience while the latter were able, with this special attention, to keep up with their peers and to learn more quickly. "But," we asked our hosts, "you must still have children who misbehave, don't you? How do you punish them?"

At this point we moved to the discussion room to pursue the question over tea. One of the Little Red Soldiers who accompanied us laughed aloud at this and the others deferred to him. "I am a little naughty," he said, blushing slightly. "Contradictions exist between me and this teacher." He pointed to the teacher seated next to him, who laughed and nodded in agreement. "But I think if there are no contradictions," the little boy went on, "then there is no struggle between people and there is no progress. Once in a classroom when I wrote in Chinese on the blackboard, I made a mistake. The teacher corrected me in the class, but I was proud and couldn't accept the mistake. When I saw this teacher again in the hall, I made a face at him; I made my eyes as big as eggs and rolled them around at him. But this teacher was very patient with me and took me into his office to explain about the mistake and why we should admit and understand our mistakes. He allowed me to criticize him and through this

meeting we became close friends. In our country teachers
and students are equal. We can criticize each other, teach
and learn from each other, and make progress together."

As our little friend finished his story, his teacher commented, "Sometimes when a teacher criticizes a student,
he is wrong and should recognize this in front of the class.
Anyway, if he doesn't, the students will hold a rebellion.
We teachers welcome the students to give their opinions."
Obviously a basic shift had taken place in the philosophy
of education during the Cultural Revolution, transforming
the very nature of the institution and the people charged
with the responsibility of building the new China. No longer was it the sole responsibility of the student to get his
education from the school. Instead it had become the
shared responsibility of the school, the teachers, and even
fellow students to educate each other. The line between
teacher and student has become blurred to the extent that
authority now rests more with knowledge than with position. When a student has difficulty learning, he or she is
not singled out for blame or ostracism, but instead, all
concerned—teachers and peers—take the responsibility for
the problem and seek a mutual solution. When a student is
sick and unable to attend school, a team of students visits
his or her home for tutoring.

We heard other specific examples of mutual assistance
and cooperation, but what impressed us most was the
spirit that underlay the entire discussion: the sense of
camaraderie and mutual trust that was so evident among
students and teachers, the shared pride in their accomplishments and the faith in each other, in their collective
ability to learn, to grow, and to meet any challenge.
Throughout the day we observed a great deal of physical
contact between teachers and students: arms around each
other as friends, "equal," as our friend had said.

Listening to the stories our hosts told, it seemed to us
that a key to their relationship was the openness to criticism that both teachers and students exhibited. Each
month the teachers regularly exposed themselves to the
critical evaluation of their students and followed these sessions with a written self-evaluation. We asked how they

felt about this practice, suspecting from our own teaching experience that it could be not only unnerving but threatening to their teaching ability. Not so, they said, criticism/self-criticism is not viewed as a struggle for power within the classroom, but rather as a way of achieving a genuine unity of purpose. The health teacher added, "Teachers will praise a student for pointing our weaknesses out. This will build good educational relationships and structure."

For many teachers this must have been a difficult and even painful change, but believing it to be right, they struggled to learn new ways. The science teacher said, "Before the Cultural Revolution, I didn't want people to criticize but now I realize its importance. Sometimes I was very impatient with the students, but that was all right because I was the teacher. Now I should change that. Students are free to criticize me and help me." Since this was stated in front of three of his students, we appreciated his frankness, and we went on to ask him more about the science program in the primary schools.

Science being a cornerstone of the revolution, it is very important that all students both understand and practice it, but science—laboratory or experimental science, as we usually think of it—is not formally taught until the fifth grade. Until that time the children must learn 3,500 characters for reading and writing, master basic mathematics, and learn to read blueprints (a course added after the Cultural Revolution to give the children a useful technical skill that utilizes their mathematical training). The teachers told us that mastering these skills, especially the complex character system, was enough to expect in the early grades. In fact, science teaching begins much earlier in less formal ways, but it is a process that builds from application to research, from practice to theory. The first exposure children get to science comes through the "spare-time activities," extracurricular activities that all the children engage in according to their interests and abilities. In yet another example of the social integration of Chinese society, we found out that many of these activities—ranging from building rockets and taking apart machines to playing ping-pong—were organized by retired workers from the community who volunteered their time to work with the school children.

We asked the children to elaborate on these activities and were taken outside the central classroom building to a courtyard surrounded by a long one-story building where many of the spare-time activities were carried on. We saw ping-pong being played in one room. In a separate room children were doing brush painting and embroidery. In another place we watched thirteen-year-old children learning to give haircuts. Their "clients" were children of the kindergarten school (two-and-a-half-to-six-year-olds), who were sitting and chatting with each other while waiting their turn. Farther down the courtyard we found a carpentry activity taught by a volunteer retired carpenter from the neighborhood. The children were learning basic woodworking skills while they repaired broken and worn-out furniture from the school building. As for science, when we left the carpentry area and stepped into the courtyard we could hear the roar of an engine. Some of the children with their experience from blueprint-reading classes had taken it upon themselves to build scale-model airplanes, complete with small gasoline engines. Others were putting together model boats with battery engines. To the background noise of a completed airplane, we watched as two children set off one of three rockets which had been set on a small launching stand in the center of the yard. A match held to a short fuse sent the skyrocket zooming high over the houses of the surrounding neighborhood. At the top of the flight a parachute popped out, opened, and drifted down to a nearby street.

Inside, on the opposite side of the yard now, we watched as pairs of ten- and eleven-year-old children practiced with acupuncture needles. They sat poring over small acupuncture books, needles poised in hand or already placed in particular spots. Here the children were working on themselves to gain an understanding of a number of points and their effects. There is, of course, a great deal of emphasis on agriculture, and one group of students has learned to produce the chemical fertilizer "920," which they use to grow vegetables. Others have learned to make soap, which is used by both the school and the community. In each case, theory is directly linked to practice, and the fruits of study are productive social contributions in which the students and teachers take great pride.

It is not clear to us just what is meant by spare time. These were not solely after-school activities, but were going on around us throughout the day. Children in Happiness Village attend school six days a week, 9:00 A.M. to 5:30 P.M., with a long lunch break. Lunch hour is 11:30 to 1:30 during the winter, and 11:30 to 2:00 when the weather is warm. The lunch break makes a longer total day, but the reason for these hours is simple. Provisions for the children of working parents are a high priority, and the children are engaged in school-related activity for the time the parents are at work. Some children go home to lunch because grandparents, older siblings, or parents have coincidental lunch hours. Others stay at school and eat and relax there.

The spare time activities seem to provide varied educational, physical, and cultural opportunities for all the times the children are not in class. These activities also give children and teachers more opportunity to get to know each other. The Happiness Village school relies heavily on retired people to work with students on many projects, giving older people an opportunity to continue sharing their much-needed skills. In these activities and throughout the formal curriculum, the children are encouraged to ask questions, for the teachers believe that knowing how to ask the right questions and being able to see a problem from many perspectives are the roots of scientific method. And it is the method more than a body of knowledge which they wish to convey to their students, so that the students will go on to use science in every area of study. Over and over again we were told that science is problem-solving in service to the people.

In the fifth grade science classes begin formally on a weekly basis. We asked the science teacher to describe the curriculum, and he told us that he teaches basic information on machinery, agriculture, water conservation, and other areas in which science theory can be joined with common experience on a fundamental level. For a lesson on fire, members of the local fire team are invited to show students how to start and extinguish fires. Back in the classroom, the teacher discusses with the children the how and why of combustion. In the study of electricity materials from the immediate environment are used. The specific electrical current in Shanghai (220 volts) is described and along with this follows a discussion of safety precautions to take when working with electric circuits. The teacher provides this information so children can learn about assembling and repairing the lighting system in the classroom. He first demonstrates how to take the lights apart and put them back together and then the children all practice this procedure. Once they master these skills, they are called upon to fix the lighting when problems arise at home or at school. The children in this school took responsibility for the repair of the broadcasting and lighting systems.

To help with the basic understanding of dynamics, children are taken to the sports ground, where there is a cart filled with earth, common materials from everyone's experience. The students take turns pushing and pulling the cart and are asked how they think the load can be made easier or more difficult to move about. Back in the classroom, the teacher explains the principles of how and why things appear heavier or lighter to us. The children not only learn some aspects of physics but, once again, can actually apply the science so that common work is made easier. In the science training at Happiness Village the emphasis is on doing as many concrete experiments as possible so that the theory of science is understood on a practical level, and therefore becomes knowledge to improve production and everyday life.

Here too, in the formal science classes, we found many direct links to the surrounding community and to production. Workers from nearby factories come to the school to share both their skills and their experience as workers. We met a factory worker who was teaching the students how to make electrical motors. A carpenter taught model building. Another man taught the making of semiconductor devices. There is also a link with a nearby telegraph station, where the students go to learn how to send telegrams. Through these experiences the children gain not only scientific knowledge but also a deep respect for labor and for working people. They are shown from the beginning how important science is to everyday life and how ordinary people can understand and use it. Without being mystified or awed by the "magic" of science, they are learning that through science they can help build the new China. Science is taught as it is practiced: as a tool forged by the people's labor, to be used for the improvement of their lives.

Peking Number 15 Middle School. At the Number 15 Middle School we were met by about a dozen members of the school, including the vice-chairman of the educational group, the doctor, teachers, a factory representative, and students, including members of the Red Guard.

The school, a fifteen-minute ride from Tien An Men Square, was built in 1952. It includes a complex of several buildings on a good-sized campus, and has 2015 students and a staff of 137, including 87 teachers. There is a Party branch, consisting of eighteen teachers and staff, and a Communist Youth Leader group of twelve teachers. There are 205 student youth leaders in eight branches. A thousand students, half the number in the school, are members of the Red Guard. (Of the 1000 who are not members, 600 are first-year students and not yet eligible.) They apply to the organization and must be recommended by fellow students. Selection is based on the students' work and on their desire to serve others and improve in all levels of moral, intellectual, physical, and cultural development; like the Little Red Soldiers, the Red Guards provide recognition for student attainments and play a model role for other students. The day-to-day management and administration of the school is conducted by a three-in-one revolutionary committee, including old, middle-aged, and young members.

There are five years to the middle-school programs: two or three years of junior middle school, roughly equivalent to our junior high school, and two or three years of senior middle school, like our high school. At Peking's Number 15 Middle School every grade had courses in politics, Chinese literature, math, foreign language, and physical training. Additional courses were given in physiology, chemistry, physics, history, geography, hygiene, agriculture, music, and art. The school year consisted of thirty-three weeks of classes, four weeks of agricultural work, four weeks of industrial production, and one week for a cultural festival; the rest of the time was for vacations and work at home. Twice a year the students and teachers were organized into criticism/self-criticism sessions, to correct each other's mistakes and learn from each other.

Our tour enabled us to observe several different kinds of activity going on around the campus. In the main classroom building we observed a physiology class, in which the lesson was about the structure of the eye. We learned that this went hand in hand with good eye care. Each day the whole school took two fifteen-minute breaks for eye exercises designed to strengthen the muscles of the eye and promote good health habits.

In a physics class we saw something of classroom procedure. The teacher had been explaining a concept accompanied by a demonstration. Equations were written along the front blackboard and colored chalk charts of sine and cosine curves were held up during the explanation. As the teacher went along we could see some students lean over to their neighbors as if they were asking for further explanation. After his discussion he called on a student to come forward and demonstrate how the electric light at the front of the room operated. When this was finished he threw out a problem related to an aspect of the physics involved in the electrical circuitry. The students broke into a lively discussion about how to solve the problem. From the back of the room we could see heads turning in all directions as groups of two, three, four, or more children worked with each other to obtain solutions. Students who were confused were not left out because they couldn't help get to the answer quickly. On the contrary, it seemed as if these children were sought out and included in the enthusiastic group dynamics by their fellow classmates. The teacher, who was smiling at the blackboard, waited for the buzz to die down and then called on a number of students around the room to present and explain procedures for solutions. As we left the room the teacher asked the whole class if some members were still confused and there were some affirmative replies, so he threw out a second problem for group discussion. We were pleased to see this aspect of classroom behavior. With the exception of music classes we had so far usually seen quiet classrooms where an average of forty children would sit listening or where one-to-one discussions between teachers and students occurred. In this classroom we got to see the sharing of information and the reliance on group solutions in practice.

Outside in the courtyard we saw classes in physical education, with students engaged in high jumping, relay races, coordination games, tumbling, and a type of badminton. In the school clinic we visited a health class under the supervision of a doctor. On one of the walls of the room was a blackboard with beautiful bright flowers drawn with colored chalk and the sign "Welcome American Friends." On the opposite wall was a large collection of dried traditional Chinese herbs gathered by the students on a field trip to the hills outside Peking. They had collected the herbs and brought them back to arrange a wall dictionary of Chinese medicine. The doctor told us that in the spring he and some students would take another outing to the hills and collect more herbs. We learned also that some of the children in the class were qualified to give inoculations in the event of epidemic in the area.

The health class was in session when we entered, and the students, divided into groups of two, were practicing acupuncture on each other, using points in the neck, head, ears, arms, and hands. They were all studying with either an acupuncture doll—a foot-high plastic doll with the acupuncture points of the body clearly displayed—or a chart of the human body with the points marked on it. They also had books describing various results of placing needles in particular points. Three boys were working with an electrical acupuncture needle stimulator. This machine, recently invented to save the labor of hand-twirling the needles, is especially useful during long operations or for procedures which involve a number of needles at once. It is a small device about the size of a portable radio that puts out low-voltage (about 6 volts) pulses of electricity that create an effect similiar to that of rotating the needles mechanically.

All these children were getting direct experience with scientific procedure. They were learning to use it, to understand it, and to gain confidence in themselves. The children worked with the needles in a matter-of-fact way and many smiles could be seen. They truly appeared to be enjoying themselves, and when questioned they were capable of explaining to us the procedures and the particular effects of acupuncture at various points. They were all being trained in the fundamentals of Chinese medicine, not only so they would understand it but so they could practice it in the event of sickness or accident when a doctor might not be immediately available. It meant that a large segment of the younger generation was becoming trained paramedics.

We also visited the two school factories on the campus. The first production unit was involved with the manufacture of "semiconductors." The process took several steps, including the use of a vacuum oven, several large pieces of equipment for bonding the semiconductor element to a plug, and a fairly elaborate setup where students test the finished product. The unit was in effect a contracting operation for a large electronics factory that had probably supplied the equipment and raw materials and would use the product. Each first-year class spends a month in the factory. During this period, instead of attending classes, the children work six hours a day and spend two hours a day learning the science theory behind their work. In this case, the factory is directed by a retired woman worker who originally helped produce semiconductors at a larger state factory. Other workers from that factory also act as supervisor-teachers at this smaller facility, teaching some of the theory classes.

The second production unit on the campus is a chemical factory in which the children produce silica gel as a desiccant (a drying agent found in such things as radio and television chassis to protect sensitive parts against moisture damage). Children do this work for a month in their second year of school, spending six hours a day in the physical production and two hours in theory classes related to the product. Although it was early March and chilly, part of the factory unit was outdoors in a sunny earth courtyard. Here we saw a group of boys gathered around a huge vat of water and some boxes of small brown bottles on the ground. Each student was busy scraping labels off the bottles. The glass containers were then carefully washed and set out in the sun to dry, so that the bottles could be reused. The next step involved the making of the silica gel. Here pairs of girls were mixing two chemicals together. Another process was done to neutralize this material and then the liquid silica substance was poured into metal trays (resembling nine-by-thirteen-inch baking pans). When this had thoroughly hardened into one solid block, a team of eight children broke the block into small crystals. The little chunks of hard silica gel were now ready to have a cobalt indicator added. This is necessary so that when the crystals have as much moisture as they can hold, the silica will change color and will remind the user that new crystals should be added to protect the materials. The indicator, which turns the crystals a deep blue, is baked in a brick oven to dry out well. When cool it is put into the brown bottles and made ready for distribution.

Siting small factories, staffed mainly by students and directed by experienced workers, on school campuses is part of the way the Chinese are restructuring education to enable students to put into practice many of the theoretical principles learned in the classroom. Such combinations also educate students directly in the life of working people. Similarly, a vegetable plot attached to the school helps the students as they grow some of their food, to learn how to apply science to agriculture and acquire a few basic farming skills.

After a performance of songs and dances by some of the older students, we had a discussion about educational policy. We wanted to know some of the changes that had been effected at the Number 15 Middle School by the Cultural Revolution. We were told that the old teaching methods of spoonfeeding, cramming, and "encyclopedia training" are no longer considered good educational practice. Education now combines theoretical work (classroom physics, for example), productive labor (the school factories, health clinic, agriculture), and proletarian politics (giving children a respect of the laboring people of China by engaging them directly in the production process among the workers and the peasants). As far as we could tell, Number 15 had no tracking. All children learned physics and all children learned factory and agricultural work, because both theoretical information and practical experience were considered important for all the children.

The twice-yearly exams have also been changed. The emphasis is now on the ability to analyze and solve problems, not just to memorize facts. Our hosts told us that students are given the questions before the exam and have a chance to discuss them with their classmates; and that the highest scores are given, not to the students who answer every question by repeating what they learned in class, but to those who bring forward new and creative solutions.

The role of the teacher has changed too. Teachers are now expected to make extra efforts to help students who are performing at a low level. First they try to find out why a student is having difficulties. If the student is in poor health, the teacher and/or a team of students will go to his home to tutor him. Other students may have a great deal of work to do at home and cannot spend enough time on their lessons. The teachers visit these families to discuss such situations and to see if changes can be made to provide for more study time. Another extra effort is made by the students themselves. They are expected to help each other, with the more advanced ones coaching the slower ones. It is considered part of learning how to serve the people. But even with this extra attention, there may be a few students who are unable to catch up, and in this school 1 or 2 percent of the students stay in class for an extra year.

Of course many of these changes are still in the experimental stage. Shortcomings occur and are expected to continue. For one, the Number 15 school cannot meet some of the needs for good teaching because there are still classes with more than fifty students. Yet it seemed to us that the schools are developing toward meeting the needs of the people, at the middle school level just as on the other levels of education, through a constant process of criticism and self-criticism among all those involved.

Tsinghua University. Tsinghua University, in Peking, is about a twenty-minute drive northwest of Tien An Men Square, in an area of scattered buildings and farms. Mostly composed of contemporary buildings, the university had a somewhat unfinished appearance because of construction and reconstruction since the Cultural Revolution. Upon meeting our hosts for the day, we were escorted to a small meeting room where we introduced ourselves and were given a brief history of the school, with emphasis on the changes wrought by the Cultural Revolution.

Tsinghua is a university of science and technology comprising eleven departments and forty-eight specialties. The departments include electronics, industrial automation, high precision instruments, mechanics, electric power, engineering chemistry, engineering physics, civil engineering, radio engineering, and water conservancy. There are presently 2,600 teachers. Before the Cultural Revolution the student body totaled 12,000. During that period enrollment stopped and the pre-Cultural Revolution students graduated in 1970. Tsinghua now has first- and second-year classes totaling 4,500 students.

The university was founded in 1911 with indemnity money, "owed" to the United States for damage to American property in the Boxer Rebellion, by Americans whose purpose was to educate overseers among the Chinese. The Chinese reported the American in charge of this project to have felt the use of the university as the best way to maintain American control of the area. Like other Chinese universities Tsinghua made some attempts at educational reforms in the late 1950s, but in 1961 these reforms came under attack from "the Liu Shao-ch'i line" of the capitalist-roaders. By 1965 the Cultural Revolution had begun in Peking with big-character posters criticizing the university administration. Tsinghua students were in the forefront of the movement (as William Hinton vividly describes it in his recent book, *Hundred Day War: The Cultural Revolution at Tsinghua University*).

Sharp differences combined with a lack of political experience resulted in a heated and ultimately violent split into two factions at Tsinghua. It took the intervention of city workers and the People's Liberation Army, on July 27, 1968, to stop the struggle and begin a resolution of the differences. In January 1969 the revolutionary committee of the university was set up to carry out the experimental work of educational transformation. Fundamental to the changes taking place was the process of carrying out Chairman Mao's directive, "Education must serve proletarian politics and be combined with productive labor." The first step was to stop admitting students directly from the middle schools and require all students to come from among the workers, peasants, or the People's Liberation Army. The university is free, and students with five years of work experience continue to receive the same salary while in school.

Tsinghua students now spent 80 percent of their time learning science and technology, which includes working in the factories; 15 percent studying Marxism, Leninism, and Mao Tse-tung Thought; and 5 percent in doing farm work and "learning from the Army." Consistent with national aims for all Chinese universities and colleges, Tsinghua now had an "open door" policy of education. This, we were told, includes operating a truck factory and electronics assembly at the university, and maintaining contact with outside factories by having students and teachers work in them. Advanced students can also work in outside laboratories. It is said that students with such experiences of practical work find lessons on theory easier to follow. Factory workers have access to the university through adult classes and so have the opportunity to learn the theory behind their practice. And both students and workers share life experiences in order to learn about each other, thus defoliating what in American society we might call an ivy curtain dividing one group from the other.

Our tour of the university began in the halls of the Department of Civil Engineering. Tacked to the walls were building designs done by the students and teachers. One was for the Museum of Chinese History and Chinese Revolution across from the Great Hall of the People in Tien An Men Square. It was done in cooperation with the Institute of Design, with the main draft done at Tsinghua. Blueprints and specifications for a number of buildings were displayed, including the main building at the university, showing heating, plumbing, wiring, and so on. Students and teachers had taken part in the construction, checking and correcting the design work as they progressed. A design for a residential area had been made after the people who lived there were asked for their opinions and suggestions. The design of a power plant had been done by veteran worker-students who were all over thirty years old. As in other cases, we were advised that the design work had shortcomings and errors. For those designs posted on the walls, there was a direct way to deal with this issue: a sheet was attached to each design so that other students and teachers could give their opinions. A stated objective of the department was to arouse the people to give opinions on its work.

We were escorted through an acoustics laboratory designed by members of the university and used to test the sound absorption of materials. The materials used in the Peking subway had been tested here. Another laboratory is used for designing musical theaters. A small electronics production unit that we saw was used as both a plant and a classroom. At the time of our visit the students were in other classes, so that only university workers were present. Of the fifteen working on the power unit stabilizers, fourteen were women doing detailed electronics work. One of them stopped to explain that she and her fellow workers study part time to get some background in circuit principles so that they know how their work is used. The regular students also take part in this work, giving the workers an opportunity to serve as on-the-job teachers.

From here we proceeded to the university library, which holds over a million books. The librarian, Shih Hung Wa, was a very friendly, animated man with a Ph.D. in sociology from Harvard. Among the displays we saw were oracle bones, still showing characters from thirty-five hundred years ago, and books that were from seven hundred to eleven hundred years old. Also on display were works of Marx and Lenin in Chinese, works of Mao Tse-tung in minority languages and in Chinese, and books by American writers, including *The Indochina Handbook,* by the Committee of Concerned Asian Scholars, and several books on the American radical movement that had been translated into Chinese.

We had lunch in a student cafeteria which was, as one would expect in any country, one of the most active and noisiest spots on campus. We stood in line with the students, taking bowls from under the tables and rinsing them before and after our meal. First we passed huge mounds of rice in straw baskets from which we served ourselves, and then hot braided steamed bread, a pork dish similar to a pâté, a variety of greens, and cold fruit for dessert. As we sat down to struggle with our chopsticks, we noticed that most of the students were using spoons, apparently to eat more quickly, as they stood or sat in groups and talked excitedly, possibly about their school work but most likely about the strange group of foreigners in their midst.

After lunch we visited a dormitory and split into two groups for discussions in student rooms. One group met with six women students. Of the six, one was in the army, another in the navy, one had been a worker in die casting, and the others were from peasant backgrounds. Comrade Ma, the student in the navy, was the daughter of a cadre and had graduated in 1968 from the middle school attached to Tsinghua University. She joined the navy and, after two years, was recommended by her commander and comrades to attend the university. She had been one of the earliest Red Guard student activists, part of the movement that played a central role in maintaining the ferment of the Cultural Revolution.

The students from the countryside were about twenty-four or twenty-five years old and had worked for three to five years before they were recommended for university by the people of their area. Even their course of study had been suggested by the local people. These young women were all advanced students studying automation control; they had come in 1970 and would be finishing this year. They expected to go back to their original positions in the countryside and were excited about the contributions they hoped to make, even though they knew that local needs might require their being assigned to other areas. But it had been difficult for them to adjust to the demands of higher education and they were equally emphatic in expressing their determination not to allow any classmates to lag behind. One of the students from the countryside told us how it had been for her:

When I entered the university, I only had an education equal to the first year of junior middle school; it was very difficult. The poor and lower-middle peasants cherished great hope in me, and I was determined to catch up with the other comrades. Students and teachers helped me a lot. Teachers often came to the dormitory at midnight. If I did not understand the first time, they were patient and would explain a second, third, and fourth time. Eventually I caught up with the other comrades.

She spoke very excitedly and quickly and got ahead

of the translator. Her classmates laughed along with her, and when she had finished one of them told us that she was now the best student in the class.

Impressed by her achievement, we went on to ask what things were like for women students in the sciences. With marked pride they responded that nearly half the student body was female and there were no special privileges for male students. Women were represented at all levels in the university, and Comrade Ma was herself a member of the Party branch. We expressed skepticism, for we had observed a disproportionate number of male scientists and teachers, but we were unable to provoke qualifiers from our companions. It was true, they said, that most teachers were men now, but that was a holdover from pre-Cultural Revolution and even pre-Liberation China. When the current generation moved into positions of leadership, sex representation would equalize. Meanwhile, representation on committees and policy-making bodies was balanced as well as possible. One student enthusiastically proceeded to tell us of their plans to celebrate International Women's Day on March 8. She recounted its significance, its origin in Chicago, and the importance of the struggle for the emancipation of working women.

From this discussion with the women students we proceeded to a long group session on the Cultural Revolution at Tsinghua. Comrade Hung Wei, who had been studying at the university for a year when the Cultural Revolution began, described the educational policy at that time as "revisionist," in that it compartmentalized knowledge, separated theory from practice, and fostered elitism. In ten years of study, Hung Wei had never made contact with workers or peasants. He gave an example of a student specializing in botany who had never been in the countryside. On one occasion this student was telling peasants how to grow walnut trees without realizing that the tree he was speaking under was a walnut.

Eight hundred of the twenty-six hundred teachers had been students before the Cultural Revolution. Most of the other, older teachers had undergone reeducation at a May Seventh Cadre School. Over a period of several months to a year they had lived with peasants, working with their hands and studying Marxism, Leninism, and Mao Tse-tung Thought. By doing so they learned to identify with working people and understand their new role in society. Some of the teachers had gotten their reeducation in a factory, but only those who were not in good health stayed at the university.

A professor who had been teaching for twenty-five years said that he had started as a student before the Revolution. At that time the subject matter taught at the College of Arts and Law was copied directly from the United States and was both written and studied in English. Scientific and technological education was simply modeled on the Massachusetts Institute of Technology. After Liberation, starting in 1952, teaching methods were copied from Moscow and Leningrad universities, with materials printed in Chinese coming from the Soviet Union. Now they used and produced their own materials, much simplified and revised continually by workers, students, and the professors.

At this point one of our hosts quoted Chairman Mao's observation: "In the problem of transforming education, it is the teachers who are the main problem," and the discussion turned to the effect of the Cultural Revolution on the teachers themselves. Professor Liang, a small, gray-haired professor of precision machinery, quietly rendered the following account of his experiences:

Before the Cultural Revolution I was satisfied with my teaching, but my students weren't. After the beginning of the Cultural Revolution my main direction became the same as the students'. So now teachers like myself also take an active part in the Cultural Revolution.

But when students first put up the big-character posters criticizing the educational system, there was some disagreement between teachers and students. For example, my students raised a criticism that I educated students who were divorced from the workers and peasants. They said that theory was separated from practice, and that these students would become the elite. At the time, I did not recognize and accept all these criticisms.

After the arrival of the propaganda team composed of workers from the factories, I went with a small group of students to some factories with the idea of trying to reform our education. It happened that one of the factories to which we went made optical instruments, and that two-thirds of the technicians there were my old students.

At the beginning there were some gaps between the factory workers and myself. I did not understand them at that time. They called me "Professor Liang." Later, they recognized that we were really willing to serve them. They said that the students I had trained all looked down on the workers. Some of my former students, for example, made a new instrument in that factory, but not until after the design was made did they ask for opinions and suggestions from the workers. It turned out none of the suggestions made by the workers were taken by them. They were just superficially asking for opinions, but then did things in their own way. So far as I know, the suggestions made by the workers were very good. It turned out that my students were failures with their new instruments, which were useless. The workers showed them to me. I could not believe that the students were trained by myself. After analyzing the situation, I came to the conclusion that the students were trying to do high-precision advanced science, and neglected the concrete conditions and needs in that factory. I think that their world outlook had been a capitalist one, so that they did not pay attention to the suggestions of the workers. At that time I worked together with some students and we made a new instrument. It was a very useful one. We arrived at it with the workers themselves.

Only after this period did I realize that the criticisms made by the students during the Cultural Revolution were right. Only since then will the workers tell me everything that is in their minds. Now they never call me "Professor Liang"; instead, they call me "Old Liang." We have become good friends and still have close contacts. My students at the factory have also made great progress with the help of the workers.

As old Liang finished, others took turns telling their stories. We heard that in the past teachers felt responsible only for preparing and presenting their own material, leaving the students immediately after a class was over. Now, feeling responsible for the students' understanding as well, they linger after class to simplify and explain themselves in response to student questions. They also discuss teaching methods with each other. There was the case of a math teacher who used to go very fast in class so that he could fulfill his assignments. As a result his students had a hard time following him. The other teachers discussed the problem with him and got him to slow down, so that he was more comprehensible to the students. Twice a month there are special meetings for teachers and students to exchange criticism and opinions. The two groups take turns chairing the sessions.

Of major importance since the Cultural Revolution is the question of political education. The faculty at Tsinghua stressed the importance of teaching students from a firm class standpoint. There is a strong feeling that students must first be revolutionaries, then scientists. As Professor Ling of the Electrical Engineering Department told us:

Part of my work is Party organization work. Even before the Cultural Revolution I taught two courses involving politics. Teachers like ourselves should learn politics and teach it as well as scientific knowledge. We are working with the students in the countryside, as well as in factories and physical training—what we call "Long March" training. Teachers always take part with their students and often go to the dormito-

ries. Now the relationship of teachers and students is
. . . one of comrades-in-arms on the same front.

As the discussion drew to a close, we asked about the
organization of the university as a whole: how was it administered? We were told that it was now run by a revolutionary committee of thirty-one, including seven members
of the workers' propaganda team, six university cadres,
one representative of the residential compound, and four
or five students. The remainder were teachers and other
workers. There were almost 3000 workers at the university, half working in plants and factories and the rest in administration. Before the Cultural Revolution they had not
been represented on the governing bodies of the university. Now the revolutionary committee met as a whole
once or twice a month and had more than a dozen standing committees meeting, once a week. Some of their responsibilities included political movements and education,
educational transformation, administration, and the daily
running of the university.

Besides the revolutionary committee, there were depart-
mental committees selected with student participation.
They sent representatives to the revolutionary committee
and helped it by conducting investigations; making suggestions; and taking care of political activities, physical culture,
and other matters. The workers at the university were
preparing to form a workers' group in addition to the existing residents' revolutionary committee and the committee
of the Communist Youth League. In principle, the Party
branch or committee, with members from the departments
and the worker and teacher groups, was above all these
organizations. It became clearer during the course of our
visit to various institutions and factories that the revolutionary committees are responsible for implementation,
and that policy is set by the Party.

Salary ranges at the universities and research institutes
tended to be higher than for other workers. Different
wages are not usually given for different jobs, but for
length of service. For teachers, the range began at 56
yüan a month for new graduates and went up to 330 *yüan*

a month for older professors. These older intellectuals, whose wages were even higher before the Revolution, may have been accorded some preferential treatment so that they would stay active within their institutions. One of the most popular ideas, the three-in-one combination, is often used at the university by balancing committees with old, middle-aged, and young people. Traditionally the Chinese felt that the young had to respect the old; now they think that both old and young people can learn together from each other. By having representatives of all ages working together in three-in-one combinations, the skills and knowledge of all can be joined.

At Tsinghua, as almost everywhere we went, we were told that the educational reforms are still experimental and open to further questioning and improvement. The basic direction has been determined, but the process of change goes on.

Peking University. On March 5 some members of our group visited Peking University for further discussions of the social role and the reeducation of the intellectuals in China. This university is in the northwestern suburbs of the city, not far from Tsinghua. It is made up of traditional-style buildings in a parklike setting, in contrast to the more contemporary design of Tsinghua.

We met there with a number of faculty members and cadres, including Chou P'ei-yüan, a theoretical physicist and vice-chairman of the University Revolutionary Committee and of the Chinese Science and Technology Association, our host in China. Chou, a distinguished-looking man of seventy years, was generally soft-spoken but often enthusiastic in conversation. At times, to be sure we understood his meaning, he would add his own comments in English after the interpreter had finished.

Peking University was founded in 1898 and was a missionary school for a time. Chou P'ei-yüan began by observing that the former missionary schools in China had played a role of cultural aggression. "They trained intellectuals under the influence of capitalist culture to serve foreign purposes." He went on to say that this was only natural, given their origins, just as Oxford and Cambridge couldn't be expected to train revolutionary cadres to overthrow the British Government. In 1950 changes were made in the departments to start the educational transformation. A middle school was set up at the university to provide a four-year preparatory course for workers, peasants, soldiers, and cadres. It was suspended when all the middle schools started to admit more students from these backgrounds. Since the Cultural Revolution, the university had begun to directly enroll students who are workers, peasants, and soldiers. Extra classes were given for students with relatively little academic training.

According to Chou, the process of educational transformation is now thought to have taken a wrong line under the leadership of Liu Shao-ch'i, who espoused uncritical support of the Soviet model. At that time Mao Tsetung had also called for learning from the Soviet Union, but favored learning the good and discarding the bad. The Chinese now view education in the Soviet Union as a system that fosters elites. Although the October Revolution in Russia was significant, the Russians did not have a cultural revolution, and thus no fundamental social change. Their schools now train elites for an intellectual aristocracy. China had a long tradition of this, going back almost three thousand years to Mencius, a disciple of Confucius, who thought that mental workers should rule physical laborers: "Those who work with the heart shall rule. Those who work with hands shall be ruled." The objective of higher education in the Soviet Union is to train scholars and authorities. Liu Shao-ch'i called for the training of Red Experts, with the emphasis on experts. That line is now regarded as leading to revisionism and the restoration of capitalism. The entire educational system was influenced by it: curriculum, teaching methods, and material. Under the Soviet influence the length of study in arts and letters was four to six years. Since the Cultural Revolution it has been shortened to three years or less.

Intellectuals can now play an important role in the revolution if they integrate with workers and peasants, and Peking University's integration is particularly interesting because one of the first progressive movements in China, the May 4, 1919, movement, started there under the influence of the October Revolution. The past history of the university became clearer when Chou P'ei-yüan told us his own story:

I was seventeen years old in Shanghai when the May 4 movement took place. Along with other young people in Shanghai I took part in it. I was studying then at a missionary middle school attached to St. John. Because I took part in the parade, I was expelled by the principal, who represented U.S. imperialism in China.

I entered Tsinghua College, which was a preparatory school for sending Chinese students to study abroad. From there I went to the United States for further study, earning B. A. and master's degrees from the University of Chicago, and a Ph.D. in theoretical physics from Cal Tech. I believed then that education and science would save our country. This was reformist and not revolutionary thinking.

In 1927 I was at Stanford University during the summer when Chiang Kai-shek betrayed the revolution. At that time students on the American West Coast were divided into two parts; I stood side by side with those who opposed Chiang Kai-shek. Three of my classmates from Tsinghua later became members of the Communist Party. One of them returned to Peking and did underground work. He was betrayed by a renegade, arrested, and executed. I realized that the Chiang Kai-shek government was reactionary and anti-people.

Influenced by reformist ideology, I returned in 1929 and engaged only in scientific research and teaching physics. I had no connection with the Chiang Kai-shek government; neither did I have the consciousness to appreciate the importance of the liberation movement of Mao Tse-tung and the Communist Party. This state of consciousness was common among Chinese intellectuals. I did not inquire into politics and I did not support the revolutionary movement, even though I didn't like Chiang. I was divorced from politics and was primarily concerned with my own work, teaching and research.

It was only after Liberation that progressive intellectuals came to see the importance of the liberation movement led by Chairman Mao. Only then did we learn to see its great significance.

I was excited when Liberation came. I thought the Chiang government was corrupt and hopeless, and I had great hope in the new government to create a different environment. The feelings of intellectuals at that time were different from those of workers and peasants. Liberation saved the workers from the abyss of bitterness and suffering, so they were grateful to Chairman Mao and the Communist Party from the bottom of their hearts. In comparison, intellectuals like ourselves led quite decent lives before Liberation, so it was impossible for us to have the same feelings as the workers and peasants. The increasing prosperity of the country built up our feelings somewhat closer to theirs. We felt more drawn to the Party and Chairman Mao. Quite a few high intellectuals joined the Communist Party and contributed their efforts to building socialism in China.

From 1929 to 1949 I taught at Tsinghua University, but had never engaged in administrative affairs. After Liberation I was appointed dean of the university. At that time I did not realize the significance of the position. The dean should train successors to the revolutionary cause and the building of the country. In 1952 I was transferred to Peking University as dean. Here too we actively took over the Soviet experience. We thought that Soviet education was the socialist type and were engaged in copying their educational system. As the Americans say, we were all "copy cats." In 1959, after ten years of education, I joined the Party, and in 1965 I was appointed vice-president of the University. During the Cultural Revolution I was criticized in the big-character posters that attacked the erroneous line pursued by the capitalist-roaders at Peking University.

After the entry of the workers' propaganda teams into the university, we began to realize the mistakes in our work. To facilitate our reeducation we ran an experimental farm in Kiangsi Province similar to Tsinghua's farm and like the cadre schools. At that time I was very anxious to go and volunteered, but the comrades thought that I was too old and did not permit me to go. After the propaganda team came, I realized the mistakes of my work and made self-criticism. It was a good opportunity for me to remold my knowledge. On September 27, 1969, the revolutionary committee of the university was established and I was elected vice-chairman by the masses.

This is the whole process of my ideological remolding, starting from the May 4 movement up to the present. The situation of many intellectuals was similar to mine.

At this point the discussion broke into groups of twos and threes. We went outside and continued our conversations while strolling through the grounds of the university. The walk took us through woods and alongside a good-sized lake, beyond which was a many-tiered pagoda. In reality it was the university's water tower, one of the most esthetically pleasing water towers we had ever seen. One group held an interview with Chao En-pu, who had been a student at Peking University during the Cultural Revolution, in which Chou P'ei-yüan served as the interpreter.

Questioner: Did you need reeducation in view of your outlook based on your own training before the Cultural Revolution?

Chao: Although I was a student before the Cultural Revolution, I feel that no matter whether one is a teacher or student, he needs remolding of world outlook. If a teacher establishes a correct world outlook, he can serve education. Before the Cultural Revolution, education was essentially capitalist, bourgeois, and revisionist. I was accustomed to the old ways of education and life. My father was a physician for the railway. I had essentially established a bourgeois world outlook. If not remolded, I would be bad as a teacher, so I needed remolding too.

Q: Do you feel that most of the teachers have successfully made the change, or do some of them still have problems and need further remolding?

Chao: We recognize that some ideological remolding is necessary for everyone. Thought remolding cannot be accomplished within a short time; it is a long-term task. We say, "We have to learn till old and remold till old." If we don't use proletarian thought to remold our ideology, bourgeois ideology will come into our heads. That is why we cannot let loose the remolding at any time. The problem of the intellectuals is how to continue thought remolding all the time ... The vast majority of teachers have undergone significant change in their ideology since the workers' propaganda team came to the university. Because feudalistic influence lasted for thousands of years in our country, and was followed by thirty to forty years of bourgeois influence, it will take a long time to overcome the feudal and capitalistic influences on teachers. I would make the point that it is impossible to have good thought remolding for everybody. We can only say that there has been a good beginning. We have only embarked on the way to unity with the workers, peasants, and soldiers. This road has to be followed for one's whole life.

Q: Is it possible to have complete success with old teachers, or does it take a new generation to complete the educational transformation?

Chao: In the course of the educational revolution, there is a need for new blood in the ranks of the teachers. Proletarian education should have successors. So far the number is not too great. Of the new graduates this year, we will have to retain some as teachers in the university. For the older teachers the task of ideological remolding is heavier. But if they can establish their stand for serving the people, then they also can contribute to the educational revolution. The old teachers are well experienced and have a higher academic level; under the correct political leadership and with the correct political line, they can accomplish much. For example, we have a seventy-eight-year-old professor, Feng Yu-lan, whose specialty is the history of Chinese philosophy. Before the Cultural Revolution he always made propaganda out of the philosophies of Confucius and Mencius. Now he uses Marxism, Leninism, and Mao Tse-tung Thought to reform his writings and thinking. As an initial step he has drawn up two plans, one to be carried out before he is eighty, and the other after he is eighty. Every week he writes many new lines of teaching material.

A professor of chemistry went with some comrades to the Number 3 Chemical Plant in Peking. They took part in labor with the workers and at the same time compiled teaching material on physical chemistry. This type of chemistry is very abstract and difficult to understand, but when they took part in the work they found that they could write about the theory and practice in an organic way. As they now put the theory it can be easily grasped by workers and students. There are many examples like this at our university, so we say that after the Cultural Revolution the youth of the old professors has been revived.

There are some 200 professors and associate professors, about a tenth of the 2,200 faculty members. Many of them have taken up teaching and research responsibilities and they also form an important force in the educational revolution. In leadership we have the three-in-one combinations of old, young, and middle-aged. Every age can make a contribution. Even in the Party committee of the university and the Party branches of the departments we have the older generation.

Q: Is there criticism of teachers by students and by other teachers?

Chao: We promote the spirit of criticism and self-criticism. The object is to help the individual progress. Teachers can criticize students and students can also criticize teachers. There is a principle of mutual help and mutual education. Teachers can also criticize each other.

Chou P'ei-ÿuan: A very important prerequisite in our criticism is that there is a foundation of comradeship. We are comrades-in-arms, that is why we help each other.

Q: Are there any shortcomings?

Chao: Because our educational revolution follows the line of Chairman Mao, we have achieved great accomplishments. But due to our lack of experience, what we have done is not sufficient. Many tasks and problems still exist. For example, the Department of Arts and Letters has to take the whole society as a factory. We still have to find the correct formulation for taking the whole society as a factory. The problem of how to combine theory in the classroom with practice in the society still needs to be implemented. There are other questions of how to write adequate teaching material for the needs of socialist construction, and how to bring about a teaching method that is enlightening. Educational revolution is a long task of strategic importance. We are still in a state of experiment.

Chou P'ei-ÿuan: I have the same feelings. We face the same problem in the science departments. We have established the university, run factories in it, and we have opened its gates to society. But we are still working on implementing the principle of integrating theory with practice. There are still many problems.

Futan University. At Futan University, in Shanghai, we met with a leading member of the University Revolutionary Committee, teachers of genetics, biology, nuclear physics, chemistry, mathematics, and English, and students who were workers and peasants. As at Tsinghua, the meeting began with a brief introduction. Futan is a university of liberal arts and sciences, founded in 1905. It was one of the main universities in China before Liberation. Of the thirteen departments, the seven in liberal arts are Chinese literature, journalism, history, philosophy, international politics, political economy, and foreign languages. The six science departments are physics, chemistry, biology, math, nuclear physics, and optics. In addition there are scientific research institutes and laboratories including the Institute of Genetics, the Mathematics Institute, the Linguistics Laboratory, and the Historical Geography Laboratory. The staff numbers 2935 teachers and workers, including 151 professors and associate professors, 292 lecturers, and 1331 assistants; the rest are administrators and other workers. During the Cultural Revolution there was a four-year shut-down in enrolling students. Since December of 1970 two groups of students totaling 1776 have been enrolled from among workers, peasants, and soldiers.

We visited a factory producing integrated solid state circuits, an optics laboratory, and the computer unit. The factory production line is used for students to gain practice. In addition the students also have some laboratories which serve the three-in-one purpose of allowing the students to do some practice, to do production work for society, and to do some research work on new circuits. The equipment in the laboratory was not very new, but all of it had been made by students. At the time of our visit there were no students there, but five women workers (about one-third of the workers are women) were doing diffusion and photoetching for semiconductors. The workers also do some study at the university and the courses they take include technology of semiconductors and semiconductor circuits. They have only had a high school education, but after working for two years they may enter the university.

The optical laboratory was started in 1960 to do research on making electric light sources in accordance with Mao's teachings of self-reliance. It is a developmental laboratory, with the results sent to a factory for large quantity production. These laboratories represent a three-in-one combinations of factory, institute (laboratory), and university; and of teacher, worker, and student. All the light sources researched and produced are used in equipment. Some of the sources we saw included an "axeson" high-repetition lamp, a 25-kilovolt lamp, a photoluminator lamp, a metal fluoride lamp, and a movie projector lamp. The worker who showed us through the lab told us the following story of the beginnings of the laboratory:

In 1960 a student broke the lamp in a piece of university equipment imported from the Soviet Union. We asked the Soviet Union to send us another lamp, but we were told that the only way we could get it would be to buy another unit of the equipment. But nothing was wrong with the equipment so why should we buy another? We only needed a lamp. I said not to. I did research and made a lamp. From this start, we now make all our lamps.

This worker-scientist has become a leading expert in electrosources and has been an invited participant at several international meetings.

Our principal host during the tour of the laboratories was a member of the Department of Nuclear Physics and we had some opportunity to discuss nuclear physics and research with him. During the Cultural Revolution, he told us, the Physics Department was divided into three parts: solid state physics, optics, and nuclear physics. There are seventy members in nuclear physics and fifty in nuclear chemistry, doing mainly support work for the nuclear physicists. At the moment there are thirty students in nuclear physics and thirty in nuclear chemistry. Whereas it took five years before the Cultural Revolution, the students now finish in three years, even in nuclear physics. This is another development that is regarded as still in an experimental or testing stage. Perhaps three years will not be enough. It may end up as three and a half or four, but the principle is that it should be as short as possible.

Most of the research in nuclear physics is basic. Some tasks come from the nuclear physics institute, such as studying radiation damage of solid state detectors, irradiation of seeds for agriculture, and testing of electronic equipment using a Van de Graaff generator, but not much research is being done on nuclear power. Our physicist host went on to say that there was also not much of a push for building nuclear reactors for research, although there was some research on fast breeders. Very little was being done on fusion, this being a very difficult and expensive field, and even the work on fission was not considerable.

There was also very little solar energy research, our host told us. Most energy research was in oil and a considerable number of oil fields had been found. Gasoline and oil used to be supplied from the Soviet Union, but this had stopped. In 1959 buses and cars carried large tanks of coal gas on top because there was no gasoline. Within a year of the discovery of the oil fields all these tanks had been removed. The coal gas (gas made from coal) was made at two large plants in Shanghai, but the Chinese were not thinking of it as a fuel for power production. Like other scientists we talked with, this physicist was aware that power sources and production are considered big problems in the United States, but this is thought to be due to overconsumption that can be avoided in China through careful long-term planning.

After our tour, one of our members discussed university administration with Tang Ching-wen, the "responsible member" of the revolutionary committee. His comments were in reply to questions about university organization and political activity. There are two hundred Party cadres in the university. Cadres spend two afternoons a week studying Marxism, Leninism, and Mao Tse-tung Thought; teachers, students, and the "broad masses" spend one afternoon a week. In addition, people study in their spare time.

Communist Youth League members number 1676, or 95 percent of the students. They work among young people as helpers of the Party. There is a Party committee in the university and each of the thirteen departments has a general Party branch. Decision making is done through discussions based on a two-in-one principle—leading cadres and masses, Party members and non-Party members. The opinions of the masses are absorbed, summarized, and returned to them for further discussion, Tang said. When it came to establishing the revolutionary committee, many discussions were held and opinions were recycled many times.

The revolutionary committee is made up of a number of three-in-one combinations: old, middle-aged, and young; teachers, students and worker-administrators; worker representatives, PLA, and revolutionary cadres. When it was formed in 1968, it consisted mainly of thirty or forty students with a few teachers. Now there are forty-two members: ten leading cadres, six workers-PLA, sixteen teachers, and six students. The committee is elected by the masses and gets its power from them, so it is expected to represent the opinion of the masses. The revolutionary committee is under the leadership of the Party committee, which makes policy.

Other members of our group discussed present educational practices at the university with Yang Fu-chia, a nuclear physics teacher; Chang Ho-lang, an English teacher; and Wang Shuang-lan and Ling Kuo-hsing, English students. Since all of them could speak English, this discussion was conducted almost entirely in English.

Questioner: Will the students tell about themselves as students?

Ling (a young man in his middle or late twenties): I entered the university in 1970 and have studied English for two years. Before coming to the university, I had not studied English. I cannot speak it very well.

Q: What did you do before entering the university?

Ling: I was in farming. After two years of farm work I was selected to be a barefoot doctor. I was a barefoot doctor for two years. Then I was selected for the university.

Q: Had you applied to come to the university or were you sent?

Chang (a pleasant woman in her mid-thirties): He had wanted to study at the university. The peasants also wanted him to study at the university. The leadership of the university considered these two aspects. The leadership from the university came to the farm and discussed it with him.

Yang (a man of about forty): Before the Cultural Revolution, students took exams to get in. Now, the students ask to come. The masses in his group also should say that he should go to the university. Also, people from the university interview him.

Q: Was English your interest or did you have other interests?.

Ling: The leaders of my production unit selected me to be a doctor. But before I had this medical knowledge, the leaders wanted me to do work in English, because the people need me to do it. So I do this work.

Q: After English, will you continue to study? Biology? Medicine?

Ling: The state needs me to study foreign language. So I have changed my job.

Wang (in her mid-twenties): I came from Sinkiang. When I graduated from middle school, I went to the countryside to receive reeducation by the peasants. After more than two years the leaders and peasants asked me to study in this university, so I am glad to come here, although I think it is far from Sinkiang to Shanghai.

Q: Did you study English before coming here?

Wang: I did not study English before entering the university in December 1970. Of course I met with many difficulties in my English study in the beginning. The first lesson the teacher taught us was "Long Live Chairman Mao." Before I had studied English how can I shout this slogan in English? But I cannot open my mouth, so I lost my heart. I thought to myself, "How can I study English well?" At that time a master worker, a member of the workers' propaganda team, found me to have a talk. She said to me: "You should study English well to talk to foreign guests." So I told her about what was in my mind, that because I didn't understand English, I cannot shout this slogan. At that time the teacher found me and helped me to pronounce it. That evening all our classmates and the teachers and workers came to our bedroom to help. I was very glad at that time and I was determined to study English from then on. Up to now, of course, I met many difficulties, but the teachers and students and workers often help me. I still think my English is very poor. Sometimes I cannot get my meaning across to other people.

Ling: Especially, I met difficulties when I began. My pronunciation is not good. My accent is very poor. I lost my heart. At that time I began to get up early and read the text many times. Teachers always help me in my room after class and correct my pronunciation. Since then I have made a little progress. With deep feeling, I shall say that my English is very poor but I have confidence to master English because the situation requires it.

Chang: They didn't speak English before coming to the university. They are working very hard. The students help each other.

Q: How difficult are the studies?

Chang: There are two periods every morning for English and two periods every week for political study.

Yang: They also study Chinese literature, philosophy, and international politics.

Wang: Sometimes we have self-study and meetings in the afternoon.

Chang: Also swimming and recreation.

Q: What sort of production work or farm work have you done while at the university?

Wang: In 1971 we went for two weeks in the countryside to help the farmers cut rice. During 1972 we often went to the docks and loaded and unloaded ships. Sometimes we worked with the workers, sometimes studied English. The first time we went for about three months, the second and third time for more than two weeks.

Yang: They often go to the docks. It gives them a chance to contact foreigners. They meet and talk with sailors. They still have a month and a half of vacation time.

All the students apologized for their English. While in many cases they were still somewhat slow and awkward, they could generally understand us and make themselves understood. Both Ling and Wang communicated effectively in English even though they may not have been as polished as they would have liked.

One of the major limitations on the number of foreign visitors to China is a shortage of interpreters, and the

Chinese have embarked on a crash program to train interpreters in all segments of the society. Many of the shop assistants at the Shanghai Friendship Store, a department store for foreign visitors, were students studying English at the Shanghai Institute for Foreign Languages. Several had been studying for less than half a year but already had a pretty good command of the language. While in Shanghai our group was accompanied by four or five students from this institute, which gave them the opportunity to observe more experienced interpreters at work and practice their English by interpreting informally. The master worker's talk with Wang about learning to talk with foreign visitors, the sending of students from the countryside to study English, and the building of large additions to presently unfilled hotels for foreign visitors in Peking and Canton are all suggestive of a program to meet an expected influx of foreign visitors. Our conversations with Ling, Wang, and other students would indicate that they are making good progress.

Chang: I graduated in 1963 and taught at Futan before the Cultural Revolution. Although I taught English before the Cultural Revolution, the methods of teaching were very poor then. Of course my method of teaching was very poor too. The methods of teaching now are quite different. Then, we just taught in class and just asked the students to read books in English. Now we lay emphasis on oral practice. Of course the system before the Cultural Revolution was bad, but I was not conscious of it at that time. Now I should say I was not satisfied with it. We seldom went to their dormitories to help the students before the Cultural Revolution. Now I go often to the dormitories to work with them. It is not awkward. I live near the university, just opposite it. It is very convenient for me to go to the dormitories. The students also come to my home if they have the time.

Q: Were you uncomfortable with the changes? What about student criticisms?

Chang: In class we sometimes have criticism. The students criticize the teachers, and if the teachers have opinions of the students we can also criticize the students. In ideology we help each other, so it is not difficult for me to hear their criticism. I think it is a good way to improve my work. If the students don't make any suggestions or if I can't hear their criticisms, I can't improve my teaching.

Yang: The worst thing in English was that we could not speak before the Cultural Revolution. We just read.

Chang: When I was a student, the teacher did not lay emphasis on speaking. So I was poor in speaking. Now I'm trying my best to speak more.

Q: In addition to sometimes going to the docks for short periods, in what other ways do you "take the whole society as your factory" in teaching English?

Chang: When on the docks we work side by side with the dockers and also study English. It also helps us in ideology. In addition, all our teaching material is selected according to the needs of the whole society. We read English newspapers and discuss them. We also go to the Seamen's Club to practice.

Q: In the United States, physicists are often among the worst examples of those who do not understand the need for practice and the need to understand politics. What about physics in China before and since the Cultural Revolution?

Yang: My interest is research work. I do very little teaching. I was the head of the laboratory. The main criticism I got during the Cultural Revolution was that I always determined myself the things I must do. I had no mass line. Now I am still the head of laboratory, but I discuss the research problems and decide everything with the masses. The research problems also have changed since the Cultural Revolution. Before we often did some work from the literature and references. Now we often go to factories or some institutes to know what people want. For example, we are doing research on methods to detect cancer by using radioactive tracers. Before the Cultural Revolution we never knew we could use our methods in such an important field. Some methods are quite useful in the hospitals. In such ways we combine our skills in practice.

Q: What were your feelings about taking direction from the masses?

Yang: At first I was not used to taking direction from the masses.

Q: What about differences of opinions?

Yang: We have further discussion. I absorb the right part from their opinion and discuss the wrong part with them. Then we got to a unified idea. I would say, in such a way the masses know much about why things are done the way they are.

Q: Is it better now?

Yang: I think so, such methods are an improvement.

Q: Do students in nuclear physics do research or have classes?

Yang: They have classes. Once a year they go to the factory. In the first year they go to an electronics equipment factory to see how the workers make equipment for analyzing radioactivity. Before the Cultural Revolution they only got some theoretical knowledge.

Q: What about your teaching?

Yang: Before the Cultural Revolution I had very little. Sometimes two classes a week. Right now I have no classes. I may have some in one or two months. Last year I had none. Before the Cultural Revolution I only taught in classes. After classes I never met with students. I could not know them by name.

Q: Do you enjoy meeting with students?

Yang: Yes. Since the Cultural Revolution the students study very hard. They have a very obvious sense of purpose. We can learn good character from them.

Chang: We should learn from each other.

Chungshan Sun Yat-sen University. At Chungshan University in Canton, we talked with P'u Chih-lung, a professor of entomology. Much of what was discussed with him concerned insect research connected with agriculture and is in-

cluded in the chapter on research institutes, but some of
our interview dealt with specific changes that had taken
place at the university as a result of the Cultural Revolution.

Chungshan University reopened in 1969 and the first
post-Cultural Revolution class graduated in 1973. As elsewhere in China, the university and the students are not
what they were before the upheavals of 1966–69. P'u Chih-
lung described how his students had changed: "There are
now more students from peasant backgrounds," he said.
"In the last two years some of the students have been
graduates of junior middle school. Before, most of them
were from high middle school. Now they have three
years' practical work in agriculture or in factories." As a
result, students usually spend more than half a year making
up courses. The Entomology Division at Chungshan currently has two grades, a freshman class with thirty students
and a junior class with forty. There is no sophomore class.
The standard period of undergraduate education is now
three years. The Biology Department as a whole now has
about 470 students in two grades.

We do not know the detailed course of the Cultural
Revolution at Chungshan, of course, but we did learn that
eventually a workers' propaganda team from local factories came to mediate the struggle among the teachers and
students. Most of the universities and institutes had been
host to one of these teams at some point during the Cultural Revolution. At Chungshan representatives of the
workers' team were still present at the administrative level
and within the departments. They make suggestions, we
were told, about the operation of the university and participate in the political education of teachers and students.

The writing and preparation of course materials is now
performed cooperatively by several teachers working as a
unit. They convene to discuss proposed courses and divide
among themselves the work of writing chapters for texts
and preparing laboratory exercises. When the work is
done they reconvene to discuss all the materials together
and solicit students criticism and opinion. Occasionally the
teachers also solicit the comments of commune techni-

cians. P'u himself thinks that it will be necessary to seek student opinion constantly and rewrite class materials every year.

The teachers follow collective course preparation with collective teaching. For example, in the Entomology Division four teachers join together to give a course in biological control. Among its advantages, collective teaching does away with a great deal of overlapping of subject matter in different courses, which P'u said was a serious problem before the Cultural Revolution.

At present, classes at Chungshan are relatively small, usually numbering forty or fifty students. In the Entomology Division students take courses in three basic areas. "Core" courses include mathematics, physics, chemistry, and politics. The material in each core course is adjusted to the needs of the students enrolled. For example, there are different elementary courses for biologists, geologists, and people in other specialties. At the next level of specialization, fundamental courses include zoology, animal physiology, botany, plant physiology, microbiology, and genetics. Finally there are specialty courses like insect taxonomy, applied entomology, insect physiology, insecticides, and entomological techniques. The division has a teaching staff of thirty people, including assistants and technicians.

"In the universities the most important task is education," P'u told us. But it is clear that neither the students nor teachers are cut off from the rest of the world. The Entomology Division regularly sends teams to various points in the countryside and maintains a fixed experiment station on a commune near Canton. Several teachers are always in residence at the commune, working for weeks or months at a time with the peasants and particularly with the commune's own science groups. On occasion the peasant technicians themselves come in to town to use the division's facilities in solving technical problems. Students work at the experiment station and must go to the fields every semester. In total, students spend about a fifth of their time in the countryside or in factories related to their studies. P'u noted that before the Cultural Revolution there was no regular system for sending students and teachers to the countryside and thus they did not go often.

We asked P'u about the current state of thinking concerning postgraduate education, a subject closely bound up with the whole idea of professional science. Right now, he said, the division hopes that their new college graduates will go to the countryside and supervise entomological work at the county or commune level. In the past many graduates went straight to work in research institutes or universities. The division is seriously considering admitting graduate students in one or two years, but it appears that it won't take students right out of college. As P'u told us:

> We think that, practically, the new graduate students should be graduated from the university or college and required to have several years of practical experience. And also, of course, part of the graduate students will come from the workers or peasants, if they have some prominent experience in a certain line. But whether or not we will offer a degree, we cannot decide. That's up to the central government.

This last remark is particularly interesting in light of the view expressed to us at the Institute for Chemistry in Peking that they were not going to grant higher degrees because such degrees broaden the gap between the holder and the working masses.

The professors in the Entomology Division are still discussing the length of graduate training. Before the Cultural Revolution graduate training lasted three or four years. Now, P'u Chih-lung said, they may not fix a specific number of years, especially for worker and peasant students. But everyone seems to agree that postgraduate students should be admitted. At least some graduate students are eventually expected to fill teaching posts in the universities.

P'u added that before the Cultural Revolution the entomologists at Chungshan offered only one course, general entomology. At that time entomology was just a subsection of a larger zoology division. Now, because entomology plays such an important role in agricultural development, the program has been elevated to independent divisional status and must offer many more courses, which requires more teachers. It is also conceivable that sometime in the future Chinese scientists may go to other countries to study particular problems, but this possibility is still remote at present.

No area of education, and ultimately of Chinese life, it seems, was left untouched by the Cultural Revolution. Gradually the staggering scope of this undertaking was beginning to dawn on us: underlying the political, economic, and social theory was a sweeping political movement of integration that extended from the pinnacle of government to the interior landscape of the person-on-the-street. The goal is a perfectly unified organism; the "enemy" includes every division, every boundary between classes, groups, and individuals, every category that both includes and excludes. We began to understand what was meant by the development of the "socialist consciousness" which is so often cited as the foundation of the society. More than a philosophy or an ideology, it is a unifying process drawing together the disparate elements of Chinese history and tradition into a grand synthesis of Marxism-Leninism and the ongoing experience of the Chinese people as they use scientific method to remold their world. Because capitalism is seen as a fragmenting principle, all tendencies toward division are regarded as capitalistic, whether they involve the social organization of schools or the intellectual organization of scientific disciplines—hence the description of book learning apart from active involvement with the world as "revisionist," or the tracking of students into ability groups as "following the capitalist road." All hierarchies are suspect.

Science in China is obviously more broadly defined than it is in western culture. It is a process of thinking and developing rational knowledge through practice. As such it should not be something mysterious and special, but a natural part of everyone's experience. From our observations and discussions it seems clear that science in China is regarded as part of the mass culture, based upon people's experience and one of the methods people use to solve problems—part of everyday life.

In the course of our tours of Chinese schools we had seen manifestations of the struggle to "put proletarian politics in command" everywhere. Before the Cultural Revolution the tendency toward creating a management elite based on expertise had threatened to remove the government from working-class rule. Now, however, politics came first and technique second. The class struggle, production, and scientific experiment had been made integral parts of the people's educational experience. Everyone in education—students, teachers, and administrators—was expected to engage in some aspect of production, both as a practical learning experience and as a means of unifying with the working-class base.

Before the Cultural Revolution, students had become divorced from the working people. They were shut off in universities and had little opportunity to gain practical knowledge. Admission was based on examination grades in the higher middle schools. Even a hierarchy of middle schools had developed, which favored students from middle-class backgrounds. Students from the countryside could not compete on the same terms with students from the better city schools that provided cultural and intellectual advantages. In addition, children of Party and administrative workers often went to collective boarding schools that had been established even before Liberation. At that time they were regarded as caring for the children of people involved in a difficult struggle for the future of their country. More recently, however, these schools had served to provide privileged treatment for the children of cadres. For the most part, they were the ones who went to university. Enrollment of students of working-class and lower and middle peasant backgrounds was low. At Peking University, for example, it was less than 40 percent in 1962.

In many ways the complaints about the Chinese education system that surfaced during the Cultural Revolution were similar to those voiced by protesting American students at almost the same time. The old method of teaching was basically a cram method. There were sharp contradictions between students and teachers, and each went their separate ways outside of class. A great deal of the learning expected of students was highly abstract and had little relationship to their concerns or the problems faced by the society. The cry of American students for relevance echoed similar sentiments in China.

Now students in China engage in some productive work throughout their educational careers. Most schools, including many primary ones, have productive work taking place on their premises. Students also spend some fraction of their school year working in factories or in the countryside. Upon completion of lower or higher middle school, the students become part of the country's work force, as workers in the factories or the countryside or in the armed forces. After two or more years of work they may apply and be selected by their fellow workers for possible admission to a university. Thus university students now come from among the masses and have a working background. They are first working people and second university students.

It seemed clear to us that relationships between teachers and students have been greatly improved. Teachers are familiar with their students' programs and even go to the dormitories to help them. Since the educational backgrounds of the students are not all the same, some having only attended lower middle school while others have completed higher middle school, time is allowed for review and more help and coaching is given to those who need it. Other students also offer their help so that no one lags behind.

Much of what has been done is regarded as still experimental, and just the first step on a "Long March." But students and teachers are truly remolding their outlook to identify with the workers and peasants. When we visited the Number I Normal School in Ch'angsha, we were shown an inscription made in 1950 by Mao Tse-tung, a former student and teacher there: "To be a teacher of the people, one must first be their pupil."

6 THE HEALTH CARE SYSTEM

It was a sunny March afternoon in Shanghai and we were driving back to our hotel after a visit to the Shanghai Jail. We sat in the back of the Chinese-made car with our interpreter Ch'iang Ch'i, gazing out at people riding bicycles, walking, going shopping or home. The scene was becoming familiar now: people of all ages dressed in pants and jackets of various sorts; grays, browns, blues, occasionally a bright yellow patterned jacket or a maroon scarf. All of a sudden we heard something different. It was the sound of cymbals, drums, and strange stringed instruments. Glancing ahead, we saw what appeared to be a demonstration. A group of about twenty-five people were marching down the street playing instruments, carrying red flags and big-character posters. Everyone was smiling, the women, men, and children who were marching, and others who joined or stood off to the side reading the posters and enjoying the sight.

Ch'iang Ch'i told us: "It's a medical propaganda team, from the local street committee. They often go through the streets informing people about health and how to prevent illness. The signs remind people that the weather is changing," she said, "and urge them to wear enough clothing and use traditional Chinese medicine to prevent colds.

Once again we were amazed at the involvement of everyday people in the drive to promote health in China. As a registered nurse, Judy had been trained in health care and "prevention philosophy," but in the United States, where health care delivery is largely restricted to professionals, the potential for public involvement in prevention has hardly been explored. In China she was to see a way to practice some of her own classroom ideals. Throughout our visit we were told that the major task of health workers in China is prevention. It is accomplished through this vast force of nonprofessional people who extend the reach of professionals.

During our stay in China we visited three hospitals in Shanghai and Peking, and a number of street clinics and clinics attached to communes, factories, and schools. We met many people on these visits, some directly involved in giving health care, others receiving these services, and discussed with them their feelings and their participation in health promotion. We heard the theory and saw the practice, and from it we concluded that "prevention work," so often used rhetorically in the United States, is a reality in the People's Republic of China.

The organization of health institutions in China is based on a division of labor. Clinics, which are integral parts of neighborhoods, factories, communes, and schools and often staffed by people from these units, do routine medical examinations, preliminary diagnosis, treat common disorders, and do health teaching with the community they serve. These local facilities refer people with more serious medical problems to higher levels in the health system. In large cities, in addition to general hospitals there are specialized facilities such as ear, nose, and throat, and maternity hospitals. These hospitals also train health workers for their outpatient clinics.

Cities in China are divided into districts, and districts into street committees that comprise as many as 70,000 people living in one area. Depending on their size, street committees have clinics or cooperative medical centers to serve the needs of their residents. The health workers in these clinics have either been trained in the hospitals or are paraprofessionals, called "barefoot doctors" after their namesakes who earlier extended the reach of medicine to the countryside. These barefoot doctors, trained by medical personnel at the clinics, treat colds, sore throats, carry out birth control propaganda, immunize children, and do hygiene and sanitation work. Essentially they treat the basically healthy individuals, freeing the hospital to use its personnel and equipment for serious cases.

Further examples of medical decentralization are the clinics attached to factories and schools, which function much like the street clinics, although in a large factory there may be doctors and nurses as well as paraprofessionals, and, there are often beds for extended care. If there is a serious illness or accident, the hospital is utilized. This kind of organization allows most people to be treated at their workplace or in their community. As a result, the staff of the hospital emergency room is not presented with a constant stream of minor ailments because people have elsewhere to go for treatment.

In rural areas we found the situation different because of the wide geographical distribution of people. Before Liberation the people in the countryside had almost no health facilities, and those that did exist were there to serve the rich. Between Liberation and the Cultural Revolution great strides were made in getting better treatment and prevention to the people, but it was disproportionately better for city dwellers. Joshua Horn, an English surgeon who spent over a decade working in China, describes the development of the health-care system in his book *Away With All Pests*. Now there is a major drive in the countryside to train health workers from communes who learn skills to serve the health needs of the peasants and, in turn, train others. In each provincial capital, we were told, there is at least one hospital where doctors, nurses, and other health workers are trained before returning to the communes. These professionals, assisted by medical teams from the large cities, then train barefoot doctors and midwives chosen from the peasants for part-time medical work. These paraprofessionals are then responsible for providing simple health care and teaching on the level of the production brigade. When a difficult case is encountered at the local level, it can be referred to the commune hospital or, if necessary, the hospital in the county seat.

The purpose of this structure, in the rural areas as in the cities, is to develop medical self-reliance. Since the small health units are linked to more specialized, centrally located hospitals in a systematic pattern, there is decentralization and, at the same time, a cooperative interdependence among all the health care facilities.

Street Clinics. One afternoon some members of our group visited the Wan P'u Street Committee in a part of Shanghai that had been a center of gambling, prostitution, and drug addiction before 1949. Here the effects of imperialism and its exploitive nature became very real to us as we climbed the old stairways to the former rooms of prostitutes, had former dens of opium shown us, and heard the stories of ex-addicts.

The committee office is in a small, uncluttered room right off the street. We were greeted there and told that this particular street committee represented 51,000 people living in the area. It has nine residential committees, which are voluntary groups organized for the specific blocks in the section. Also within its area are nine dining rooms, six nurseries, and various schools and service centers. Most interesting in our pursuit of medical practices were the nine cooperative medical centers, although other aspects of the committee are discussed in the chapter on planning.

We walked two blocks to one of the medical clinics, which was in a storefront. There we were met by five women barefoot doctors who, after four months of training in the local hospital, had been working in the street clinic for the past two years.

The clinic had a front room furnished with a desk, chairs, and large cabinets for medicines, both herbal (traditional Chinese) and western. Colorful posters, mostly for health teaching, decorated the white walls. We asked what the clinic's purpose was, and one of the barefoot doctors told us, "Prevention is our main task; to serve the people in this residential area."

The clinic opens at eight in the morning and about thirty patients are seen each day. Children and adults are given immunological vaccinations to prevent disease. Birth control propaganda, as well as the supplying of contraceptives and instruction in their use, is done at the clinic or in the community by the barefoot doctors. When someone feels ill he or she comes to the clinic for an examination. If the problem isn't very serious, the barefoot doctors dispense medicine and often give acupuncture, treatments for headaches, stomachaches, and sore throats. If a serious problem arises the barefoot doctors take the person to the hospital. "Even if the patient is unconscious," one of them told us, "we still use acupuncture on the way to the hospital." Later we learned a bit of practical acupuncture technique: halfway between the nose and mouth is a point that helps with shock and fainting. If a needle is not available, pressure by fingernail may be applied there until the person awakens.

When we asked about situations in which people were unable to come to the clinic, they replied, "If someone has high blood pressure, for example, and cannot come to the clinic, we will visit the home, give the treatment, and do some teaching about the condition. We are always willing to go to people's homes."

The question of medical records, which can be problematic for health facilities, is handled very easily at the clinic level. People keep their own records and bring them to the clinic when they are sick or are called for preventive vaccinations. This system involves the patients in their own medical care. They are responsible for their own medical records; they read them and know the status of their health. How different this seemed from the enormous record-keeping system in American hospitals, clinics, and private doctors' offices. In the United States there is a virtual ban on patients' reading of their own medical records, ostensibly to prevent misunderstanding of the seriousness of the descriptive terminology used by doctors, but of course it is the terminology itself and our lack of understanding of it that sets up the problem. We are left with a sense of powerlessness about health, a sense of mystery about the way our bodies function, and an awesome faith in what doctors do for us. It is a dependence that clearly serves the medical profession more than it serves us.

The eight other cooperative medical centers under the jurisdiction of the street committee were all doing similar work, according to our hosts: basically screening and prevention, so that the work of the hospital could be concentrated on patients who were seriously ill. In addition to direct health care, the clinics were involved in organizing community residents in activities such as the parade we had seen, and educating the community about health through the distribution of posters and discussions.

Factory Clinics. After our general tour of the Shanghai Machine Tool Works, we divided into three groups to discuss specific questions. One of the three met with health personnel and workers to talk about the services provided and the problems of occupational health at the factory. This factory, discussed in the industry chapter, has 6,000 workers and staff members. We learned that there were five health stations at the plant, each one serving about a thousand workers, and that there was also a sanatorium with 104 beds. In all there are forty medical workers: twenty-eight nurses and twelve doctors. Three of the doctors were originally workers in the factory who had been chosen to study medicine. They began their training in the factory clinic and were then sent to a hospital—in all, a one-year initial training period. After two years of practical work in the factory clinic they had been sent back to the hospital for an additional six months of training and study. Now they were back working in the clinics. Their preparation has consisted of a repeated pattern of practice and study, practice and study.

Factory clinics treat ordinary sickness such as colds, stomachaches, seasonal ailments, and small wounds. Workers can come to the clinic at any time during the day, and medical treatment is free for them. Their relatives can go to the clinic, but they generally pay half the cost of the medicine they receive. The workers at the machine tool factory also get their hospital registration free (the usual fee is 10 *fen,* about 5 cents). If a patient at this clinic is seriously ill, he is sent to one of five hospitals to which workers from the factory can go. For these workers medical treatment at the hospitals is free. The relationship between the health teams at the factory and the hospitals is a close one; they are involved in research work together to study the effects and prevention of occupational health hazards.

Besides treating sick people, factory clinics are involved in a considerable amount of prevention work. At the tool factory clinic every worker is given a chest x-ray once a year. Workers whose jobs bring them into contact with certain materials, such as nickel, are given blood tests at specified intervals to check for toxicity. Some chemical compounds of nickel damage the liver and spleen when swallowed, others cause dermatitis. One specific compound, nickel carbonyl, causes lung damage and can cause cancer. It is used in production of highly purified metals. The details of the processes using nickel or the surveillance program weren't discussed. Spreading information is another part of the prevention work. The medical teams here used the public address system and put up big character posters to educate the workers about wearing protective clothing and equipment, and taking other safety precautions.

There is also a special women's clinic in the factory, with a woman doctor. Once a year the women are screened for cervical and breast cancer. This clinic also conducts birth control propaganda. Here too we were reminded that women in China get fifty-six days of maternity leave with pay. When a woman returns to work she can bring her baby to the factory nursery, where she has time off each day to breastfeed and be with her child.

If a worker at this plant is sick and needs bed rest, he can either stay at home, if there is someone to care for him, or in the sanatorium at the factory, or in a hospital. For up to six months of sick leave he gets his full salary. Staying in the hospital would cost 40 *fen* a day (20 cents), while the factory sanatorium would cost 20 *fen* (10 cents).

One woman worker told us, "Before Liberation, if a worker was ill the bosses didn't want him to work and didn't pay him. Recently one worker had a tumor in her stomach. It cost 2000 *yüan* to remove (about $1000) and the state paid the whole operation. The workers say 'Socialism is good. It pays for our medical needs, and insures our health.'"

The discussion included a lively exchange about sex roles in the health system. When Liu P'ei-mu, one of the male clinic doctors, mentioned that five of the seven doctors were men but that all twenty-eight nurses were women, Judy asked why all the nurses were women. One of the (male) translators laughed at this, and the two male doctors present smiled, but a woman who worked in the clinic looked annoyed at their amusement. She explained: "In some other clinics and hospitals there are some male nurses, but here they are all women. This factory is a basic unit, not like a hospital. There is not a very clear distinction between their positions and they sometimes exchange work. The nurses give medical treatment and the doctors go to the shop."

Judy wasn't satisfied: "Why is there such a distinction between men and women?" The whole host group started discussing the matter, then the woman comrade continued: "In some hospitals there are more women than men doctors, and in the medical schools there are more women than men. In this factory, it just happens to be the other way. After the Cultural Revolution, the situation changed, and we pay more attention to women, not just as medical workers but as cadres, teachers and so on. But here, all the nurses were graduated before the Cultural Revolution. Women do more medical work than men."

Judy answered that, "In the United States also women do more medical work than men, but they get paid less." The clinic worker responded, "In our country that isn't so. An experienced nurse gets 100 *yüan* or more, while a new doctor gets paid 46 *yüan*. The highest paid doctor now makes about 100 *yüan*, doctors who were trained before the Cultural Revolution get about 60 *yüan*, but an experienced nurse makes the same as an experienced doctor."

This exchange illustrates a few points often repeated. Sex differentiation and typing exists in many fields, but is much less pronounced among young people, especially those trained after the Cultural Revolution. There is much emphasis on and many examples of women doing jobs formerly dominated by men, but there are many fewer examples of men doing jobs thought of as women's work. Ruth Sidel goes into this subject in considerably more depth and with broader documentation in her book, *Women and Child Care in China*, published by Penguin Books.

During the discussion we shared with our hosts some more of our own observations. As everywhere we went in China, our criticisms and suggestions were asked for and appreciated. In this case we commented that although medical equipment in China was not as advanced technologically as in the United States, it appeared that both the utilization of existing equipment and the relationship of people to people are so advanced that health work is clearly moving toward serving the needs of all the Chinese people. Even at our small meeting workers took part in the discussion along with the medical personnel and added their opinions about the health service. This interaction bridges the gap between people who are professionally trained and those who are not. It helps to eliminate professional elitism, the idea that people who are not academically trained have nothing to contribute. Time and time again, whenever we visited a medical institution, we witnessed on the part of staff a similar respect for people and a desire to learn from them. Of course, it was also made clear that medical workers do have special skills, and that their goal of educating people in the prevention of illness is pursued while they continue to treat existing medical problems. But we were impressed with the repeatedly stated philosophy that health knowledge belongs to all the people, not only to the few whose special training could otherwise set them apart from the people.

Hua Shan Hospital. When we visited Hua Shan Hospital, a teaching hospital attached to the Shanghai Medical College, on March 14, we were greeted by a cross-section of its workers, including nurses, doctors, professors, medical technicians, students, and ambulance drivers. Some of them were members of the revolutionary committee of the hospital. As elsewhere, this is the body that supervises the daily running of the institution.

As we entered the hospital we were led through a beautiful garden, in the traditional Chinese style, into a long one-room building. The garden, we were told, and all the other land on which the hospital stood had once been owned by a very rich man. This man had built the sanatorium and the intricate gardens with their carved wooden buildings for his only daughter, who had tuberculosis. Today the attractive wooden buildings, looking like teahouses, are used for classrooms and meeting rooms, while the garden provides relaxation and serenity for the patients and staff. A new concrete building now serves hundreds of patients, where before there were facilities for only one.

During our brief introduction, we were told over tea and cigarettes that the hospital has 607 beds and almost 800 workers, including 260 nurses, 215 doctors, more than 100 medical workers, and 160 people in administration. Although there are no barefoot doctors on the staff, they come to the hospital for study and training, and there are experimental classes for them at the medical college. Some of the hospital departments we heard mentioned during our introduction were internal medicine, surgery, neurology, dermatology, Chinese traditional medicine, and acupuncture and moxibustion (moxibustion is a traditional herb burning technique associated with acupuncture).

Our hosts told us about the workings of the hospital in a series of broad-ranging statements, one of which went like this:

During the process of the Cultural Revolution we acted according to Chairman Mao and put stress on the rural areas. We've already sent fourteen teams of doctors, nurses, etc., to rural areas, as well as to border and mountain regions of our motherland. These teams involve five hundred medical people. Of the medical workers greeting you today, many have done this work.

During these years we scored some achievements in curing diseases using combinations of Chinese and western medicine; for example, pneumonia, heart disease, and side effects of infantile paralysis. We've also achieved gains in acupuncture. At the end of 1972 we had done more than 2300 operations with acupuncture anesthesia. The efficiency of the operations is about 90 percent; but we think our work has just begun and we have a lot to do. After your visit, we would like your suggestions.

Today we would like to show you some operations with acupuncture anesthesia; removal of a brain tumor, gastrectomy [removal of part or all of the stomach], and, if there is time, a laminectomy [a back operation involving discs], removal of a neck tumor, and an operation for cancer of the jawbone.

After further descriptions of work at the hospital, our group was taken to see one of the operations. All ten of us, plus our interpreters and friends from the Foreign Affairs Office, were taken to the women's and men's dressing rooms in the main building, where we put on white gowns, masks, caps, and special boots, for our safety and that of the patients.

We were then ushered into the operating room, in the middle of which was a plain operating table. Three surgeons and a nurse in gowns, masks, and gloves stood over the patient, whose head was shaved and draped with sterile towels. Two other members of the medical team were holding her hand. Their role was to give the patient personal support and to watch her condition during the operation by taking her blood pressure and feeling the rate and quality of pulse. The patient was a schoolteacher, a thirty-three-year-old woman who had complained of headaches and convulsions for a year. She had been diagnosed as having a brain tumor; a craniotomy (opening into the cranium) to remove the tumor was to be performed.

On one of the walls of the operating room were two x-ray films of the woman's skull. One of the woman doctors who had greeted our group led us over to the films and outlined the tumor, explaining the procedure, risks, and possible outcomes—depending on whether the tumor was benign or malignant. Something struck us about the room: it was very simple. There were only one or two cabinets for supplies, and one small tray of instruments beside the operating table. Judy had recently watched a craniotomy in a college hospital near New York City. There had been an amazing amount of equipment. Still, it seemed to her that the biggest differences between the Chinese and American operations were in the type of anesthesia used and in the relationship of the staff to the patient and each other.

On another wall was a chart of the human body outlining the acupuncture channels and the various points. The patient was already anesthetized (technically, analgized, since the acupuncture effect here is analgesic rather than anesthetic) by one acupuncture needle in her cheek, but she was awake and alert. During the operation we walked around the table and peered into the drapes. The woman looked at us and acknowledged our presence. The surgeons, in the meantime, were deftly cutting through the top layers of scalp to the bone, through the bone, and removing the tumor itself. Unfortunately, they later indicated that the tumor was probably malignant.

Here we were, ten Americans, nine of whom had no medical training in terms of sterile operating room technique, standing with our notebooks and cameras in the midst of a craniotomy in the People's Republic of China. The Chinese seemed more comfortable with our presence in the operating room than we were. Our anxiety about possible intrusions into the sterile field, so important to preventing infection, was allayed by the reassurance that the medical team's calm and competence conveyed.

The operation itself—the patient awake while her head

was being cut open and the tumor removed—was impressive to us. Although the surgeons and nurses worked quickly, they took time to talk to her. They showed respect and compassion and solicited her response to the procedure. It was the first operation any of us had ever seen in which the team effort included the patient as an integral part of the team.

The first especially interesting thing about the craniotomy operation was the surgical use of acupuncture anesthesia, which we had seen in experimental use and whose theories we had discussed with several researchers. Only one needle was used in the craniotomy, but other operations we saw, like the gastrectomy, performed on a young man, involved as many as eight needles. We were told at this hospital that the number of needles varies with the location of the operation and the individual person. If the patient is uncomfortable, more needles may be inserted, or the frequency with which they are turned may be increased. The needles require vibration to be effective and can be connected to a very low-voltage electrical source as an easily controlled substitute for manual manipulation. We were also told that there are certain benefits to acupuncture anesthetic when used effectively, with the cooperation of the patient. There is a smaller postoperative risk of pneumonia because the patient does not face the problem of the copious secretions that follow general anesthesia and the use of tubes inserted to maintain ventilation. The recovery time is markedly shortened because the patient is awake and can begin functioning earlier. The patient himself, since he is integrated into the procedure, tends to have more understanding and less fear of pain. The acupuncture technique is believed by some to have a homeostatic effect on circulation, which would account for the lower risk of bleeding during the operation. As a result, fewer transfusions are required and there is less risk of incompatibility reactions.

The other important difference was the working relationship between nurses, doctors, and other members of the health team, including the patients. In the United States the hierarchy among health workers, especially among doctors and nurses, and nurses and aides, creates antagonisms which may hinder the care of the patient. There is often more tension than trust between co-workers and, as a result, less of the creative teamwork that would better serve the health needs of the people. One nurse in China told us:

> Before the Cultural Revolution there was a large gap between nurses and doctors. The nurse had practical experience, but couldn't cure the patient because of restrictions. For example, if a patient felt pain, the nurse had to wake the doctor to give the medication. Now this has changed. Doctors and nurses represent a division of labor; the goal is the same: to serve the people wholeheartedly. So the relationship between nurses and doctors is a relationship of comrades.

Nurses now take part in medical work that was traditionally the property of physicians (and are now recruited for training *as* physicians). They can perform diagnostic punctures, such as spinal taps, physical exams, minor surgery, and acupuncture treatments. The emphasis of the Chinese medical system is on medical workers learning and acquiring new health skills, and on the mass of the population improving the overall prevention work. Nurses and doctors are in the same study groups and offer criticism aimed at improving their work together. In the past, we were told, doctors often developed ideas that made them feel all-important, thereby diminishing the work of their medical colleagues. Now, however, doctors take part in physical labor. In many cases they thoroughly clean the operating room once a week, to "lower their airs."

Nurses' training is the same as for other students. It follows a simple principle put forth by Chairman Mao, that school instruction must be shortened and education revolutionized. The period of schooling for nurses is two years. The students have either finished junior middle school or are graduates who have trained in the countryside for several years. They are trained at a special nursing school and at a school run by the hospital. The teaching method at the hospital is mainly concerned with practical experience. The nurses study while working, and are taught theory and skills linked to their practice. One of the nurses said:

> When students come to classes they spend half a day in the workroom, taking part in medical work and learning how to support the patient. The other half of the day is devoted to learning basic theory. In the workroom students serve the patient immediately and in this process they learn medical skills. After half a year students are acquainted with the work room and nursing-medical skills. After a whole year they can work in the daytime or at night, and solve some problems independently. This teaching method is high-speed ... and combines in a shorter time the necessary knowledge.
>
> We act according to Chairman Mao's teaching that we should pay more attention to medical work in the rural areas. So the nurses don't only study how to support the patients, they also learn some skill in curing diseases. When they go to the countryside they can use these skills to serve the broad masses of poor and lower-middle peasants. In the cities they can learn more about their nursing work, how to support the patient. There are close links.

The relationship between students and teachers seemed to have the same openness we had seen before in schools, factories, and hospitals. Since the Cultural Revolution, students and teachers meet together for criticism/self-criticism sessions and have discussions on how to improve education. They try to break down the old enmities and fears that existed between them. Teachers are to learn from the students as well as teach them. There are still examinations, especially practical ones in medical treatment, but the teachers regard the results as reflections of their own work as well as that of the students.

At Hua Shan Hospital basic medical training for doctors has been reduced to a three-year course. Like the nursing program, it links theory and practice in its curriculum. Students are chosen from among the workers, peasants, and members of the People's Liberation Army. They must have a high political consciousness, an understanding of the life of the masses, and experience in class struggle, production, and scientific research. The students not only study medicine but also help to reform the medical college, struggling against old elitist ideas and habits. This struggle, we were told, would contribute to better understanding of technical knowledge.

There are no rigorous limitations of practice related to academic degrees in China's health program. When students finish nursing or medical training they work with the people according to their experience and knowledge. If a nurse has considerable experience, and is skilled, she or he can carry out medical tasks traditionally performed by physicians. Often nurses who have become experienced on the job, and have gained more knowledge, can function much like doctors. In medicine, as in other areas of Chinese society, there is a flexibility of function born of scarce resources that we do not see in the United States, where nurses and paramedics are prohibited by law from performing many simple medical procedures that lie within their sphere of competence. Some relaxation in these restrictions being considered here, especially in the area of midwifery, is due in part to lobbying by the women's movement, but by and large the medical profession resists such reforms as incursions on their prerogatives.

We met one young man who had formerly been a barefoot doctor and was now back in the hospital, studying for another period of almost three years to become a full physician. Although most barefoot doctors don't become physicians, this one being an exception, many do return to hospitals for updated knowledge and to acquire new skills. It is more common for nurses to become doctors, either while working on the job or by returning to a medical institution after selection by fellow workers.

The management of Hua Shan Hospital is no exception to the rule that politics are deeply inbedded in every facet of Chinese life. The hospital is run by a revolutionary committee of fourteen: three cadres (administrators), two workers, two nurses, and seven doctors. Four of these people are women, and six are members of the Chinese Communist Party. The Committee implements the policies that have been decided upon by the Party branch in the hospital, half of whose members are medical workers, the others being administrators and members of the "workers' propaganda team of Mao Tse-tung Thought." All the workers in the hospital are organized into political study groups, in which discussions of readings as well as criticism/self-criticism concerning hospital work, are carried out toward the goal of better serving the people's health needs.

Peking Maternity Hospital. Maternity care in the People's Republic of China reflects the growing equality and dignity of Chinese women. The Peking Maternity Hospital was built in 1959 to promote the health of women and their newborn. It has a staff of 398, of whom 250 are doctors and nurses. Ninety-eight percent of the medical staff are women. Obstetrical and gynecological care in the United States is largely administered and delivered by men, but the Chinese seem to believe that women are more comfortable discussing the status of their health with other women, who can understand more fully the functioning of their bodies.

The hospital is divided into several different departments, one of which is an outpatient clinic of thirty beds. There women rest for two or three hours after an abortion or the insertion of an intrauterine device. If a woman has an abortion she is entitled to two weeks' vacation from work to regain her health. The main function of the outpatient clinic is to provide family planning services to prevent the need for abortion. IUD (intrauterine device) insertions are done in the clinic, after which women have two days off from work. IUDs are usually inserted two months after a birth and are not changed for five to ten years unless there are complications. The clinic also dispenses birth control pills, which are widely used in China. The pill usually prescribed now is taken once a day for twenty-two days, until the menstrual period. Research is currently being done on pills taken once a week, once a month, and once every three months. Research is also under way on the use of prostaglandins, a class of hormone that may be applicable to male birth control by immobilizing sperm; as in the United States, it is proceeding slowly. Tubal ligations, in which the Fallopian tubes are tied, are done in the operating room, and vasectomies are performed in the general hospitals of Peking. One of the doctors told us that there are more tubal ligations than vasectomies, and indicated that more propaganda should be directed at men, since a vasectomy is in some respects an easier operation. More attention seemed to be directed at male responsibility for birth control and child rearing in China than in the United States, but it seemed to us that in this area there was considerable room for improvement in both countries.

The outpatient clinic checks up on women after operations and conducts classes in prenatal care. Some individual consultation is given if problems arise, but most of the instruction is done in group classes. After pregnancy is ascertained, women are seen once a month for two months, then every two weeks, and in the last month, once a week. Topics discussed with the women include nutrition during pregnancy and the pastpartum lactating period, knowledge of the birth process, fetal development, labor and delivery, the care of the newborn, and family planning after the birth of the child.

Population and birth rate figures for China as a whole are hard to come by. Some are given by Ruth and Victor Sidel in an article in the April 1974 issue of *Scientific American*. In 1972 Shanghai reported a birth rate of 6.4 per thousand population for the central city. A small neighborhood in Hangchow had a birth rate of 5.9 per thousand. The comparable figures in two rural areas near Peking were 24 per thousand and 21 per thousand in 1971. The birth rate in pre-Liberation China has been estimated to be 45 per thousand. For comparison, the birth rate for the United States white population was 17 per thousand.

In China, contraceptive materials and information have been made available at the local level. A planned family life has been made a national goal, and the reasons for the goal, as well as contraceptive techniques have been spread by health workers trained from among the residents of the neighborhoods and communes. In our opinion, the liberation of women, as shown by the trends of movement into the job market, freedom of choice in marriage, an ending to discrimination in jobs and leadership positions and an attack on many of the ideas of female inferiority has been the major cause of the drop in the birth rate. At the same time, control over reproductive life has been a great force in the liberation of women.

In a similar way, the liberation from age as a class factor has also acted to curb family size. The pension for workers in factories and government jobs is 70% of the wage which means that parents need not worry about having many children to support them in retirement.

Another factor in reducing family size has been the decrease in infant mortality. Parents no long need to have many children in the hope that a few would grow to adulthood. In 1949 the death rate for children under one year old in Shanghai was 150 per 1000 live births. At the same time the death rate in New York City was 24 per thousand for whites and 41 per thousand for non-whites. By 1959 the death rate in Shanghai had dropped to 38 per thousand, and in 1972 it was stated to be 8.8 per thousand. The comparable figures in New York in 1970 for whites and non-whites were 19 and 26. The staff at the Peking Maternity Hospital reported a figure of 7.7 per thousand for their area.

The obstetrical department has 120 beds, plus a nursery with a hundred cribs and twelve incubators. The labor room has eight beds which, when we entered, were all filled with women in active labor. It was a bright room, with large windows and white walls. No medication is given to the women during labor, but some deep-breathing exercises are done to relax them. None of the women was screaming or appeared to be in pain. No drugs like scopolamine, an amnesiac used widely in the United States as an uninhibiting agent, are used. This contributes to the women's dignity by enabling them to have control during the birth and to recall it clearly later.

There are six delivery beds in the department, three in single rooms and three in one room. Normally no anesthesia is used except in a difficult delivery such as posterior or breech presentation. In these cases acupuncture is used. If a Caesarean section is indicated, acupuncture is usually the anesthesia of choice, although epidurals (injections of the anesthetizing agent carbocaine) are sometimes administered.

Episiotomies (incisions made to ease birth) are not done as routinely as in the United States. About 30 percent of the women delivering their first babies receive them. The percentage drops after the first birth.

Husbands are not present in the delivery room. When we asked why, we were told, "There is no need for them." The delivery room was plain and simple: women deliver in flat beds and use leg supports only in a difficult delivery. No intravenous bags and poles were in evidence. Only a suction unit and some oxygen were present in case the baby should be in respiratory distress. All other supplies are kept in a nearby closet "to avoid frightening the mother." Forceps are rarely used; if there is difficulty, the suction method is preferred for helping the baby through the vaginal canal.

After delivery, women rest in the postpartum unit for four to six days. When we visited the unit there were seven women—peasants, workers, and administrators—all in the same room, talking and smiling together.

The babies are not brought to the mother until twelve hours after the delivery, to allow her some rest. During that time the babies are fed a bottle of sugared water. From then on they are breastfed every four hours, with little or no supplemental feeding. Babies do not stay in the same room with their mothers during the postpartum period because of the risk of infection. Women usually breastfeed up to one and a half years, the hospital staff told us, and children are weaned directly from the breast to the cup.

We next visited the gynecology department, where we were invited to watch an ovarian cyst operation. The patient, a thirty-three-year-old factory worker, was anesthetized with a tranquilizer and six acupuncture needles. The operation was performed very quickly and successfully. The woman was awake throughout and three doctors and nurses stood by her head, feeding her orange slices, talking to her, and generally supporting her morale. When the cyst was removed the surgeons showed it to her and then proceeded to do a tubal ligation; the woman had three children and didn't want any more. The whole operation was done within half an hour. After the closure, we walked down from the observation theater and entered the room. The woman sat up, smiled, and told us she felt fine. We asked about the recovery period and were told that this patient would go straight to her room because with acupuncture there was less bleeding and no complications in the respiratory system.

After finishing our tour of the hospital with a talk over tea, we walked out on one of the balconies. Before us lay the temples and dwellings of the old Forbidden City and the Imperial Palace, beautiful and serene, and now a shrine to the creativity and skill of the working people of China. In a similar way, we felt that the Peking Maternity Hospital was also a shrine—to the health and happiness of Chinese workingwomen and the society as a whole. Here pregnant women were treated as healthy people and not as if they were suffering from a disease. The birth of China's young, the "bright stars of its future," was taking place in an open, warm, and cooperative atmosphere, one that was truly conducive to health and happy recovery.

Hsikou People's Commune and Protection Brigade. Our introduction to rural medicine in China was provided by visits to two communes: the Hsikou People's Commune in

Shansi Province, and the Red Star Sino-Korean Friendship Commune outside Peking. As we mentioned in the agriculture chapter, the entire Hsikou Commune, in North Central China, contains 15,000 people divided into ten production brigades. The production brigade where we stayed has 1600 members, divided into twelve production teams. We visited its clinic one afternoon to get an overview of health work at a rural commune.

The Hsikou Production Birgade Clinic was a two-story structure built into the side of a mountain. The four rooms on the bottom floor looked like reinforced caves, a common form of architecture we saw in mountainous regions. It had been built in two months during 1972 by the peasants and medical workers, who used timber and stone from the local area—a nice example of medical self-reliance.

Yang Ch'i-tzu, the young, energetic doctor, was born in Hsikou and trained in the provincial capital for three years. He led us up the steep, winding path to the top floor of the clinic. (Patients get to the top floor either by walking or being carried, as they would anywhere else in this community since the whole place is built into the side of a mountain.) The clinic is separated into a traditional section on the bottom floor and a western-style one at the top. Inside was a long hallway with rooms along the right and windows on the left, through which sunlight streamed onto the stucco walls. At the end was the operating room, built just a few months earlier. It was of adequate size, comparable to any in American hospitals, but it was extremely bare. There were two beds, a coal stove, a modern lamp, an operating table, and a cabinet with medicines and instruments. There were no intravenous bottles and no complex anesthesia equipment. The view from the windows on the far wall looked out over the homes and fields in the valley to the terraced mountains on the other side.

Yang Ch'i-tzu told us the various types of operations that had been performed in the past two months, including a gastrectomy for stomach ulcers and a Caesarean-section birth. They gave no general anesthesia but, instead, used epidurals, in which the anesthetic agent is introduced close to rather than into the spinal column in such a way that the fluid enters the spinal column and the central nervous system by absorption. (Epidurals are used in the United States but are not preferred by doctors because they take longer to administer and they keep the patient conscious.) We were told that one of the nurses from the clinic had been sent to the county hospital for three months to learn acupuncture anesthesia. When he returned, he would form a class and teach the technique to the other medical workers.

"Eighty percent of all operations in the county hospital are done with acupuncture anesthesia," Yang Ch'i-tzu told us. "When we learn it we will also use it. We can do operations, such as removing the appendix, even in peasants' homes now; but it will be much safer and easier with that new knowledge."

Next to the operating room was the pharmacy, where both western and traditional Chinese medicines are stored in large cabinets. Most of the medicines are generally procured from the county seat, but some of the herbal medicines are collected in the surrounding area by adults and children in the brigade. Like other medical workers, the pharmicist, a woman in her late twenties, was trained at the county seat for a year, returned for practical work in the brigade, went back for another year of training, and is now back to work in the brigade clinic. She told us that patients get a full explanation of their disease, along with the medication ordered. They are also taught methods of prevention. Both medical care and medications are free.

It was cold outside when we went back down the dirt path to the lower level of the clinic, and we buttoned the white lab coats we had put on over our jackets. The mountains were covered with snow from the last night's flurry. Somehow this rugged setting enhanced our appreciation of Hsikou hard work for quality rural health care.

One of the rooms on the lower level contained the traditional Chinese medicine clinic. Opposite the door, a picture of Chairman Mao hung on one of the white walls. Cha Tzu-an, the traditional Chinese doctor, was there. He was an older man, of sixty-nine years, short and squat, with a wide, warm smile and deep, pensive eyes. He was at his desk when we walked in, listening to a peasant woman and studying her carefully. He felt the pulse in her wrist and asked her to stick out her tongue, then proceeded with questions about her complaint, following traditional practice. He told us that the woman had rheumatism and ended by giving her four varieties of Chinese herbal medicine.

We watched a barefoot doctor from one of the other Hsikou brigades who had come to the clinic for a month or so of further training. He administered acupuncture treatment to three people, a woman and a boy who both had stomachaches, and a woman with a backache. He treated the woman with the backache by placing one needle in her stomach and one in each of her arms, above the inside of her wrists. He went from patient to patient, turning the needles and asking whether they felt any sensations, and if they felt better or worse.

When people in the production brigade feel ill, they come to the clinic and are seen by a doctor. If their problems can be treated by traditional Chinese medicine, they are referred to Cha Tzu-an for herbal medicine or acupuncture. If not, there is a clinic for western medicine next door. When we looked in on it a woman doctor was examining a young woman while two other women waited to be seen. The examination was held in full view of the other patients, not in private. There seems to be little shyness concerning medical affairs among people in China, and certainly there is no secrecy, such as keeping the diagnosis from a patient. Many women had come to the clinic to see the woman doctor, who usually alternates days with a man.

We met the clinic midwife, Yang She-lang, who trained in the county hospital for a year and now teaches the "responsible person" in each of the ten production brigades about childbearing. Almost all the births that Yang She-lang delivers are done in the peasants' homes. If there is some difficulty, or a Caesarean section is needed, the woman comes to the clinic. Epidurals and local anesthetics were currently used, but were to be replaced to a large

degree when the commune health workers learned acupuncture anesthesia.

Abortions are also performed in the rural areas. The
suction method is used with good results. It is a quick and
uncomplicated technique: a vacuum created in a sealed
bottle is attached to an instrument that sucks out the uter-
ine contents. A meter indicates the strength of the suction
and no electricity is needed. Because of the good birth control education, we were told, combined with the tendency
of peasants in the countryside to have more children than
urban people, abortions are not performed often. But they
are available, and they are free.

After the tour was over we met with Yang Ch'i-tzu
again for a general discussion about the work of the clinic.
He reminded us that it was built only at the end of 1972;
as a result, there was still a gap between the work it could
do and the needs of the people. He emphasized how
closely related the clinic was to the economic and political
life of the commune. After all, he pointed out, it was the
increase in production of the commune that led to the
creation of the clinic and the training of skilled medical
workers. And now that the clinic was established:

> The primary way to maintain and improve the
> health care is to create a medical team that works to-
> gether and grows together, one that isn't divorced
> from the people. The medical workers in Hsikou meet
> together six times a week: doctors, nurses, barefoot
> doctors, midwives, etc. Four times a week they en-
> gage in political study, with one hour a week for crit-
> icism/self-criticism and one hour for medical study.
> These meetings create a foundation for communica-
> tion and growth, breaking down the professional divi-
> sions between the health workers, and between the
> professionals and the peasants.
>
> In our work, the main task is prevention. We
> haven't had an epidemic of infectious diseases in ten
> years. By 1970 we had cured all the regional diseases,
> such as those of the thyroid gland. [Probably goiter
> caused by lack of iodine in diet.] Often we use tradi-

tional methods of treatment, incorporating herbs and acupuncture. We do propaganda about family planning, and have wiped out tetanus in the newborn infants. Since Liberation we have wiped out venereal disease. Now our task is the prevention of diseases that come in the spring. [Probably flu viruses but we are not positive.] Already we have seen 6,000 people and given them Chinese herbs.

The medical workers at Hsikou give preventive injections, especially to children, and distribute traditional Chinese herbs. Education is also vital to their work, especially that connected with periodic checks of the drinking water, of night soil fertilizer, and of the fruit trees. By solving the problems of diseases among the peasants they improve the general level of health and contribute to increasing production. The work of the rural medical workers molds itself to the life and needs of the peasants.

An effort is also made to broaden the understanding of health care techniques. All the middle school children here, as well as many older peasants, knew up to thirty acupuncture points, so that simple ailments like headaches could be cured by the people themselves. Barefoot doctors trained at the clinic from time to time and four of the regular doctors worked in the fields with the peasants. They thus learned people's needs directly so that the clinic could evaluate its work and change priorities as needed. Already there was planning for a thirty-bed unit by the end of this year.

Our discussion over, we walked outside into the cold, brisk air. The sun was beginning to set behind the mountains, and the fresh snow from the morning took on an icy purplish hue. We took some photographs of our hosts, who posed together in their white gowns and caps in front of the clinic they had helped to build and about which they were simultaneously proud and modest. For us it seemed almost an ideal image of rural health care, dedicated to working collectively to serve the people. It was different indeed from health care in the rural areas of our own country, where private doctors are often few and far between and have next to no paraprofessionals to enable them to meet health care needs.

The Hsikou clinic is an example of the growth in health care facilities in China's countryside which is one of the latest developments in the growth of the Chinese medical system. Sanitation work, especially the control of human wastes, an end to periodic famine, pest control projects, mass campaigns against disease and the general improvement in life in the country certainly has a profound effect on the health of the peasants. But the early stages of growth of the health care system (doctors and hospitals) had concentrated in the cities. In 1965 this pattern was denounced by Mao Tse-tung:

> Tell the Minister of Public Health that the Ministry works only for 15 percent of the nation's population, and that of this 15 percent only the lords are served. The broad masses of peasants do not get medical treatment, and they are provided with neither doctors nor with medicine. The Ministry of Public Health is not that of the people, and it is better to rename it as the Ministry of Urban Health, or the Lords' Health Ministry or the Health Ministry of the Urban Lords.

The turmoil of the Cultural Revolution put this policy into action. The most important act was to send mobile medical teams, made up of urban and People's Liberation Army medical personnel to the countryside in great numbers to train medical workers. There was also an improvement in facilities, as shown by the newly built clinic at Hsikou. There was also a growth in cooperative insurance plans at this time. The cost of medical care deserves a brief explanation. The People's Communes operate differently from most enterprises in the city. A factory worker is an employee of the state. The government owns the factory, pays his or her salary and provides medical insurance and facilities as part of the job benefits. In contrast, a commune member works land and shares in crops which are communally owned, not state owned. Before the Cultural Revolution, medical expenses were generally borne by the individual peasant and his family, although there were many cases where commune members pitched in to help out (see Horn). Since the Cultural Revolution, the pattern has been to establish cooperative insurance plans, where peasants pay in a certain amount per year, reportedly about one *yüan*. Overall, 70% of the communes have established such plans, and since these are concentrated in the more highly populated areas, probably more than 70% of the peasants are included. We could learn little of how this works in practice. Probably building a clinic or hiring a doctor is a decision made like other types of commune or brigade investment decisions.

Red Star Sino-Korean Friendship Commune. The Red Star Commune, on the outskirts of Peking, is considered a suburban commune because of its close proximity to the city. Because of this, medical care at Red Star is somewhat more developed than in remote rural areas like Xigou. The commune has 78,000 members who are divided by work into ten administrative districts. Their health needs are served by a clinic in each administrative district and a hospital for the whole commune. In addition, each of the 124 production brigades has two or three barefoot doctors who do the same work as the other people much of the time but also deal with everyday illnesses and accidents. They keep track of their fellow workers' health and do preventive work, like giving immunological vaccinations.

Once more we were told that living and health conditions are directly related to production. If pig production increases, there is more manure, which increases grain production, which raises the standard of living of the people, allowing for more medical services, and therefore improving health.

We walked through several different rooms in the clinic during our brief tour. The first one, the internal medicine room, was small, with only a bed, desk, table, and stove. The woman doctor, who had studied for three years at a medical school in Peking, told us that their main task was prevention. Clinic workers go out to the production brigades and homes every month to give inoculations and do other preventive work. They work closely on a day-to-day basis with the barefoot doctors, who provide the first line of health care. When people in the brigades get sick they go to the barefoot doctors for help. If the barefoot doctors can't solve the problem, the person is sent to the clinic. If further help is required beyond the clinic level, the patient is sent to the commune hospital.

Both western and traditional varieties of Chinese medicine were stored in the neighboring rooms. We found the room devoted entirely to herbal storage fascinating. The smell of anise floated through the cold, clear air, among the burlap bags and trays of roots, flowers, and leaves. It was a "treasure house of nature" being used to cure and prevent human ills. In the West virtually total emphasis is placed on the scientific production of medicine, and so much skepticism or scorn is directed against the tradition of natural healing (such as American Indian medical practices) that we forget that many of today's wonder drugs are synthetic copies of organic substances whose use has been documented for centuries, and do not take advantage of the further potential which surely lies in our own traditional herbal medicines.

The integration of herbs and acupuncture into western style medicine is also a very practical policy. Every time acupuncture can be used in place of a drug, the commune or neighborhood clinic becomes a bit more self-sufficient. Communes and other units grow or gather medicinal herbs, which means less work that the chemical and drug industry has to do, and less problems in shipping material to the countryside. This practice can be considered parallel to the emphasis on biological insect control methods, which are also promoted in part to free the local agricultural units from dependence on the chemical industry. The development of science and technology is determined by social goals. Also, while the drug industry is developing and spreading, the Chinese use what is already there. This is another example of "walking on two legs."

In the small acupuncture room we saw three people receiving treatment. One woman had not been able to move her arm. After five treatments, movement had returned and its range was increasing steadily. The treatment consisted of placing one very small needle in her right temple and three others in each shoulder. They were turned often during the course of treatment, which lasted about twenty minutes. The woman sat up during the acupuncture and explained her case to us, periodically stroking her young son, who was sitting next to her. We were told that acupuncture is also used in this clinic for treating mental diseases, since it decreases anxieties and hallucinations.

Across the courtyard we visited the gynecology and family planning room. We were greeted there by the midwife, a woman who had been trained by doctors at the commune for three months. She sees all the gynecology and prenatal cases and delivers all the babies, with the exception of high-risk births, either in the women's homes or at the clinic. With regard to birth control, she told us that the pill and IUD are used almost exclusively. We were deeply involved in a discussion of the advantages and disadvantages of the Chinese method of delivery, in which the rest of the group had already left and we had to take our woman lies flat in bed, when we were reminded that the leave to continue our tour.

Health and the Young. Developing good health habits in children is crucial to a program of disease prevention. The students at the Happiness Village Primary School in Shanghai meet for an hour each week with a doctor for instruction in this area. She teaches them basic health habits, such as washing their faces, cutting their hair, keeping nails trim, bathing, changing clothes, and brushing their teeth. There is emphasis on good eye habits: remembering to keep a good distance between eye and the book, reading with a good light, sitting straight—not lying down —eye examinations twice a year. Very few of the children in the school were wearing glasses. Some posters in one of the classrooms, showing a young girl performing eye exercises and explaining the steps, were a constant reminder to think about the health of the eyes. The doctor told us that the children have two short breaks during the day to do eye exercises.

In an acupuncture class thirty children were working with needles and bottles of iodine and alcohol, practicing certain points on themselves and their friends. The teacher told us that she teaches them specific points to prevent and relieve headaches, sore throats, and common colds. Besides this knowledge and the practice in inserting the needles, the class discusses the channels involved in the traditional Chinese concept of acupuncture.

Later we learned that students are also assigned to duty in the school health room. Every morning and afternoon two students work in the little clinic giving minor treatments. What an opportunity for children to learn about the functioning of their bodies and the maintenance of their health, at the same time demystifying the role of professional health workers! The integration of children into health work extends disease prevention to the most basic level, because they are the people who carry the future of a country's health. This aspect of China's health care, combined with prevention and treatment in the rural and urban areas—the emphasis everywhere on both self-reliance and cooperation—forms an impressive and exciting program.

Mental hospitals can reveal vital information about a society. Like jails, they house the people who can't operate within the social rules deemed necessary by the dominant culture. We wondered who these people were in China, what rules of thought and behavior they had violated, how they were experienced by others, and what environmental stresses could account for their aberrant feelings.

Our answers to these questions are based on two visits to a mental hospital in Shanghai and two interviews with psychologists at the Psychological Institute in Peking. Beyond the obvious constraints of limited data, we call the reader's attention to a problem peculiar to psychiatry—that of terminology—which contributes to the unusually subjective nature of this chapter. Language was a minor problem throughout our visit to China, but in this case our difficulty extended beyond mere translation. Words like "personality," "psychosis," "emotion," and "therapy" are meaningful within a particular cultural context. They do not survive verbal translation as adequately as words like "enzyme" or "gene." There was simply no way of knowing whether a common professional language insured that the states of mind so described were experienced the same way.

For example, although apparently rejecting much of

western psychology, the Chinese use the western system of diagnostic categories to describe their patients. People are labeled "schizophrenic," "neurotic," "hebephrenic," and so on. On the other hand, the Chinese do not use the word "psychotherapy." Rather, they speak of "heart-to-heart" talks, "education in ideology," and "political study." What do these phrases mean? How are these interpersonal events different from their counterparts in western psychotherapy? What do they have in common with it?

On March 13, 1973, we visited the Shanghai Psychiatric Hospital for Treatment and Prevention. Its complex of white buildings in the suburbs of the city, built in 1958, was beautifully landscaped with fruit trees and other shrubbery. As we approached we were greeted by four members of the revolutionary committee, three doctors and a nurse. They stood at the entrance, wearing white coats and caps, smiling broadly and clapping as our cars approached, a welcome banner at their side.

Inside, the hallways were bright and everything was spotless and simple. Sunlight streamed through the windows onto walls painted turquoise and white. There were none of the ominous or depressing intimations one feels on entering a state hospital at home, nor the antiseptic, all-business atmosphere of glass, aluminum, and linoleum of the fancy private hospital. It seemed like a friendly place.

Over the usual welcoming tea and cigarettes we received a brief introduction to the hospital. It has 996 beds divided into thirteen wards, seven for men and six for women. (A significant departure from inpatient populations in the United States, where women considerably outnumber men). The staff of 585 include 61 doctors and 261 nurses. The patients have all kinds of disorders: the majority are schizophrenic, some have "symptomatic psychoses," and others are epileptics. (It was unclear to us why epileptics are treated here, and not in a medical hospital.) A small number of patients are diagnosed "neurotic" and "psychoneurotic." There is a sanatorium attached to the hospital and an outpatient department treating an average of 400 patients mostly diagnosed "neurotic" or "psychoneurotic."

The treatment combines traditional Chinese and western methods. Acupuncture and traditional herbal medicines are given, as well as synthetic chemical tranquilizers like chlorpromazine. During treatment patients are also given "education in ideology," in which they are taught to have a "correct attitude" toward their illness. (The use of political study in mental health treatment is, we were to discover, one of the distinguishing features of the Chinese system.)

"The environment here is not like a jail," one of the doctors told us. "Patients engage in physical labor, cultural events, and physical culture; and the medical staff works in urban and rural areas doing preventive work as well as attending to the inpatients." The staff attempts to treat mental illness in rural areas and factories by "teaching the masses about mental illness." They also train factory doctors and barefoot doctors to treat people with mental disorders."

With this introduction we left the reception room and began our tour of the hospital. The first four patients we saw were seated at a small table receiving acupuncture treatment. One doctor was monitoring a small machine to which acupuncture needles were wired, while another doctor and nurse inserted the needles and watched the patients. Everyone was relaxed. While two patients waited, needles were inserted in the ear lobes or temples of the other two. They sat there, smoking or just sitting, while the needles were stimulated electronically by the doctor at the machine. (This gentle electronic stimulation should not be confused with electric shock treatment. The impulses, unlike those of EST, are very mild.) As we watched, one of the doctors accompanying us tapped the shoulder of one of the patients who was receiving acupuncture treatment, and spoke quietly to him. A moment later the man began to speak. It took us a few moments to realize that he was telling us his story. His speech had the tone of a recitation—as if he had given his account many times before.

He spoke rather slowly, without much animation but in a clear and logical manner.

I had TB, and when I came back from the hospital I was not clear in my mind because of it. I was worried that I wouldn't recover. In general, I had hallucinations: I believed that my brain was controlled by electricity, and that everyone could hear what I thought. I was afraid my thoughts were being overheard and, because of this, I stayed outside my house, walking around. Eventually my wife reported my actions to my work unit, and the leading member of my unit took care of me and sent me to the hospital. When he and other comrades came to my house to see me, I thought they had come to murder me. When I arrived at the hospital, I thought it was a place dealing with mental illness and I was afraid, because I didn't believe I suffered from mental illness. After a week of acupuncture treatment I no longer heard any sound in my ears. I had been unable to sleep, but after a week I could sleep. In the old society I would have disappeared; in the new society I can recover.

The doctors told us that this patient had been in the hospital a month and would be ready to leave in a short time. His symptoms, as restated by the doctors, were hallucinations and the presence of a thought disorder. His diagnosis: schizophrenia, hebephrenic type. When asked why he was being treated with acupuncture, the doctors told us it helped eliminate the hallucinations.

Continuing our tour, we walked through a large recreation room where about a hundred men and women patients were playing games—cards, miniature basketball, and "sink the ship," and others. Other patients were reading picture books and magazines. The ratio of patients to staff was striking: there were only about ten staff members in the room, yet the patients were self-directed, organized, and reasonably quiet. No one was aggressive or called attention to himself by exhibiting bizarre behavior. This observation was so noteworthy that we asked if everyone in the room was medicated. They replied that most of the people were on low dosages of tranquilizers. It was clear from the attentive expressions of the patients and their level of physical activity that these people were not "doped up." The games being played all required a high degree of concentration and motor coordination. No one was vegetating in front of a television set. We were told that such games were deliberately designed to focus attention, that when one concentrates on external activity, there is less room for hallucinations.

The patients, although cooperative, and behaving appropriately, did look somewhat "off balance." (It was clear that we were in a mental hospital.) Some were bouncing their feet in a kind of jittery way, as hospitalized patients often do; others looked vague, though not "vacant"; and some looked at us suspiciously. (With good reason—who were we anyway?) But it was usually easy to make contact with them; a smile and a nod always evoked a similar response.

We went into one room in which men and women patients were making baskets out of colored nylon thread, a rather intricate task. When completed, the baskets had designs of colored flowers arranged in a bouquet. Everyone was quiet, although not somber. As the patients worked, a nurse brought over a young woman patient who presented us with two baskets. She walked slowly and smiled shyly. After making the presentation she lingered with us, holding the hands of someone in our group, seemingly unaware that the interchange was over. A nurse gently turned her around and led her back to her seat.

In another room we observed a discussion between a patient, three doctors, and an aide. The patient, we were told, "was worried about not doing enough work, even though the leading members of his unit felt that his work was good and really appreciated him." (Every morning doctors have similar discussions about cases, usually with the patient present.)

When we entered the lunchroom we found the walls covered with bulletin boards and blackboards. One of them displayed poems written by the patients, including some praising the Party and criticizing "revisionism." Another bore a set of regulations written in colored chalk and taken from the old Red Army's "Eight Points for Attention," set to music and still a People's Liberation Army song: "Don't steal," "Return what you borrow," "Don't damage things," and so on. There were also the words to the *"Internationale"* and a study plan for the day.

We visited a smaller room, for serious cases—those that require the presence of a nurse around the clock. About six patients and three or four nurses and aides were sitting on cots. The doctors told us that one of the patients, an older man with gray hair, who sat reading, had been a "responsible member" of a mine team in another province until he was struck with carbon monoxide poisoning while working the night shift. He was treated medically for a year and a half, but was transferred to the mental hospital because his muscles remained rigid, he was incontinent, and he still suffered memory loss. At the hospital he was treated with acupuncture, vitamins, low dosages of tranquilizers and Chinese herbs. His muscles had since relaxed. As his story was being told, the old man laid his book down and smiled broadly, his eyes twinkling. He bent his arm at the elbow to demonstrate that he was no longer rigid. When we got up to leave, he stood up and was slowly following us down the hall, still smiling, when a nurse came to gently turn him around and lead him back to the room. We were told that another patient in the room, who looked completely catatonic, had experienced a "failed love affair" and had slowly withdrawn over a period of two months. The people around him had not realized he was ill until he stopped eating, at which point they brought him to the hospital. Since entering he had been given acupuncture treatments and had begun to eat again, although he was still stiff.

Continuing in our tour, we saw a group of about eighty male patients in another room making toothbrush covers. Three articles written by patients were posted on the bulletin board: "Long, Long Life to Chairman Mao," "Make Progress along the Long March," and "Unite to Win Victories." On another blackboard was the list of duties for the patient chosen to head the ward: "Hold high Chairman Mao's thought," "Behave oneself," "Assist medical personnel," "Organize the patients." Another sign explained the reasons why work was included in the treatment program: "The significance of treatment by labor: a) political aspect, b) medical good results, c) economic."

Outside, a group of female patients was playing a complicated game of jump-rope as two nurses turned the rope. Some male patients and staff members were playing netless volleyball. Everywhere we looked patients and staff were in close, friendly contact. The staff impressed us as being very gentle and patient, often touching the patients and putting their arms around their shoulders. (It was noteworthy that the patients did not make this kind of contact with each other, even though it is a common mode of relating in China.) On our way to another building we passed a large herb garden where the hospital grows some of its own medicine. In the warmer weather it is tended by the patients and staff.

Inside again, we observed a political study session. About twenty female patients and a nurse were seated at a table reading an article by Chairman Mao. The patients took turns reading sections out loud and discussing them. Although some were visibly distressed, they were all extremely attentive. A doctor told us that patients often have "unrealistic thoughts" and that reading and studying Chairman Mao helps to focus and "correct" such ideas. A patient was speaking to the group as we entered. "Before the Cultural Revolution," she said, "I didn't take part in the struggle; but during it, I did. In the past I had a poor attitude toward criticism. When people criticized me, I thought about it and it made me sick."

We were ushered into another room where about twenty patients and nurses were singing together. We were offered seats, and before we knew it a performance had begun. There was a small orchestra of Chinese traditional instruments, two of the players staff and the others patients. Two rows of men and women faced us. One stepped forward to announce the first song. For the next ten minutes the ensemble played and sang. There were some solos and two dances as well. The performance was excellent, one of the best we had seen in China. Everyone sang beautifully, with style and verve, and the orchestra was marvelous. One had to look very closely to notice a slight tremor in the hands of one of the singers, or a vague look, when not singing, in another.

We then returned to the reception room, where we divided into two groups to discuss more fully all that we had seen. One of the doctors told us that all the patients had "both physical and mental causes" to their diseases. We were surprised to learn that there were patients in the hospital with brain tumors, cancer, infections of the blood vessels, and heart disease. Before Liberation, our hosts told us, there were patients with syphilis, other venereal diseases, alcoholism, and drug addiction, but all these afflictions had since been eliminated in China.

When asked what was meant by a "mental cause" of a disease, a doctor gave the following examples: "An incorrect attitude toward criticism/self-criticism, meeting difficulties in work or study that can't be solved, problems in managing love relationships, an inability to handle contradictions [problems] among colleagues and co-workers, or suffering from great shocks."

To illustrate one of these themes, he provided a case study. An engineer responsible for the design of large ships became increasingly worried that the accidents which occasionally occurred were the result of failures in his design. He experienced a lot of tension over this and couldn't sleep. As his anxiety grew, he began to feel that every aspect of his life had to be in order. During this period he got married. At the wedding the guests presented him with sweets. He refused to eat them because they were not handed or displayed to him in the right order. He thought that people around him had certain objections to his behavior, and were saying "bad words."

He began to hear sounds and refused to go home, staying at his workplace but not resting. People in his unit began to worry and consulted with his family. They learned that he would often spend many nights not sleeping, to "put things in order." He was suspicious of objects on the table, believing there was some order and meaning to their placement. Finally his family and colleagues sent him to the hospital. Upon examining him, the doctors observed that he had hallucinations and symbolic thoughts and ideas. His condition was diagnosed as schizophrenic by the outpatient doctor, and he was admitted to the hospital at the family's request and with the agreement of the medical personnel.

This case history is familiar to anyone who has had contact with mental illness diagnosed as paranoid schizophrenic. Unfortunately, we were unable to determine the precise nature of the theories the Chinese bring to bear on problems of this nature. All we can state with certainty is that this pattern of distress, common to many individuals hospitalized in the United States, is shared by their Chinese counterparts.

We asked one of the doctors if the hospital staff did any family therapy. He replied:

Medical treatment is not enough for patients. The masses who live and work with them should have a correct attitude toward the situation. While working outside the hospital we do specific propaganda work with the patient's family, friends, co-workers, and neighbors.

Before the patient leaves the hospital we give him or her some theoretical education about how to prevent a recurrence of the illness and we also inform the relatives about the medication and how often the patient must return to the outpatient department. We believe a long period of medication after discharge prevents a recurrence. We also tell the relatives and co-workers to pay more attention to the patient and to take better care of him or her, because we believe that if we pay more attention to the patient's daily life it will consolidate the good results of our treatment and prevent a recurrence.

Sometimes patients make reasonable demands of comrades in the community and of their family, and we ask those involved to grant these demands. For example, a woman patient had been a shop assistant before being hospitalized. When she was ready for discharge, she was afraid that her memory was not as good as it had been and that she would make mistakes on her job. Because of this, she asked for a change of work. We conveyed her feelings to the leaders of her department, believing that her request was a reasonable one, and they reassigned her. After six months she felt she had improved, and was given her old job back.

In response to a request for an example of an "unreasonable demand," the doctor smiled and said:

Unreasonable demands usually reflect that the person is not fully recovered. Usually when the patients leave the hospital their units will reduce their work and give them more time to rest. Some female patients recover their health but are afraid to go back to their jobs, afraid they will be looked down upon by the others. We consider this a wrong idea. We visit the factory or office to tell them not to look down on such patients. We also talk to the patient and study together with him or her. We try to teach the patient to accept that he or she has a mental disease, and how to develop a correct attitude toward it. We tell our patients that it is important to take part in socialist construction and to prevent a recurrence of their disease.

Our hosts told us that families, neighbors, and co-workers are consulted during the patient's hospitalization and are asked for information regarding the patient's habits and problems. Members of the patient's neighborhood revolutionary committee are sometimes invited to the hospital to tell the staff how the patient manages in the community, and members of the family often help in talking with the patient about things that he or she may have difficulty telling the doctors. Similarly, when staff members have difficulty conveying their wishes or ideas to the patient, his or her family may be asked to intercede.

Families and colleagues do not, however, attend staff discussions about the patient or participate in therapeutic discussions with him or her. Although there is clearly a high degree of community involvement in the treatment program, the patient's social network seems to be viewed as an adjunct to the process rather than as an object of treatment itself.

This network is also centrally involved in getting the patient into the hospital at the outset. As in the United States, it seems to be the case that a person gets hospitalized when those around him or her are made so uncomfortable by certain kinds of behavior that they no longer feel able to maintain their relationship with the distressed individual without some outside intervention. A doctor explained, "When people in certain departments find someone who can't act in normal ways, his comrades and family bring him to the hospital. Many patients when they are seriously ill don't want to come out to the hospital," he said. "The doctors, comrades and relatives educate and persuade them to come. First they ask them to have an examination in the hospital, then they make them live there."

He gave us an example:

A man had backaches, and began to have disturbing thoughts in his mind. These periods become worse day by day. He felt that someone was always talking about him, and that his brain was controlled by others. He had been a factory worker but was unable to continue his work. As a result of his condition, he began to talk strangely to his wife. She thought this was not normal and she gave her opinion to the leaders of her husband's department. His comrades at the factory sent him to the hospital. They told him he needed a rest and should go to the hospital.

In the beginning he didn't think he was ill, so we can say he was a little forced to come here. It was not voluntary. If you talk with him and consult with him now, he agrees it is good that he is in the hospital. Most of the patients are like this. When they first arrive, they don't think they are ill, but after talking with their leaders and hospital personnel, they usually agree to come.

A few patients behave very seriously and are very excited. With such cases it is very difficult to get them to agree to enter the hospital. Some people must force them to come here. We sedate them when they first arrive, and in a few days, when they are not so excited, the doctors and nurses talk to them and tell them they are ill and it would be a good idea to stay in the hospital.

This intimate connection between the hospital and the community also seems to include the penal institutions. When asked about patients who commit crimes, the doctors told us that if a minor was committed by someone who was emotionally disturbed, the individual was first sent to the hospital, not to jail. One doctor told us about a worker who beat another worker and wounded him. The leaders and co-workers in the factory felt this situation was too serious to be handled within the factory, and asked their comrades in the court to come and investigate. In their investigation they learned that previous to this assault the worker in question had not been behaving normally, and so the man was sent to the hospital instead. The doctor told us that there were some cases when members of the court "do not pay attention," and a person who was emotionally disturbed was imprisoned, but that as soon as the jailors noticed that an inmate was not acting normally, they transferred him to the hospital prior to serving his jail sentence.

Just as the prison authorities are likely to transfer an inmate who has emotional difficulties, people in the patient's neighborhood will send such a person back to the hospital rather than report him or her to police officials if the person bothers others in the street or commits a similarly minor offense. The doctors remarked that "since we pay attention to the patient after he leaves the hospital, and ask the neighbors, relatives, and comrades to take care of him, such problems rarely occur."

In all these accounts of what we might call "involuntary

hospitalization," what is significant about the Chinese approach is that legalistic points of reference are not relied upon exclusively in making such decisions. It is a common expectation that people will behave toward each other responsibly and with kindness. Thus people close to the patient, as well as those who administer the psychiatric and penal facilities, are simply expected to make humane and responsible decisions. When errors are made, other responsible citizens are expected to correct them and to engage in constructive criticism with those at fault.

One of the doctors involved in the discussion was currently spending most of his time in factories and rural areas. He told us that he teaches medical workers in the factory clinics and on the communes about the treatment and methods of prevention of various mental disorders. The health workers are also invited to the hospital to learn about typical cases of emotional disorders. Since these medical workers study and work with members of a particular factory or commune, they know their comrades very well, and are especially suited to help them, he told us.

He illustrated his point with an example:

A thirty-year-old woman worker had a love affair difficulty, and as a result she began to believe that all the men in her factory were falling in love with her. She stopped paying attention to her work and spent all her time walking around the factory. The medical worker at the site treated her and gave her medicine, but she didn't seem to improve. When the doctor visited her family he learned that her mother was blind. Not believing she was ill, the patient lied when her mother asked her if she had taken her medicine. After this the medical worker returned to the patient's work group and did some propaganda. Her comrades began to take the responsibility for giving her the medication twice a day, and she started to improve. She is now able to work and study once again with her comrades.

We asked how her comrades were able to convince her that she was ill. The doctor replied that a close friend of hers had a "heart-to-heart talk" with her, saying, "You can't sleep well, you should take your medication so that you can sleep." We asked if the friend tried to tell her that she was mentally ill. "No," he replied. "Her comrades didn't tell her what was wrong, they didn't suggest that she was mentally ill, they just told her. 'You need to sleep.' "

In this case the immediate problem was solved by social investigation and follow-up work. The family, co-workers, neighbors, and medical workers are all expected to play an active role in the process. They told us with pride that they had no professional social workers to do the job that belongs to everyone. Like the tale of the distressed engineer, however, the story of this young woman raised more questions than it answered. To illustrate the great difficulty we and our hosts encountered when we tried to share ideas about theory, the dialogue that followed the doctor's description of this young factory worker is reproduced verbatim.

"What do you see as the cause of her disorder?"

"I've already told you—a disappointment in love."

"Yes, that was the precipitating event. But what do you see as the relationship between that event and the woman's bizarre reaction to it?"

Another doctor responded somewhat wearily, seemingly feeling that this question too had already been answered.

"According to our investigations of schizophrenia, 60 percent of the cases are caused by psychogenic factors"— incorrect attitudes, personality, unresolved problems, etc. "This, however, is not the fundamental cause, it is simply one factor leading to mental disorder. Two to 4 percent of the cases have organic causes." Here the doctors suggested viruses as an example. "In 30 percent of the cases, we can't find a clear cause."

This explanation is very similar to the context within which psychological disorders are viewed in the West. In the United States distress patterns are often categorized as organic (biological and genetic), nonorganic (psychogenic), and situational (environmental). We were unable to go beyond this mutually shared general orientation to discover how the Chinese used such a model when analyzing this specific case history, but as our discussions proceeded one theme kept emerging. While western psychological models placed a high premium on emotions, the Chinese seem to consider "attitudes" a central variable. As one doctor explained, using the Chinese aphorism, "One divides into two. "In mental activities, some thoughts are right and some are wrong. There are normal aspects to the patient's thoughts as well as pathological aspects. For example, patients who suffer from paranoia can still manage to keep their daily life in order. Often other people don't even know such a person is a patient." he added, "We use the normal to overcome the pathological. Thus, if the patient is conscious of his or her illness, the hallucinations may still exist, but the patient has a correct attitude toward them."

Similarly, when asked what they regard as a "cure," the doctors replied that an essential characteristic was that the patient could "recognize and analyze his or her disease." The other major determining factors they listed were that the behaviors that were exhibited during the illness are gone, and that the patient is able to work and live at home.

This belief that incorrect attitudes are a major source of psychological difficulty, and that the development of correct attitudes will result in a remission of the disorder, is reflected in the use of education in ideology and political study as two of the major verbal forms of psychological treatment. A third form, heart-to-heart talks, is simply frequent and unscheduled intimate and supportive chats between the patients and nurses or other patients who are elected by their comrades to be leaders.

Shortly after patients are admitted to the hospital and a case history has been taken, they meet with a doctor to begin education in ideology. The doctor tries to determine the nature of the patient's ideas about the world and then attempts to help the person develop a correct attitude toward the illness. "First we try to help the patients recognize that they are ill, and in what ways their symptoms reflect that illness," a doctor explained. "Then we tell them why they are ill; what the causes of the illness are. These explanations help patients develop a correct attitude toward their illness."

He gave an example to illustrate his point:

A twenty-one-year-old female patient named Wang, from a lower-middle peasant family in a Shanghai suburb, took part in a water conservation project on a production team. At a study meeting in which the group discussed Chairman Mao's essays in order to help them determine how they could increase their production, Wang arrived without the essays and was severely criticized by her team leader. Wang could not accept the criticism and began to suspect that other team members were talking about her. This was untrue. She started to believe that she was seen as a "bad element." She started assaulting other people and calling them names. At this point she was sent to the hospital.

When we learned of this case, we concluded that besides medical treatment, we needed to help Wang develop a correct attitude toward what had happened. Medical workers, doctors, and nurses studied the works of Chairman Mao with her, paying special attention to the articles "Analysis of the Classes in Chinese Society" and "Serve the People." As she studied Wang began to recognize that the poor and lower-middle peasants are the main force of the revolution and that these classes firmly believe in the policy of the Party.

We studied together some quotations from "Serve the People," giving special emphasis to the sentence, "If we have shortcomings, we are not afraid of criticism." Gradually Wang came to recognize that the goal of criticism is a good one, and that by not paying sufficient attention to the study of Chairman Mao's works, she had not been able to develop a correct attitude toward criticism. She became determined to return to the team, to study seriously and to develop a correct attitude toward criticism.

Without direct observation of a political study session, this description by the doctor may leave the impression that such study is no more than restating in rote fashion certain political slogans. This is not the case. Although it is important to the Chinese that people affirm the basic tenets of their social system (just as Americans are encouraged to affirm the ideals of their society), the Chinese place an equal emphasis on helping people develop the cognitive tools necessary to think for themselves. They place a high premium on logical, rational, and inferential thinking. Thus political study in the hospital setting is, among other things, an attempt to "use the normal to overcome the pathological"—to help the patient rediscover his or her own reason and reasoning faculties.

This stress on developing the necessary cognitive skills for the subsequent development of correct attitudes is reflected in another anecdote. "There was a patient in the hospital with paranoid suspicions," a doctor told us.

She thought her food was poisoned, and had not eaten for a week at the point at which she was admitted to the hospital. A nurse had a heart-to-heart talk with her, telling her that not eating was bad for her health and that if she did eat she would contribute to the revolution. The patient was then willing to touch the food, but would not swallow it. The nurse decided to continue her propaganda work by setting an example. She ate the food herself, eating what the patient had refused to eat. After this example, the patient ate her first meal in the hospital.

Paranoid thought disorders of this nature seemed to be the most common disturbance of the patients here. When we asked the doctors about this, they agreed and told us that the majority of their patients were considered "paranoid schizophrenic" (also one of the most common diagnoses in the United States, and next most frequent was "hebephrenic schizophrenia" (a diagnostic category rarely used in our country any more—our equivalent is "chronic undifferentiated schizophrenia"). People in aggressive states outnumber those who are depressed (very few) or manic, and least common are catatonic and anxiety states. Suicide, senile psychosis, and childhood schizophrenia are "extremely rare." We asked about homosexuality and were told that this was also "very rare in China" and was treated in the outpatient department by "social reeducation."

There is no question, a psychologist at the institute in Peking told us, that "mental diseases reflect the social system." He too commented that there is hardly any senile psychosis or childhood schizophrenia in China. Social attitudes toward the old and the young help to explain the low incidence of psychological distress among these two groups. Both young and old people are held in high esteem. The young, according to Chairman Mao, are "the budding flowers of the Revolution." Everyone cares for them, we are told, friends, neighbors, schools, not just their parents. Similarly, old people in China are free from the basic problems of security. After retirement a worker gets 70 percent of his former wages, there is no unemployment, medical care is provided, and there is a tradition of honor and support given parents by their children.

As a result of the total eradication of opium addiction, alcoholism, and prostitution, there are no new cases of alcoholic, drug, or syphilitic psychosis. The vast changes in the face of China since Liberation, accomplished by putting an end to the exploitation in the old society, have clearly played a central role in eliminating many clinical syndromes that are still common in the West.

When asked how they diagnosed schizophrenia, the responses of the Shanghai hospital staff indicate that the doctors share a common frame of reference with western psychiatry. They cited incoherent thinking, logical disorder, breaks in ideology, and ambivalence as the significant variables. The first three phrases suggest the signs and symptoms of what we would call a thought disorder, although one could only conjecture about the meaning the Chinese attached to the word ambivalence.

We asked whether they felt they had been successful in treating their schizophrenic patients. They told us that a number of these patients "get the disease again," but that their treatment has improved since the Cultural Revolution. Before that time the hospital's only treatment was the use of tranquilizers. They did not use acupuncture or traditional Chinese medicine, did not attempt any ideological education, and did only limited work with the patient's relatives and work units.

A small study, recently completed, illustrated the difference in their success rates before and after the Cultural Revolution. They told us that in 1965, out of 104 patients in one ward, 40 percent relapsed after a year. They were not rehospitalized, but they had to be seen in the outpatient department. In 1972, out of 128 patients on the same ward, only 14.8 percent relapsed during the same time period. These statistics, even though vague, suggest a significant difference in rates of relapse, although the behavioral criteria for the term "relapse" were not clear.

Research in the United States has isolated three factors which are considered the most crucial in keeping people out of the hospital. In order of importance these are: continuing medication after discharge, family cooperation and involvement, and work. Interestingly enough, as the Chinese doctors quoted their own findings they stressed the great emphasis they now place on insuring that their patients keep taking medication and on educating their relatives and co-workers to watch for a recurrence of symptoms and to monitor the medication.

They told us that the average length of stay in the hospital was seventy days, and that patients when discharged are maintained on 200 mg. per day of chlorpromazine. (The average in-hospital dose is 300 mg. per day, a moderate dosage by American standards.) In Peking we were told that the average period of hospitalization is thirty days. In New York State it is forty-five days, but where the length of each stay for Chinese and American mental patients is roughly the same, the total length of time patients spend in hospitals differs markedly because of the extremely high rate of relapse in the United States. In New York hospitals 75 to 80 percent of the patients are readmissions. The obvious inference from this is that reforms in American hospitals have not extended to the outside community, and until they do we are only shuffling statistics by cutting the length of each stay.

The full spectrum of in-hospital treatment in China includes medical, interpersonal, political, and occupational components, as well as cultural and recreational activities. Medical treatments include Chinese herbal medicine (as many as ten or more herbs are combined to treat one patient, although the staff is trying to reduce the number through research to determine which herbs in what combinations are the active ones), tranquilizers (including the Chinese equivalents of Taractin, Stellazine, and Thorazine), and acupuncture. The doctors told us they believe that disappearance of symptoms following acupuncture treatment is physiologically based, not merely the result of psychological suggestion. They cited as an example a patient who strenuously objected to acupuncture treatment but nevertheless received it. This patient also had a symptom remission. Interpersonal and political treatments include education in ideology, heart-to-heart talks, political study, and an active political life in the hospital. Cultural activities include song, dance, poetry, and art, while productive labor involves tending the hospital garden and doing other projects inside the hospital.

The daily schedule begins with medical treatment in the morning, followed by various activities in the afternoon. A typical day starts at 7:00 A.M. with a news broadcast; from 8:00 to 10:00 there are medical treatments; before lunch there is free time; after lunch there is a nap; from 1:30 to 2:15 P.M. large groups read newspapers or study the works of Chairman Mao; after 2:15 there are collective activities like basketball and volleyball. Three times a week there are family visits with the patients. Once a week patients and doctors clean the ward thoroughly. In the spring manual work is done in the herb garden.

The hospital has a many-leveled, interdependent structure. It is administered by a revolutionary committee of fifteen, four of whom are women. Doctors, nurses, cadres, and representatives of the workers' propaganda team are all represented. The group meets biweekly, with extra meetings when necessary.

Each ward is led by three staff members: a doctor, a head nurse, and an elementary medical worker who looks after housekeeping activities. There is a short meeting every morning for the night and day shifts to exchange information and discuss the daily routine. Every month there is a meeting of the ward staff for criticism/self-criticism. They discuss how to improve their work and raise the level of service to the ward, and how to better consult patients and their families for opinions and suggestions.

The patients are organized as well. Leaders are elected in every small group of eight to ten, and there are two or three leaders in each large ward. The ward leaders meet once a week to make decisions about the daily routine. One is responsible for study, one for cleaning, and the third for occupational therapy. Study programs are discussed with the head doctor and nurse and then taken to the patients for discussion. Special classes called recovery classes are formed for patients leaving the hospital, to discuss how to continue recovery outside.

The staff of the outpatient department includes eleven doctors and nine nurses. Patients are expected to return two weeks after discharge, and then about once a month. Patients primarily come in to receive their medicine, but if there is a "recurrence" they talk to the doctors as well.

In addition to the treatment of patients, the hospital also trains psychiatrists. They receive courses in mental disorders, categories of diseases, and taking case histories, as well as traditional Chinese medical knowledge. Most of the teaching is done in connection with clinical experience, not out of textbooks. There is a division of labor between the doctors and nurses, though they "support each other's work." The doctors' responsibility is to cure disease through diagnosis and medical treatment. They collect and write case histories, determine treatment, and educate the patients in ideology. Doctors are also expected to do "service"—to clean along with the patients and to serve their food when the nurses need help. The nurses give medication, attend to the hygiene of the patients and have heart-to-heart talks with them.

This visit to the mental hospital had enormous impact on many of us. One of our older male interpreters commented as we left that the experience brought tears to his eyes, because, he said slowly and with feeling, "they take such good *care* of them." It is hard to describe the kind of patient and tender caretaking we saw, except to say that the hospital had the atmosphere of a place one could conjure up in a children's story—a safe, benevolent "home" where people in white uniforms take care of others who don't feel well.

The level of cooperation, task-directedness, dignity, and appropriateness of behavior between patients and among patients and staff was remarkably high. There was no evidence, either, of intrastaff rivalry. If there were class divisions among the staff, they were not visible to us. Although there was a division of labor within the medical staff, their mutual respect and cooperation seemed genuine. Moreover, since their clinical training is essentially practical, with people learning from experience and from the experience of others, the processes by which learning occurs are visible and available to everyone. Professional skills cannot be mystified when they are so accessible. As one of the psychologists we talked with in Peking told us, "We motivate medical personnel and patients to activate their initiative to fight the disease in cooperation."

The apparent absence of deep class divisions within the hospital (and on the outside) provides the patients with a consistent set of messages about the nature of reality and of socially appropriate behavior. Those whom we observed seemed to share a common view about the nature of the good life, the moral tenets of social behavior, the qualities of personality to value and cultivate, the general political direction of their nation—even a cognitive strategy for solving intellectual problems. This formidable social consensus is clearly a central feature in the success of hospital treatment.

The nurse who got her patient to eat the food the patient believed was poisoned is a significant example. The intractability of paranoid delusions is a common phenomenon in western psychiatry. Why didn't the Chinese patient "decide" that the poison in the food transformed itself while the nurse was eating, but retained its toxic qualities every time the patient ate? The patient seemed to relinquish the idea so easily, and accepted consensual rules of logic in doing so. Similarly, the mere suggestion that by eating the patient would "contribute to the revolution" had an effect on her behavior. It seems that this shared view of reality, conbined with a trust in authority figures, sometimes makes ordinary reason and small doses of social pressure adequate to deal with psychological disturbances that confound medical practitioners in our country. The Chinese assumption that reason, logic, and a desire to "serve the people" will prevail seems to work therapeutically.

The stress on the cognitive and rational is also reflected in the directness with which the Chinese doctors deal with their patients. There is apparently no notion of withholding an insight until the patient is "ready for it." Staff members say what they think, believing the listener has the capacity to absorb it. Moreover, treatment centers on ideas, not feelings. Western psychology seems to operate on the belief that unless a lot of feeling is spilled, a person will be unable to assimilate, accept, and generate a new set of ideas. The Chinese do not share that view. Rather, they maintain an abiding faith in objective reality comprehended by applying the tools of dialectical thinking. Teaching those skills to distressed people, they believe, will enable the distressed individuals to use that orientation in digging their way out of their morass.

This emphasis on thought and study also seems to reflect a different attitude toward the place of human emotion in interpersonal relationships. Restraint and dignity, rather than emotionality, seem to be the cultural norm. This is not to say the Chinese are not "feelingful" people.

There are wide variations in personality, but not the extreme variations of attention-producing styles that are common in the West. We found our hosts to be warm, playful, earnest, disciplined, pained, or angry as the situation demanded, but emotions of the greatest magnitude seemed to be reserved for political matters ("matters of principle") rather than issues between people.

It is when individuals talk of the old society that one sees great flashes of feeling. An old woman we talked with cried as she told us of life before Liberation. Others, when speaking of political oppression, showed restrained but intense anger. When talking of serving the people, on the other hand, they looked joyful and determined.

It seems (although the barriers of language and culture make all generalizations suspect) that "personal" relationships do not have quite the valence of "political" ones. There were many patients in the hospital whose case histories included references to "failed love affairs" and "difficulties in love," but our Chinese hosts and traveling companions rarely discussed such matters with us. Our interpreters, a young man and woman in their mid-twenties, seemed more interested in their jobs than in love and marriage. On the street, when passing a couple (a rather uncommon sight) one does not observe the kind of sexualized intensity of manner that seem so natural here. It may be that China's present need for hard-working, skilled people is felt with the same kind of emotional urgency that we place on love relationships. The patients with love affair problems in the hospital suggest that there are some people in China whose vulnerability to personal relationships and need for that kind of intimacy are not satisfactorily rechanneled into their work.

If one looks at a mental hospital as a resting place for those who have trouble adapting adequately to the cultural norms, then those for whom personal love has too much valence are joined by those who cannnot successfully manage their reactions to criticism. Difficulties in handling criticism are not the special problem of hospital patients, although they seem to feel it more acutely. There is great stress in China on "being good." People are always looking at themselves for instances of bourgeois or selfish attitudes, and it must be very distressing to feel that one is viewed by others in such a light. Thus even when others are not overtly critical, those whose internalized "superego" is very harsh may well imagine that the criticism is coming from outside when it is coming from within. The boat designer and the man who needed assurance from the psychiatrists that his work was well received may be exhibiting this kind of projection.

It is to the difficulties of assimilating criticism constructively and working through the accompanying anxiety that political reeducation in the hospital is directed. If one of the roles of the hospital is the socialization of people when the general society has failed, then the mental hospital in Shanghai provides a sanctuary where people can be taught a correct attitude toward this crucial mode of relating. The use of political study as a vehicle for thought and behavior change makes sense in this context. The study of Chairman Mao's works is an integral part of the life of every Chinese citizen. Mao's thought is both inspiration and conscience, conceptual framework and emotional context for the Chinese people. Thus using political material to help refashion one's personality, to mediate interpersonal problems, to increase production, to think through a problem, are common features of Chinese life. Its use in the mental hospital is in no way unique.

Indeed, life inside the hospital is very much like life on the outside. As one of the psychologists in Peking remarked, "Patients in the hospital live like other patients in regular hospitals, and like people on the outside. They are not detached and isolated from society, but lead a collective life. They have close relationships with doctors, nurses, and staff, have discussion groups, and study Chairman Mao's works. Their life is the same as it is for all Chinese. Thus the patient doesn't have to adjust to normal life, he is living it already." This lack of disruption in familiar rhythms of life, coupled with the inclusion of members of the patient's social network in the treatment program, must be a major factor in getting people out of the hospital and keeping them out.

American psychiatry has recently begun to recognize the importance of this way of working, but attempts to incorporate such practices into hospital policy in our country still founder. What makes the Chinese situation unique is that hospital personnel can *expect* to have leverage with the people and institutions in a patient's life. If the family and colleagues of a patient are asked to take better care of him, it is assumed they will. People expect to take care of one another, and to extend themselves when called upon. A psychologist in Peking said, "Relationships between people, as Chairman Mao teaches us, are to serve the people. Thus people are always concerned. They care for and help each other. Relationships are warm, you feel you are warmly received by everyone." Not all Americans share that cultural tradition, as mental health workers trying to mobilize community support for their patients will wearily attest.

The system of responsive and responsible human social networks in China probably accounts for the seemingly low incidence of hospital admissions. Shanghai and the extended area around it have a population of approximately eighteen million people. This region is served by two mental hospitals, the one we visited, which treats "acute" patients (those whose psychotic episodes are brief and/or infrequent) and another treating "chronic" patients (those who have been disturbed for long periods of time). Each of these facilities has only 1000 beds. A little arithmetic tells us that is one bed for every 9,000 citizens (compared to a 1:1,500 in a state hospital in New York City). This striking ratio suggests either that the incidence of severe emotional distress is quite low or that distressed persons are cared for outside the hospital. Our investigations of Chinese community life suggests that both are true.

Ross Speck, an American psychiatrist whose work with the social networks of schizophrenic families is receiving wide attention in the psychiatric community, has suggested that the degree of mental illness decreases when people have large social networks actively intervening in their lives. In China individuals participate in and feel responsible toward many subsets of interpersonal networks: their families, both nuclear and extended, their work units (with whom they engage in political study and criticism/self-criticism on a regular basis), their street and neighborhood committees in the cities or their communes, brigades, and production teams if they live in rural areas, and often other social groupings as well. People are simply not alone, and it seemed to us that there was very little social alienation.

In the United States social networks are smaller and have a tendency to work at cross-purposes. Neighbors, friends, co-workers, and relatives often don't know each other, and rarely feel responsible for one another. Each network subset operates in a partial vacuum, developing its own, often contradictory mores and values. Without common goals, there can be no "higher moral authority" with which everyone concurs. The Chinese, on the other hand, operate within network structures that are mutually supportive and highly self-conscious. Relationships between individuals and social groups, and between these and the state, seem meaningful and purposeful.

Because people are organized to meet common needs themselves, they do not feel dependent on a national or regional delivery system, and thus do not feel impotent in directing their own lives. Adults are organized into study groups and children into socialization classes, both of which connect individuals to each other and to the larger society. They receive direction in their work and study from superordinate levels of network organization (the Party branch in the area, the municipal revolutionary committee of the city, and so on). These directives are constantly being clarified and discussed among the people at the local level. Thus individuals feel a part of a complete coordinated system of social networks. Even the job of reclaiming deviant social behavior, which we in the United States leave to the mental health and criminal justice systems, is most often kept where it really belongs, integrated within a community of comrades. The neighborhood committees themselves are composed of citizens elected by their peers and serving at no pay. They are often people who are forgotten in many societies: the old and the housewives. As these people are mobilized to deal with common social problems, they too are given avenues to contribute to their society and can reclaim a sense of their own dignity.

Because city life, even in China, separates people and disrupts social patterns that develop in villages and towns, the neighborhood committees provide the link that keeps urban people connected. Since part of their job is to monitor interpersonal relationships within the neighborhood, they act as a kind of early intervention team specializing in problem solving. By bringing peer group pressure to bear on those involved in such disputes, they help temporary adversaries find a compromise, and potentially violent or destructive relationships can be brought under control before they become unmanageable. Individuals are not left alone to brutalize each other but are brought into contact with their community, which accepts responsibility for dealing with them. It is these activated social networks that can probably take a large share of the credit for keeping people emotionally healthy.

There is always a highly conscious audience for people's actions. With the exception of one's dream and sex life, almost all behavior is considered part of the public domain. If parents are mistreating a child or co-workers are arguing, there are groups or individuals not directly involved who see it as their revolutionary duty to help mediate and resolve the difficulty. Similarly, those caught in the disagreement expect others to help them through it and accept their responsibility to be criticized, if appropriate.

Since the population in Chinese cities is very dense, the American variety of privacy, even if it were a cultural norm, is practically impossible. When neighbors or families quarrel, everyone knows about it. The neighborhood committee learns either indirectly or through a request for help from one of the quarreling parties. Frequently a delegation of a few members visits with the participants in the dispute and arranges a series of meetings with all concerned.

For example, in Shanghai a married couple began to quarrel because the husband felt his wife was not spending enough time at home. During the day she worked in a street factory and she spent many evenings in meetings at the local school. When the husband returned from his job he was very tired and resented having to do the housework. Sometimes he lost his temper and there was "sharp mental struggle" (intense arguments) between them. His wife felt that her work was serving the people and did not want to give it up. "Both of us lose our tempers easily," the wife told us. "After a while we even came to blows, and I demanded a divorce" (highly unusual in China).

The neighborhood committee learned of the problem from neighbors and had a talk with the husband. They pointed out that the wife's work was indeed serving the people; that her work at the school was educating young people, which was very important. After a few meetings with both of them, the wife began to pay more attention to her housework (although she kept her evening work) and her husband began to help out more—he even started sewing clothes. A member of the neighborhood committee proudly told us, now "both husband and wife work for the revolution and at night they do housework together."

For such outside intervention to be successful, it is clear that people must accept the legitimacy of external mediation and must share common goals and methods of analyzing problems. Here again the teachings of Chairman Mao provide the common ground. Everyone in China seems to operate within certain consensual ground rules that are often taken from Mao's writings. The phrase "cure the illness, save the patient," for example, admonishes people that correcting mistakes should not be the basis for personal attacks. Similarly, "one divides into two" implies that everyone has shortcomings, even those doing the criticizing. It is the responsibility of the criticizer to look at the strong points of the one being criticized. "We must look at the other's strong points to discover our weak points," one of our Chinese hosts explained in classic dialectical fashion. Thus during mediation of disputes everyone involved is expected to make self-criticism as well as argue his or her position.

In Mao's article "On the Correct Handling of Contradictions Among the People" he makes an important distinction between "contradictions among the people" and "contradictions between the people and the enemy." Contradictions between the people and the enemy are considered "fundamental," and occur over "matters of principle." They cannot be compromised except at the expense of the revolution itself. Enemies of the people must be removed. On the other hand, "contradictions among the people" are not usually over matters of principle, but over "matters of everyday life." Arguments between husband and wife over child-rearing practices, for example, or between neighbors, should be resolved in a spirit of friendship and compromise, using the idea that one divides into two. Factions, disputes, and splits among groups are regarded as errors of ultraleftism, and in such instances too the neighborhood committees or some other mediating body is expected to intervene to help find a correct solution. Using these commonly shared principles, people manage to come to terms with each other even when feelings of bitterness threaten to explode the situation.

The neighborhood committees deal with problems of divorce, abortion, and death, as well as marital squabbles and quarrels between neighbors. We were told that different personal habits were not usually considered sufficient reason for divorce. In such cases the committee advises the couple to correct their mistakes and become reconciled. In cases of physical fighting between husband and wife, the committee directs its attention at protecting the position of the woman, and their first effort is usually to educate the husband. Most cases of fighting occur among young couples, we were told, because young husbands are more likely to neglect their household chores and go out with their friends. Left to carry the burden of housework alone, the wives feel neglected and unfairly overworked. The committee tells the couple that both must do the household tasks and neither has the right to leave them to the other.

With respect to abortion, the committee's policy in cases where a married couple has failed in birth control and doesn't want a child is to recommend the abortion—

assuring the hospital that this is the wish of both parties. There are a few cases of abortion because of illegitimacy, but marriage is usually regarded as the preferable solution.

In cases of both divorce and abortion, the wife's attitude is regularly given the greater weight. Care of children after divorce is settled by discussion, but it is preferred that the woman take them.

Although the street and neighborhood Committees discharge a special function in urban China, much of their practice is mirrored in other social organizations. The study of Chairman Mao's writings, for example, is a regularly scheduled part of the work week in factories, offices, and communes, as well as a central activity in the schools. Similarly, criticism/self-criticism occurs at least once a month (and often at two-week intervals) in every social institution, and in times of trouble, in the home as well. Thus the whole society spends considerable time focusing its attention on its own processes. Order, rationality, good will, and cohesion are the fruits of such painstaking attention.

Even in such a humane and responsible environment, however, some people become sufficiently disorganized and distressed to make their community feel the need to hospitalize them. Why certain people in certain social settings become so overwhelmed that they begin acting in ways that prompt others to remove them remains an incompletely answered question in all societies. The medical model, an orientation that has been the cornerstone of western psychiatry, is based on the assumption that people acting in highly unusual ways have an "illness," which like a physical illness needs to be diagnosed and treated by medical personnel who may cure it. In the West such a view has often resulted in the belief that mental disorders exist independently of culture and social systems, since such aberrations are seen as existing "inside" the distressed individual.

These ideas are now being challenged by new ones insisting that deviant behavior can be made intelligible only if one looks at the social system in which the individual lives. These ideas assume that human beings do not exist in a vacuum but are members of interconnected social systems that play a large part in determining their emotional lives. In recent years western psychiatry has had to consider the effects of social systems, from families to nation states, on the individual. If one redefines the treatment unit to include all the people who surround a patient, especially the family, the patient's bizarre behavior begins to make quite a bit of sense. The work of R. D. Laing, Donald Jackson, and Gregory Bateson among others has shown that a person's family of origin or his or her adult nuclear family can affect and even create psychosis. Thomas Szasz, the author of *The Myth of Mental Illness*, has written that since no one has been able to scientifically establish any physical basis to behaviors labeled "psychotic," the term is simply a label of degradation used to discredit those people whom others find threatening. Laing argues that the person in visible distress is merely responding to subtle messages he or she is receiving from others, and unless everyone involved in the system can be "monitored" the "psychosis" will persist. If one extends these ideas, then it is not just the family that should be regarded as the treatment unit but the entire interpersonal context in which the person is situated: the social network and, beyond that, the entire social system.

These two seemingly mutually exclusive views appear to have been integrated in Chinese psychiatry. The doctors we talked with seemed to believe that there is a biological or "constitutional" component to mental disorder. They used the words "disease" and "illness" and discussed possible physiological causes of schizophrenia. At the same time they maintained that the larger social system has a powerful effect on individual psychology. The low incidence of many distress patterns more common in the West (childhood schizophrenia, senile psychosis, alcoholic and syphilitic psychosis, and so on) provides considerable support for a point of view that goes beyond individual psychodynamics, while biochemical and genetic research findings in this country and abroad suggest that physiological factors may be operating as well.

Just as their theory is eclectic, Chinese methods of

treatment reflected the same broad approach. Social and political ideas as well as drugs and acupuncture are major aspects of their hospital treatment. Although they do not "treat" whole families or networks—this work being done by the community itself—medical personnel maintain close contact with the people closest to the patient, using their influence to improve relationships between patients and their whole human environment.

8 PLANNING AND STREET COMMITTEES

Plans are an important aspect of life in China. Especially since the Cultural Revolution, the whole approach to planning seems to reflect a growing emphasis on participatory democracy for eight hundred million people. We saw considerable evidence that plans are not just made at the top and handed down in the form of quotas to be fulfilled, jobs to be done, and benefits to be gained. People at all levels are asked to make plans; increasingly the government asks them what quotas they are setting for themselves, what jobs they can accomplish, what benefits they wish to gain.

Our trip was too short and too varied for us to gain a complete picture of the overall planning process in China, to tell how all the pieces fit together. We did have the opportunity, however, to see enough pieces of the puzzle to get a general impression of how things work. Rather than try to fit them all together neatly, this chapter will simply present some of the things we heard in discussions with members of national and city planning teams, as well as with people planning at the neighborhood level.

In Peking we spent a pleasant morning with three members of the State (National) Planning Council who were working with environmental questions. These planners rep-

resented diverse backgrounds. Mr. Yeh was a chemical engineer, Ms. Wang was a medical hygienist, and Mr. Chu
Ka-p'ei a leader in a division of city planning.

They explained that the problem of pollution, so grave
in other countries, was a relatively new one in China and
that they were still in the early stages of studying it. This
struck us as a bit modest, since it had been apparent
throughout our visit that ecological concerns have been part
of planning for some time.

Before Liberation, we were told, the distribution of industry was unreasonable in human terms, concentrated in
the three major cities on the east coast. As a result
Shanghai, Dairen, and Tientsin were almost unlivable,
their waters poisoned by solid and liquid industrial wastes
and their air foul with pollution. After Liberation, thousands of these city factories were physically dismantled
and carried to suburban areas or rebuilt in China's interior, and those remaining developed new processes to re-
use or remove polluting substances. Now planners attempt
to scatter new industry evenly throughout the countryside
where wastes cannot concentrate and are more easily discharged. In each new location a set of industries is built
together to facilitate multipurpose use and economically
efficient production and disposal. Balance in industrial development between coastal and interior areas is considered
very important, not only ecologically but also as part of
the long-term campaign to reduce differences between life
in the city and in the countryside.

Our hosts noted the example of the Taching oil field, a
model industrial site. Taching is a huge complex that includes a spacious residential town surrounded by supportive agricultural lands. This arrangement physically inte-
grates workers and peasants in a single area, so that often
the peasants growing grains and vegetables are relatives of
the oil-field workers. This, we were told, is good for production and convenient for the people. It also means that
industry develops without disrupting the social fabric of
the countryside with mass migration to the cities, a far cry
from patterns of development in most of the rest of the
world. The Chinese have found that the planning of new

cities is far easier than the modification of old ones. For example, in new cities planners can consider wind patterns when they locate new industries; old cities that have inherited industrial plants upwind from housing are stuck with them for the time being. Even post-Liberation planners had to learn these things, and we were told that at first many mistakes were made, such as putting new industries too close to residential areas.

"Chairman Mao always stresses the comprehensive use of materials to turn harm into benefits," Mr. Yeh pointed out. The Chinese hold that all materials must be utilized for human benefit, and they now make strong efforts to develop new processes for using all materials not previously considered useful. Many factories have developed sideline industries to utilize "wastes." For example, a pharmaceutical plant producing antibiotics has found that poison by-products they once buried can be used in making dyes, solvents, and weed killers. A three-in-one team of workers, technicians, and cadres achieved these results by conducting experiments according to the model "from simple to complex." This model, alluded to in many discussions of education and production, describes the process of beginning with simple or easy problems and systematically progressing to those of increasing complexity and difficulty. Sometimes the new processes are economically expensive, but hazard reduction takes priority over profits.

One of our hosts had visited Sweden and France and expressed his amazement at the amount of garbage he saw there. In China, he told us, garbage is never piled up, burned, or used as fill. Domestic wastes are purchased by the government from every household and then sorted into various useful components. Fibrous materials like paper and cloth go to paper mills, metal goes to the metallurgical industries, plastic goes to the plastics factory, glass is returned to glassworks. Dust, ash, earth, and vegetable matter go to the suburbs, where they are mixed with dung or night soil and fermented as fertilizer. Fermentation kills bacteria and parasites while conserving valuable potassium, nitrogen, and phosphorus. In areas where modern sewage systems exist, solid wastes are filtered out and used the same way, while the liquid is recycled separately in irrigation. In Europe our host had seen plastics burned as wastes. When he asked about the harmful gases given off and suggested recycling, he had been told it would not be profitable.

One member of our group couldn't understand why the Chinese Government had to pay for wastes. "Shouldn't the citizens of a socialist country bring in their wastes for free?" he asked. In the United States, he said, ecology groups had vigorously campaigned to get people—many of them a good way behind the Chinese in political consciousness—to turn in their newspapers, bottles, and cans without remuneration. The woman to whom he posed the question explained that the present system of payments for garbage and trash wasn't intended for the millennium. But payments encourage thrift, and in what is still a materially underdeveloped country they give social recognition to the intrinsic value that even wastes possess. In the future, she said, as material scarcity disappears and people receive incomes based entirely on their individual needs, a different system will prevail.

In one of Peking's nine districts alone, 1,500,000 tons of waste materials are collected annually. The planners asked us to imagine what enormous quantities there would be if everything weren't recycled. We could only think of the far greater quantities of garbage and trash encroaching on our own advanced America. China, after all, is a country still far too poor to produce much garbage. Nevertheless, although we saw everywhere we went that the problem of waste is coming under control in China, we were told that it was in fact enormous at the time of Liberation, when garbage had piled up from the time of the Ch'ing Dynasty and masses of people mounted campaigns to remove it.

The task of the State Planning Council is basically to integrate the plans of city, rural, and provincial or regional councils. Local plans may make sense locally but not necessarily nationally. Central planning specialists, like the team we talked to, may travel to local councils as consultants. Ms. Wang, for instance, works under the leadership of the Public Health Department, which might, for example, notify medical schools how many doctors are needed in a particular area, depending on information gathered from local levels. Local plans are discussed by local groups and then are proposed to the State Planning Council. When they have been discussed, negotiated, and approved, they are submitted to the Central Committee of the Communist Party for further negotiation and approval, and eventually they are sent back to the local level as completed plans. Planning at the local level, for example, when new factories are to be built in an area, takes into account the need for schools, hospitals, shops, and cultural centers which must also be planned and integrated with them. There are frequent mass campaigns to plant trees, participate in building, fight pests in health and agriculture, and so on, which help teach people planning needs. Planning administrators have the task of consulting the masses of ordinary people on planning issues and their opinions are then discussed at the higher levels. The view often repeated to us is that experts alone cannot determine or solve the people's problems.

We had an opportunity to look at another level of the planning process in Shanghai, where we talked at length with members of the City Construction Bureau, which plans and is responsible for the construction of roads, bridges, water systems, and buildings. The bureau is under the City Planning Council, which in turn reports directly to the State Planning Council (each of the major cities, Shanghai, Peking, and Tientsin, is administered as a separate district, not as part of a province). Within Shanghai the Planning Group of the Construction Bureau is part of the Municipal Revolutionary Committee. The Construction Bureau has an administrative staff of two hundred and a work force of forty thousand. Bureau plans are discussed in the revolutionary committee as a whole before they are submitted to the State Planning Council. These plans are formulated through a well-organized process of soliciting ideas from the grass roots level up and sending consultants down to the lower levels of the municipal social structure.

Turning Shanghai from a semifeudal colonial city with rampant exploitation and misery into a clean, thriving, lively city for the people must rank among the greatest achievements in history. In the past people the world over had heard tales of Shanghai's starving, homeless masses and its prostitution, drugs, disease, beggars, and gangsters; the English verb "to shanghai" connotes an abduction that is seamy and deceitful as well as coercive. Coupled with this image was a complementary legend of opulence and high living by rich Chinese and foreign adventurers and profiteers. Our hotel, a vestige of the days of foreign domination, retained beautiful paneled walls and luxurious chandeliers as reminders of the past. But when we looked down on the riverside park, formerly posted with a sign forbidding Chinese (and dogs) to enter, we could see throngs of people strolling, walking briskly to work, doing their morning exercises, or sitting down for a cigarette or an ice cream in the sun.

The city had not only been filthy and inadequate for its population, it had also evolved as a random disaster from a planner's point of view. English, French, Japanese, and American concession areas were legally autonomous and each had its own transportation, gas, sewage and electrical system, without links. The city expanded from east to west with no planning for north-south trunk roads. Working people were huddled in makeshift hovels around their factories, which belched black smoke and poured effluents into ditches and rivers. The huts of straw and wood and the river sampans could not hold all the population. Even after the war with Japan, when China regained her territorial rights over the foreign concessions, the Kuomintang paid little attention to planning and reconstruction in the areas they controlled, and things deteriorated further.

When Shanghai was liberated in May of 1949, the Party and the government turned all foreign enterprises over to the people and established a principle of "independence, initiative, and self-reliance" for reconstructing their city. People were encouraged to aim high and to get better, faster, more economical results in industry. Planning and construction groups began to take a hard look at the most serious needs, enlisting mass campaigns of people to solve problems of public health and rebuilding. No great amounts of capital existed, so the people had to make use of the old in building the new. Shanghai today is still an old city in appearance, though great numbers of new factories, public buildings, and housing projects are scattered over its fifty-three square miles of inner city and 2,280 square miles of suburbs. The total population is still over ten million, despite dispersion efforts. But the city is immaculately clean, the population is fully employed, there is no hunger, there is universal education and medical care. How was it done?

The first policy was to end haphazard expansion, divide the city into industrial areas, and build an encircling complex of new towns. Other policies include family planning: the 1957 population increase rate was 4.5 percent; in 1971 it was less than .07. Young people were called upon to move to the countryside; by now up to one million have gone. Workers moved to rural areas, or at least to suburbs, to rebuild factories destroyed during war or deemed congesting.

Narrow, winding pre-Liberation roads, frequently blocked entirely by buildings, were widened, and almost a thousand miles of new roads were built. Peking Road alone, over three miles long, was blocked by twenty-three buildings, all of which were torn down by 1953. The main road from the city center to the railway station was widened from between ten and twenty yards to over forty. All the buildings lining it are new. Chungshan Road, now the main belt around the city, was built from old, narrow sections of road in a single year. Nanking Road, the main street in front of our hotel, had five buildings razed and the first floors of others cut out to permit widening, where buildings could be saved in this manner. It is now Shanghai's main shopping street, with long stretches of big department stores and smaller shops which we wandered through when our hosts and interpreters took an after-lunch break by themselves. Photography studios, exhibits, and restaurants seemed particularly popular.

Among the accomplishments since Liberation, the people of Shanghai have brought gas to over 280,000 additional households, laid vast new sewer systems underground to replace open ditches, and developed forestation projects to bring trees into the city. In some sections, where the open sewers were surrounded closely with people, whole populations had to be moved while ditches without outlet were filled in and housing was constructed. The people around one such section planted 150,000 trees and turned it into an attractive park with walkways and recreation facilities. People who had experienced the environmental hazards and problems of old Shanghai spoke of them publicly and enlisted community support in dealing with them. Campaigns ranged from cleanups and rebuilding to research in new uses for waste materials, including poisonous polluting substances.

Many old docks have been turned into riverside parks to make an attractive waterfront where one sees, while strolling, the commerce between China and countries around the world. Seventy-five "new workers' villages" have been built, with plants, housing, schools, hospitals, stores, cultural centers, bathhouses, playgrounds, and banks included in each one. Every year teams of people investigate the changing needs of each area: perhaps more vegetable markets are needed, or a new primary school. Residents are also consulted about the adequacy and design of their own living quarters. Recently building designs have been changed to provide for higher ceilings, private kitchens and baths, windows with different exposures, and so forth. All these new features reflect the ideas and opinions of the residents. The very idea of soliciting design ideas from ordinary people and responding seriously to them is rooted in the much broader Chinese political campaign to win mutual respect between professionals and nonprofessionals. The Construction Bureau itself is headed by former railroad workers and other workers, as well as civil engineers, and includes people with a wide spectrum of formal education. Before the Cultural Revolution, our hosts told us, experts divorced from the masses frequently developed wrong ideas and plans. Now the mass line is in command: expert opinions are there for people to absorb, but experts also rely on the practical knowledge of the people who are affected by the decisions.

To see the planning process at work among the people we visited street and neighborhood committees in the large cities. Urban areas in China are divided into districts, and then into street committees. The planning process in the city as a whole extends through this layered structure down to its smallest component. In addition to dealing with the daily life of the community, these local committees receive directives from above for discussion and implementation and send locally made decisions back up the structure of government. As organized as Chinese society appears to be, there is still a remarkable decentralization of activity, with considerable local autonomy among the different institutions. We probably saw more variation and less bureaucracy in China than exists in many comparable social realms in the United States.

In Peking we visited the Western China Avenue Street Committee, which oversees an area of about two square miles containing 150 small streets populated by 20,000 households, about 80,000 people. Street committees originally formed around public security areas (police districts) but, especially during the Cultural Revolution, evolved responsibilities that go far beyond security. For example, five small local street factories were developed by this committee, at first making daily necessities such as simple sewing supplies, later transformed into technically advanced enterprises, producing locks in a seventy-step process and one-horsepower-motors for such users as spraying insecticides in agriculture. They now employ 1,700 of the residents, including many former housewives.

We interviewed members of one of the smaller neighborhood committees under the street committee. This group had responsibility for a subsection comprised of three lanes with 696 households, 2,400 people. After we and our hosts had settled at the long tea table at committee headquarters, they quickly introduced us to the far-reaching changes such committees have helped to accomplish. Before Liberation, they said, most of the workers in this subsection were unemployed and living under conditions of severe deprivation. Prices inflated continually, disease was rampant, housing was totally inadequate and dilapidated, and begging was a way of life. Ditches filled with dirty water emitted a perpetual stench and carried the dead bodies of rats, dogs, and even children. Flies and mosquitoes were everywhere. When the wind blew, dust piled up a meter high and ensuing rain turned it to knee-deep mud.

None of these conditions prevails today, as we could see in walking through the neat streets and alleys where children played at jump-rope and hopscotch. The People's Government, as our hosts referred to the national leadership, had cared for the people and their immediate interests, helping them begin "the happy life." Houses were repaired, ditches filled in, dust and garbage hauled away, new roads built, prices stabilized, jobs created, and lives generally made secure. The standard of living rose rapidly.

A woman named Chang Yin told us how her parents had worked literally as beasts of burden until her father became too ill and the seven remaining family members could no longer feed themselves. They were forced out of their home and the two youngest of her sisters had to be sold. Chang Yin is married now and has seven children of her own. Five have graduated from middle school, two still attend. She sees herself as one of the millions of Chinese who have lived through an incredible transformation from abject poverty to rising standards of living and self-respect.

The neighborhood committee's thirteen members are elected by the people of their area and are not compensated. The committee's tasks are 1) to organize housewives, children, and old people for political study of both literature and current events; 2) to conduct educational propaganda among the residents and improve relationships among them, including the settlement of disputes; 3) to organize production shops of individuals or collectives to do work in homes; 4) to organize the neighborhood on questions of hygiene, both personal and environmental; 5) to organize student activities during vacation time, encouraging the mental, physical, and cultural development of youth; and 6) to organize local cultural productions.

The neighborhood and street committees supervise the running of local street factories, which are controlled by people living in each area through the local committees and for this reason vary greatly from place to place. In some districts the street enterprises consist of knitting and sewing cooperatives where the work is done in people's homes. Other places have small handicraft shops. Some street factories do light industry such as making hats or shoes, metal works, printing and papermaking, and glass production.

Street factories were first formed during the Great Leap Forward and the urban commune movement of the late 1950s. They served the purpose of integrating into the work force many previously unemployed housewives, old people, and handicapped and unemployed workers. People in the residential urban areas pooled their resources, surveyed the skills available in the neighborhood, held meetings to decide what to make, and then in the spirit of "self-reliance with empty hands" they began production. Often they got assistance from the industrial plants in the area in the form of old equipment, scrap materials, information, and training. The neighborhoods usually had little or no capital to invest in equipment, so when they began they were usually limited to doing labor-intensive work. After a few years of operation there might be enough money to invest in equipment or machinery. Now there are many such street factories, collectively owned by workers in China, making transistors, integrated circuits for computers, and even entire computers, as we have described in an earlier chapter.

Essentially the street factory movement consisted of neighborhood people getting together to contribute to the national economy and improve the quality of their lives. One of the consequences of the American economy is the great number of unemployed people whose potentially valuable contributions go to waste because the owners of businesses see no profitable way to employ them. These people are sometimes given subsistance through welfare or unemployment compensation, but their real value to society and themselves is lost. In China, street factories bring these people into production and play an important role in helping people to learn both important productive skills and reliance on their own collective efforts within the neighborhoods.

Women, who formerly made up the vast majority of the underemployed in cities, now play a primary role in the street factories. Under the old society they were relegated to a subservient position to men and to the household, but the street factory and committee movement provided an opportunity for women to unite with other women to set up enterprises that serve the needs of the new society. This was a liberating process, but as our hosts said, it was not easy. Many men resisted the emancipation of their wives and tried to prevent or discourage them from being active in neighborhood enterprises. But such attitudes were struggled with by people in the community, and men who resisted the liberation of women were changing their attitudes with time. Political discussion about women's roles helps this process along. The organization of nurseries, kindergartens, laundry services, and dining facilities makes it easier for women to take on an active public life; so does the social expectation that the remaining housework will be shared by both men and women.

We toured some of the local facilities in the Peking neighborhood, meeting with several small production collectives and individuals. In a collective where hand-embroidered children's clothes were being made, the loving concern for detail that reflected the attention that Chinese lavish on their children. Farther along we visited the studio of a group of old people who had recently been trained in classical painting by a master artist. We could see the pride of these senior citizens, not institutionalized but taught a respected new skill in their old age.

Next we were received in the home of an elderly railroad worker, on leave from his job because of high blood pressure. He served us tea in glasses as we crowded into the small house he shares with his wife, married daughter, son-in-law, and their children. His personal account of the "happy life" he leads included telling us of raising fish—he had several tanks of them, which we admired—studying, taking leisurely walks, maintaining contact with his work team on a regular basis, teaching and playing with children, and working on the local committees. He also spoke of cooking the evening meal while his wife made fishnet-weave shopping bags. "No pressure is needed in this household to get anyone to do jobs," he said. "Everyone wants to help. Nowadays much of the housework is done by both men and women in cooperation." We laughed together about the recalcitrance of some husbands, not setting as good an example as he, and compared women's liberation struggles in China and America. Throughout our talk we felt the impact of the attempts of this locally organized committee to make available for every individual in its area a life filled with productive and rewarding social activities.

When we left the old worker's home, waving good-by to the whole family, we went down the street to a local kindergarten which, like all those we visited, overflowed with bright, cheerful, confident children dressed in colorful garb who pulled us into their circle games in the courtyard, calling us "uncles" and "aunties" like family friends. Such kindergartens—described in more detail in the education chapter—bore further witness to the benefits neighborhoods derive from the coordinated activities of their committees.

Back at headquarters, around the long tea table again, we reviewed all we had seen and asked further questions about the committee's role in promoting good relations between neighbors, doing what they call "propaganda between neighbors." We heard about one case in which a man's wife died in 1967, leaving him to care for their four children. It was very difficult for him to manage all the housework and child care, so the neighborhood committee organized some of the old women in his courtyard to help. They did the cooking and made the children's clothes, in addition to their own work.

In another case, two families had quarreled bitterly during the previous year. The battle was so heated that one went to the other's home and threatened to die there, and the other reciprocated with a similar threat. Our storytellers seemed to imply that these dire threats, apparently taken very seriously in Chinese culture, really indicated each family's hurt at the other's lack of concern. The neighborhood committee was called in by one of the daughters-in-law, and after patient discussion and study the families became true friends. They now do each other's shopping, visit each other when ill, and generally demonstrate real concern for one another.

Other disputes arose when people thought themselves better than others, or spoke behind each other's backs. In such cases people were helped, through political study, to learn from each other's strong points and strengthen their own weak points. The committee members spoke of "uniting for greater victories," meaning that when people realize that the contradictions among themselves hold up progress toward common goals, and that they are of similar class backgrounds and thus not natural enemies, conflicts can be resolved.

When a serious contradiction exists between an individual and the masses, it may warrant consideration as a contradiction with an enemy, in which case the person may be labeled a "bad element" who should be turned over to the criminal justice system. Such labels are not given out lightly, since the committees pride themselves on resolving the vast majority of contradictions without recourse to police or courts. When a person who has been accused of a serious crime returns to his community from imprisonment, however, he is not supposed to be stigmatized, but regarded as one who has corrected his errors and is no longer an enemy.

One such case concerned a man who was discovered selling opium a few years after Liberation. He was sentenced to death, under a one-year stay of execution. Because he made progress toward reform during that year, he was given a seven-year sentence in lieu of the death penalty. After three years his progress had warranted parole, and he was now a fully integrated member of the community, "working to build socialism." In another case, a man who had served as an agent of the Kuomintang, having confessed after Liberation, was discovered in secret possession of a pistol. He was sent to prison for three years and then returned to his neighborhood and job as a fully integrated citizen. Both these stories were from past times, within a few years after Liberation, suggesting that such serious cases had not occurred in this neighborhood for a long time. (This seemed to be borne out during our visit to the Shanghai Municipal Jail, where we found extremely few prisoners under the age of forty.)

Further discussions with our neighborhood committee hosts centered on the care of retarded and handicapped children. We were told that such children are sent to special schools or institutions only in the most extreme cases or when there are clear advantages in intensive special education, such as for blind and deaf children. Whenever possible, their education takes place among their nonhandicapped peers and adults, to maintain their acceptance in the community and to teach other children not to regard them as inferior.

Liaison cadres are sent back and forth between the neighborhood committees and the street committees, which form the link with the Party, to discuss directives, pass on requests, and aid in the implementation of policies and plans. We got the sense of a real two-way process, where leadership was clearly exercised, but kept accountable by and responsible to the people it represented.

The transformation of Chinese cities demanded the creation of new communities as well as reorganization of the old. One example we have already seen is the residential community of the Peking Number 3 Textile Mill, where the housing development is connected to the factory and under its administration. Another kind of urban community is the P'eng-p'u New Workers Residential Community in Shanghai. It was started in 1959 with fifty-six buildings; now 17,000 people, workers from fifteen factories and their families, live in its 138 buildings.

The community has a shoe factory that employs fifty

women. The one man in the shop is from a large shoe factory that helped set up the small street factory and supplies it with raw materials. The community also maintains production facilities that make switches, toys, and machine parts. Altogether, 800 former housewives are employed in these enterprises.

The mobilization of housewives to do productive labor and to study politics has been part of the emancipation of women in China. Our hostess, Hou Fu-hsien, head of the neighborhood committee, told us:

> Before the Cultural Revolution, Liu Shao-ch'i and his followers looked down on housewives when they wanted to study Chairman Mao and other works. They said we couldn't read and write, and that our task was only to bear children, cook and shop. They said the task of a housewife was to stay home; that doing housework well means revolution. During the Cultural Revolution the old comrade and I went to a meeting held by the masses of the whole city to criticize the revisionist line. Now the housewives can answer these capitalist roaders loudly; although housework is heavy, we are not afraid of more work—low literacy will not stop us. . . .
>
> After Liberation . . . all women under forty-five years of age joined in the work. In the past, over 600 women here had no work. After the Cultural Revolution, in 1970, we united and began to take part in collective productive work. To improve the economic and political life, we organized women to work at processing shoes.

With the women working outside their homes, it was necessary to provide day care. The neighborhood committee now runs a day-care center with more than 500 children. It also set up a multipurpose service center for mending clothes, giving haircuts, and providing other services. There are sixteen shops in this new community, selling all necessary goods from cereal to hardware, and a canteen for the convenience of residents who do not wish to cook.

There are two primary schools in the community, serving 4,000 students, and one middle school with 3,000 students.

Education is the task of the neighborhood committee as well as that of the schools. In the P'eng-p'u community two hundred retired workers who volunteered to do some revolutionary work had been organized to help young people study and to tell them about the old society. We visited one of these workers at home. Wu Hsü-ming, a sixty-three-year-old retired woman, shares her small flat with a son, his wife, and their child. Besides taking part in a study group for retired workers and a study group for women, she educates young people about the old society. She told us her own story:

Before the Revolution we suffered from the repression of the Kuomintang reactionaries. Working people had nothing. Two years after my marriage, my husband lost his job. He was a shop assistant, and for several years he could not get another job. In seven years I had three sons, so living conditions were very difficult. Then my husband fell ill and had no money to see a doctor, so he just had to wait to die. After two months he did. That was over thirty years ago; I still don't know what disease he suffered. I was only twenty-seven and my sons were young, the youngest only a year old. Life became more difficult. My mother, who had six children, of whom I was the only survivor, wanted to kill herself. She drank poison from a bowl. Her neighbors found her and made her throw up so that she didn't die.

Such things happened very often. People sold their own children or killed themselves. When my children were ten, they went to work in factories and worked like men for the capitalists. Even then we had to give my youngest son to other people; we could not make enough money to support ourselves, so the family had to separate. In the new society, one worker can support three or four people, but in the old society I could not even support myself. Prices rose everyday, sometimes three times a day.

Life became better after Liberation. I got a house and could live with my sons. My first son started primary school at eighteen, and at thirty he graduated from the university. My second son joined the People's Liberation Army after he graduated from junior middle school. My third son, who was given back after Liberation, graduated from the Foreign Languages Institute in Shanghai and is now an interpreter. My sons are married; my daughters-in-law are a doctor, a teacher, and a nurse. My second son is an electrical worker, so he and I are the only workers left in the family, all the rest are intellectuals.

During our conversation we asked her how her youngest son had been returned to the family. She answered, "In 1949, when Shanghai was liberated, there were many members of the Revolutionary Army here. I approached a Party member to ask for help in finding my son. The Party responded by finding him and returning him home."

As she recounted the past she would cry a bit and shake her head, but in recounting present conditions Ms. Wu smiled. Retirement pay, free medical care, good wages all around: today's happy life could not have been dreamed of in the past.

She told us that the Cultural Revolution had at first split her family into two groups, with her on the conservative side. "I was influenced by Liu Shao-ch'i's revisionist line," she said. "I thought: I'm retired, I want to enjoy life, sit around indoors in winter and be warm, in the courtyard in summer. I was very concerned with my health. Now I have revolutionary work to do." Eventually she became convinced that the rebellion was justified, and peace was restored in the family.

In Shanghai we also visited the Wan-p'u Street Committee (whose clinic is discussed in the chapter on health care). This committee oversees a very densely populated 35-square-kilometer area of 51,000 people and has nine residential committees under it. Before Liberation there were four large companies in the area in addition to numerous houses of entertainment, prostitution, gambling, and drugs. One after another we visited the rehabilitated quarters of prostitutes and the buildings formerly owned by wealthy exploiters. Now working families occupy the buildings and, simple though many of these homes are, the people made it clear that they feel extremely fortunate to be living in them now.

Like its counterpart in Peking, this Shanghai street committee oversees factories, clinics, study groups, and schools, with perhaps its greatest emphasis on education. Here too housewives and retired workers not organized in other institutions are among its most active members. The committee also handles interpersonal disputes, described to us as falling into four main categories: those between neighbors, between husband and wife, and between mother-in-law and daughter-in-law, and conflicts over property. In all cases members of the committee study with those in conflict to help them analyze and overcome their individual differences in favor of a common goal of serving the people in a united way. Of the fifty such cases that the committee handled last year, thirty were between neighbors, ten between husbands and wives, and the remaining ten of other types.

One such case of conflict between a husband and a wife was described in the previous chapter. One of the conflicts between neighbors involved two women in the same building who had sons of different ages. The boys started fighting, and their anger spread to their mothers, who quarreled over the use of water in their building and ended up fighting physically. At that point a comrade from the local neighborhood committee tried to help. She began by getting both women to sit down and study the works of Chairman Mao and to engage in self-criticism. Since the Chairman says the people must unite to win greater victories, she asked, how could those women think they should fight each other? She spent many evenings with them and got each one to analyze in what ways she was right and in what ways wrong. She pointed out that before Liberation people lived miserably in poor, small houses; but now they lived in decent, adequate dwellings: all the more reason for less quarreling and more unity. Eventually both women engaged in self-criticism, stopped their dispute, and agreed that each should pay more attention to the social education of her own child.

The incident was an example of how the committee uses political study to raise people's consciousness and resolve arguments. Its role in such cases is to show the people that their quarrels are over matters of daily life, not basic principles, and that their fundamental interests are the same. People are expected to see that everyone has shortcomings and no one should think of himself as completely good, or the other as all bad.

In addition to seeing to the daily lives of its inhabitants, the street committee also carries out the policies of the government by mobilizing the people to study socialist construction. In one committee over eighty weekly study groups are organized to encourage the people to discuss and analyze the work of the Party. Among other things, these meetings promote unity through a better understanding and a feeling of involvement.

Education of the young is a joint responsibility of the three-in-one combination of schools, family, and society, with the street committee representing society. It organizes small groups of students and parents to maintain close contact with the schools, participating in discussions and planning with them. Retired workers and housewives conduct these groups. They meet with primary school children every day and with middle school students once a week, and they keep in touch with the teachers to exchange information about the children. For example, they keep track of homework assignments and make sure that the students have done them. If children have trouble, they are given encouragement and help. The group also tells the students about revolutionary heroes and heroines, leads them in singing songs, and organizes them to take night soil to the countryside on free days. Students are especially taught to return any money that they find in the streets. In the P'eng-p'u Residential Community last year two young children who found a hundred *yüan* ($50) in the grass told their grandmother and then took it to a neighborhood committee cadre. He asked them, "What are your names? You should be rewarded." One of the children said, "I'm a Little Red Soldier. Chairman Mao told us to return the money. He teaches us that we must turn in everything we find. It's the discipline of the People's Liberation Army."

These examples illustrate some of the ways in which the street committees create unity and social responsibility in the neighborhoods. We were told of another illustration that occurred outside Shanghai, when a workingwoman fell ill. Some of her neighbors took her to the hospital while others cared for her children. Those who worked by day nursed her at the hospital by night. During the two weeks she spent in the hospital her three children were cared for. In other cases people may have old parents and young children at home but work a long way off in another part of the city. Their neighbors help them care for their dependents. Neighbors are encouraged to care for each other as one family, and the development of friendship and care among people, so often left to chance and personal preference in our society, is one of the explicit purposes of the local committees.

The street and neighborhood committees are so situated in the social structure that they can fulfill their varied functions, bringing coordinated planning to the people at the same time they are organizing the people to create and carry out their own plans. Their overall goal is to help build a society that truly aids people in all aspects of their daily lives.

9 SUMMING UP

Discover the truth through practice, and again through practice verify and develop the truth. Start from perceptual knowledge and actively develop it into rational knowledge; then start from rational knowledge and actively guide revolutionary practice to change both the subjective and the objective world. Practice, knowledge, again practice, and again knowledge. This form repeats itself in endless cycles, and with each cycle the content of practice and knowledge rises to a higher level.

Mao Tse-tung, "On Practice" (1937),
Selected Works, Vol. I

In discussions and demonstrations of science in China, we heard science defined variously as "a summation of the laboring people's experience," as "a tool forged by the people's labor to be used for the improvement of their lives," as "a process of thinking and developing rational knowledge through practice," and as "one of the three great revolutionary movements" (along with class struggle and the struggle for production). Such concepts were difficult for us to grasp in our early encounters with them. After all we, as Americans, are more accustomed to thinking of science as a set of ideas and experiments gen-

erated in the minds of a special set of people—with somewhat mysterious talents—known as "scientists." Our Chinese counterparts told us that they too used to hold this
view, and that they had looked for "bright" and "talented"
students to train as scientists. Today the science student is
chosen more for high motivation to serve the people by
studying hard, for a willing dedication to bringing the
fruits of higher education back to the people. This change
is rooted in the basic concept that society rests on working
people, who taken together express the knowledge and
technology of that society. The scientist's job is to "sum
up" their experience, translate or abstract it into theory,
discover new problems through this summation, and teach
the theory back to the people, integrating practical experiences together with theory to solve new problems.

As we heard one example after another of the former
limitations of a science developed in the isolation of the
laboratory, and witnessed the rapid progress of a science
rooted in working people's experience and facilitated by
science workers, the concepts began to be clearer to us.
Such practice of science is inseparable from the politics
which teaches equality, cooperation, and a materialist
foundation for science—natural and social. Trying to dis-
tinguish science from politics is like trying to answer the
proverbial chicken-and-egg question. They cannot be
viewed in a cause-and-effect, primary-secondary way.
China is a preeminent example of the general proposition
that politics is scientific and science is political. Hence our
book is as much about the politics of new China as it is
about science.

Scientific achievements, such as insulin synthesis, are
brought to the people as lessons to help them overcome
feudal mythology with a scientific approach, to help them
believe that people can transform nature to meet their
needs. Scientific and technological breakthroughs at the
worker and peasant levels, such as the construction of the
Red Flag Canal, are in turn brought to scientists and intellectuals as lessons to help them overcome bourgeois elitism
with a political approach, to deepen respect for the
strengths and abilities of the masses. All the people are

thus encouraged to use their initiative, to think analyti-
cally, and to act together to transform their society in
their common interests.

Understanding is synonomous with freedom, as ignorance
is synonomous with oppression. Science, for the Chinese
people, is a methodology, a way of acting upon and understanding their world, so it must be shared by all the
members of the society if they are all to be free. Knowledge is power. Those who possess it will control themselves and their world. The collectivization of knowledge is
therefore as fundamental to the Chinese as the collectivization of material production.

Vast numbers of Chinese people are being liberated
from ignorance: feeding, clothing, educating, and healing
themselves. This, to the Chinese, is what freedom is all
about. And again the concept of freedom is at once political and scientific. Restraints on freedom are not only those
of an external authority but also those of ignorance.
Marxists hold that people are free only when they understand natural laws—the forces and contradictions of
nature—so that within these laws they can change nature
wherever possible if it is in their collective, long-range interest to do so. Primitive man, who knew no engineering
to cross rivers and no medicine to cure disease, was not
free. The feudal peasants and unemployed urban pro-
letariat in the old China were not free. But neither are the
citizens of "advanced" nations who cross rivers, are cured
of disease, and hold jobs, if they do not both understand
and control the means by which these feats are accomplished.

Here in America, as we tell of our trip, we are invari-
ably asked about the "regimentation" necessary to effect
progress in China, about the manipulation of the Chinese
people by their leaders to accomplish political ends. It is
true that New China is a highly organized society, that
large numbers of people act in unison to solve problems,
that Chinese society is "managed." The Chinese believe in
"correct ideas," that is, they elevate politics to the level of
a science. These ideas originate among the people, are
"summed up" by the leadership, and are sent back to the

people to be tested, criticized, evaluated, and transformed as with natural science theory. It is the maintenance of this constant interaction between theory and practice, between leadership and people, that is looked to for the ongoing liberation of the Chinese people. It is a system based on eight hundred million checks and balances.

The Chinese leaders continually urge the people to be self-reliant, to study their conditions, to rebel against nonrepresentative leaders, and to fight out different political ideas to test their validity for progress. The Cultural Revolution of the 1960s is the most dramatic recent example of this policy, but it was neither unique nor exceptional in the political experience of Chinese Marxists. In August 1973 the Tenth Congress of the Chinese Communist Party amended the Party constitution with the admonition that "Revolutions like this will have to be carried out many times in the future." Revolt against the leadership is thus the policy of the leadership. It is possible for such a policy to lead to leftist excesses, to forceful repression of one contingent by another, but Mao has said that revolution is not a dinner party and that errors are essential to learning. Liberation from feudal "nonthinking"—from the desire to depend on leaders to tell you what to do—is neither an easy nor a short-term task. Centuries of the habit of being manipulated must be overcome. Whether the Chinese will effectively complete their battle against the manipulation and oppression of the past depends on their continued response to the mandate to rebel against everything that is backward.

What can we learn from the models we saw in China about the practice of science in America? We look for answers to this question not in China but here in America, in the places where we live and work. We begin by asking more questions, having learned from the Chinese that no area of society should escape our scrutiny. We share only a few of the problems of an underdeveloped country, but we can ask ourselves whether our practice of science serves to promote continuing advance and freedom for all of us. Immediately we notice substantial disparities between what our science and technology could accomplish and what it actually does for us. We notice also clear distinctions among the people whom science serves. Who reaps the fruits of science? Who controls funding and therefore the direction of scientific research? How much democracy is there in the workplace of scientific practice? How many of us even understand the languages of "science" well enough to make consequential decisions about the practice of it? And if the vast majority of American people neither understand nor control their science and technology, are we truly free?

This is not to say that China is "freer" than we are or that we should blindly imitate their models. On the contrary, if we learn nothing else from the Chinese, the lesson that revolutionary change in a society must proceed from its own particular material conditions and the ongoing experience of its people is fundamental, as the Chinese learned from their experience with the Soviet model. Equally, we would be foolish to ignore the Chinese experience and learn nothing from its successes and errors. We have attempted in this book to present to American readers some of the Chinese successes. We were deeply impressed with what we saw in China and have tried to convey that excitement as well, an excitement born of watching a people struggling together to achieve a common liberation. We come home committed to a similar struggle here to achieve an American liberation—a liberation rooted in the unique material conditions and cultural heritage of our resourceful people—so that we too can learn to walk on two legs.

Appendix 1: Profile of SESPA/Science for the People

Scientists and Engineers for Social and Political Action (SESPA)/Science for the People is presently a loosely structured organization of national scope. There are approximately forty chapters or contact people throughout the United States and in some areas abroad. Although there is underlying agreement about the misdirection of science and technology in the United States, the real definition and goals of SESPA/Science for the People are determined by the actions of its chapters and project groups. Organizational structure is currently being evaluated and developed to provide a stronger basis for activities.

To better understand Science for the People's directions and potential impact, it is worthwhile to consider its history. Since the post-World War II blossoming of technology—especially for war—numerous strains of political involvement by science workers have evolved. These range from expert-led science seminars, for the "nation's leaders," and elite advisory councils, to the radical analyses and militant actions of activists. During its own development Science for the People has also encompassed several variants of thought, all of which, however, lie toward the activism and most of which prevail today in Science for the People's activities and continuing political debate.

The activities which led to the initial organization developed within the American Physical Society. Efforts to enable the members to vote, committing the APS on social issues, were consistently thwarted by the physics establishment for two years. Finally, at the APS meeting of January 1969, the dissident members, who were mainly academic physicists outraged at the Indochina war, and who by then had considerable membership support, formed Scientists for Social and Political Action. This group, in reaction to the tight, closed organization of the APS hierarchy, chose a loosely structured organization open to diverse membership and without a binding political manifesto.

Another contributing thread in the formation of SESPA/SFTP came from organizing for the March 4, 1969, "Research Stoppage" to protest war research. This action, planned since the previous November, was built at MIT, Cornell, Yale, and several other campuses and research centers around the country and again reflected the distinguishable political tendencies of science workers. The Science Action Coordinating Committee which helped organize the research stoppage activities at MIT consisted mainly of radical graduate students. This was in contrast to other groups that worked with SESPA such as the Union of Concerned Scientists at MIT and the Federation of American Scientists elsewhere, whose members concentrated on legislative reform.

In Boston there was continuing cooperation between SESPA's members, industrially employed science workers, and radical students not only on the March 4 program but also in the anti-ABM campaign and later for the first SESPA attendence at the American Association for the Advancement of Science meeting in Boston in December 1969. From this alliance a more militant and radical group resulted, symbolized by the fist and flask of our emblem and the slogan "science for the people." This group became increasingly interested in a working-class political orientation and in developing a broad critique of the capitalist system.

A major emphasis by the Science for the People organization at the AAAS meetings was soon placed on ideological issues, especially focusing on the damaging ideas inherent in racism and sexism. While SESPA attendence at professional meetings such as AAAS and the APS became increasingly visible and effective, other activities were also being elaborated. The People's Science approach, presented at the 1970 AAAS meeting in Chicago, inaugurated a political strategy whereby science workers could directly apply their skills to problems that oppressed people face. Along this line, the Science for Vietnam Project followed. In August 1970 a different major thrust of Science for the People began—the former mimeographed newsletter was upgraded to a bimonthly magazine of political discussion, analysis, reporting, and correspondence between chapters.

Another significant advance came in 1971 with the formation of the Science Teaching Group, which made its debut at the National Science Teachers Association meeting with a widely distributed critique. The Science Teaching Group has subsequently worked to counter and supplant the usual science teaching in schools with materials revealing the political connotations of topics that are typically ignored or treated as if "neutral." A Science Teaching Conference for New England was organized in March of 1973 and its workshops resulted in three pamphlets on science and society.

By 1971 Science for the People activities had become sufficiently diverse and widespread that additional publications had come into being to serve more specialized functions, such as the Science for Vietnam national newsletter as well as several local newsletters. Joint operations with other organizations have developed, including those with Computer People for Peace, the Committee for Social Responsibility in Engineering, and the Vietnam Veterans Against the War.

Finally, discussions of internal structure and national organization have begun. The Madison, Wisconsin, chapter has two paid staff members, and in Boston an interim steering committee and a paid coordinator are being tried out. A national conference is now being discussed and the general political questions implied in establishing an effective nation-wide organization are being increasingly raised in many local chapters.

Current activities are a mixture of research, discussion, publication, and direct action. They include a number of project groups:

Science for Vietnam (Chicago, Evanston, Minneapolis, Washington, D.C., Madison) exists to aid and support the struggle of the peoples of Indochina and to carry on the fight for humane and deprofessionalized science in the United States. SFVN now consists of a variety of collectives, groups, and individuals with the Chicago Collective coordinating projects and publishing a newsletter. Some examples of the work done thus far are sending packages of literature on the treatment of TB and malaria, and exposing weather modification warfare. (SFVN Chicago Collective, 1103 East 57th Street, Chicago, Illinois, 60637.)

Science Teaching Group (Boston) provides a critique of present curricula, methods, and school structure, and is developing materials for teaching science in a social-political context. Activities include NSTA conventions (alternatives and critiques), regional teacher conferences, and the Science and Society Series of teacher guides on such subjects as the "Energy Crisis" and "Genetic Engineering."

Madison Collective (Madison) is currently assembling a book cataloguing the mathematical assistance the Army Mathematics Research Center has given the military, and is pressing for a new center to apply math to the problems of the Wisconsin working class.

Women's Issue Group (Boston) began as a group of women writing articles for an issue of *Science for the People* on the use of science ideology to oppress women. It is now broadening its activities to raise women's issues within and without Science for the People.

China Group (Boston, Stony Brook, Chicago, Minneapolis, Berkeley, St. Louis) organized the Science for the People delegation which went to China and is publicizing what was learned on the trip through the publication of articles and this book, and through speaking engagements.

Industrial Group (Boston) gives support to its members in developing more effective politicizing at the workplace and a better understanding of the role of technical workers. It is building a more numerous and cohesive group of industrially employed workers in Science for the People.

Berkeley Collective has several ongoing projects, including an exposé of the Jason Division (Pentagon science consultants), a monthly radio program, a China study group, and support for the Shell strike.

The most important means of communication among all SESPA groups and members in the United States and throughout the world is the bi-monthly magazine *Science for the People*. It prints articles from people in all parts of the Science for the People constituency and is published in Boston, with a different collective responsible for each issue. The structure of the magazine collective is an attempt to set up a system in which no one is "boss" and all decisions are reached collectively (it takes more time but is more creative and challenging): everyone does soliciting, choosing articles, editing, typing, layout and paste-up. Members for the collective are chosen by a group of the past year's editorial collectives, and ideally the group is well represented from industrial academic, research, and other spheres, as well as having an equal or woman-biased sex ratio. The magazine serves to unite all those isolated individuals or groups who wish to be part of a radical science movement but are geographically cut off from others like themselves. It reports on political activities and works at developing a broader political understanding and a more critical analysis.

Further inquiries concerning the organization and/or its publications should be addressed to: *Science for the People*, 9 Walden Street, Jamaica Plain, Massachusetts 02130, (617) 427-0642.

Appendix 2: Science for the People Delegation's Itinerary in China

Wednesday, February 21. Canton.

We entered the People's Republic of China at Shumchun from Hongkong. A Chinese train took us to Canton, where after resting we spent the evening at a cultural park.

Thursday, February 22. Canton.

Visited the Peasant Movement Institute Museum and Exhibition Hall, where we learned about the early history of the Chinese Communist Party. In the afternoon we visited the monument to the Canton Uprising. Then we took an evening jet to Peking.

Friday, February 23. Peking.

A visit to Tien An Men Square and the Forbidden City. In the evening we attended a dinner given by our official host in China, Chou P'ei-yüan.

Saturday, February 24. Peking.

A day at the Red Star Sino-Korean Friendship People's Commune, about twenty miles from Peking, where we saw dairy farming, greenhouses, a school, a clinic, and small industry.

Sunday, February 25. Peking.

Spent the day at the Central District May Seventh Cadre School, about thirty miles from Peking. We saw the agricultural and industrial work at the school, and had discussions with Chinese cadres about the role of intellectuals in China and the purpose of reeducation.

Monday, February 26. Peking.

After a tour of the Tsinghua University campus, including classrooms, dormitories, dining rooms, laboratories, and library, we discussed education in China and the Cultural Revolution at Tsinghua with students and faculty.

Tuesday, February 27. Peking.

In the morning we visited the Institute for Chemistry and the Genetics Institute, and had discussions with members of the Psychology Institute. In the afternoon we went to the National Minorities Institute, where we saw classes in art, dance, music, and traditional Chinese martial arts.

Wednesday, February 28. Peking.

A trip to the Great Wall and the Ming Tombs. At the Physical Culture Institute we toured the facilities and joined in volley ball, ping-pong, badminton, and swimming. Later there was a discussion with members of the Computer Institute and a visit to the Embassy of the Democratic Republic of Vietnam.

Thursday, March 1. Peking.

In the morning there was a tour of the Institute for Zoology as well as a discussion of the goals and activities of our organization, Science for the People, with representatives from Hsinhua News Agency, Academica Sinica, and the Chinese People's Association for Friendship with Foreign Countries. Later we visited the Embassy of the Provisional Revolutionary Government of South Vietnam. In the evening we showed the Wiseman film, "Hospital."

Friday, March 2. Peking.

In the morning we went to the Great Hall of the People

for a discussion with Liu Hsi-yao, deputy member of the Central Committee of the Communist Party and member of the state council. In the afternoon some of us visited a street committee in a residential area while others toured the Peking Maternity Hospital and observed surgery under acupuncture anesthesia.

Saturday, March 3. Peking.

Four of us set off by train, bus, and jeep to Hsikou Commune, in the T'aihang Mountains in Shansi Province. In Peking, we visited the No. 15 Peking Middle School and the No. 3 Cotton Mill.

Sunday, March 4. Peking.

A day relaxing at the Summer Palace, outside Peking.

Monday, March 5. Peking.

A return visit to the Institute for Zoology, a visit to Peking University, and discussions with city planners for the Peking district.

Tuesday, March 6. Hsikou Commune.

The rest of the group traveled to Hsikou Commune, where our four colleagues had been observing reforestation, water conservancy, primary and middle schools, hospital, and a scientific field station. We all had discussions and interviews with science and technology team, peasants, and intellectuals, and did some manual labor: shoveling dirt into wheelbarrows.

Wednesday, March 7. Xigou Commune.

Meeting with Li Shun-ta, leader of Hsikou production brigade, member of Central Committee of the Communist Party.

Thursday, March 8. Lin County, Honan Province.

Visited various parts of the Red Flag Canal network on our way back from Hsikou. In the evening there was a dinner celebrating International Women's Day.

Friday, March 9. Honan Province.

A bus trip through the mountains to Ch'engchou, then an overnight train to Shanghai.

Saturday, March 10. Shanghai.

Arrived at Shanghai in the afternoon.

Sunday, March 11. Shanghai.

Visited the Shanghai Industrial Exhibition, where we saw various industrial products of the Shanghai district on display. In the afternoon we visited the Shanghai Machine Tool Plant, which is known for its emphasis on worker education.

Monday, March 12. Shanghai.

Visits to Futan University, Happiness Village Primary School, and two factories: the Shanghai Electrochemical Works, known for its efforts at recycling industrial wastes, and a factory staffed by handicapped workers.

Tuesday, March 13. Shanghai.

A tour of the facilities of the Shanghai Psychiatric Hospital. In the afternoon we visited a new residential housing area and an old one, the Wan-p'u District, and saw street committees at work.

Wednesday, March 14. Shanghai.

At the Hua Shan Hospital we witnessed five operations using acupuncture anesthesia and learned something of how medical schools operate in China. Later we made a return visit to the psychiatric hospital and a visit to the Shanghai Institute of Computer Technology—including a small neighborhood factory where computers are produced—as well as visits to the Institute for Biochemistry and the Institute for Physiology.

Thursday, March 15. Shanghai.

A discussion with Shanghai city planners at the City Construction Bureau and a tour of the Shanghai Science and Technology Exchange Station, which is responsible for exchange and popularization of scientific and technical information.

In the afternoon we visited the Shanghai Municipal Prison and had discussions about the Chinese criminal justice system.

Friday, March 16. Ch'angsha, Human Province.

Arriving by plane from Shanghai, we visited various places where the young Mao Tse-tung did political work while teaching classical literature at the Ch'angsha Normal School.

Saturday, March 17. Shaoshan.

Spent the day at the small village of Shaoshan—about sixty miles from Ch'angsha—where Mao Tse-tung was born. Exhibition halls there give an overview of the history of the Chinese Communist Party.

Sunday, March 18. Ch'angsha.

A day of resting, shopping, and hiking in Ch'angsha, then an evening train to Canton.

Monday, March 19. Canton.

Discussion on biological control of insects and a visit to the Entomology Institute. Tours of a Taoist temple and a porcelain factory.

Tuesday, March 20. Canton.

A day of sharing notes and experiences, plus a visit to the Canton Zoo.

Wednesday, March 21. Canton.

A morning train to Shumchun and from there a train to Hongkong.

Appendix 3: Science for the People
Delegation Biographies

Mary Altendorf (Minneapolis, Minnesota) is a member of the Science for Vietnam section of Science for the People. With training in natural science, she was especially interested in the exchange between scientists and nonscientists in China. B. S. from Experimental College of University of Minnesota in political theory and movements.

David Aronow (Worchester, Massachusetts) is a medical student at the University of Massachusetts Medical School. He has worked with the St. Louis branch of the Intercommunal Survival Committee.

John Dove (Brookline, Massachusetts), a computer programmer at Interactive Data Corporation for the past five years, has been active in Computer People for Peace and Science for the People, working on ways to organize computer programmers and other technical and office workers.

Minna Goldfarb (Port Jefferson, New York), a graduate student in social psychology, has worked for three years in parent-controlled community child-care centers and has done community counseling along with child-care center organizing. She is currently working on the class nature of modern progressive education movements.

Ginger Goldner (New York, New York), a psychologist and a former director of the feminist studies program at Goddard College, in Plainfield, Vermont, is now living in New York City. She is studying family therapy and feminist psychoanalysis and maintains a small private practice.

Judy Greenberg (San Francisco, California), formerly of New York, is a registered nurse now working at the U. S. Public Health Service Hospital. She has been active in struggles for better health-care, especially for women and children.

Marvin Kalkstein (East Setauket, New York) is a nuclear chemist interested in issues of social responsibility of scientists and of science and public policy. He works at Empire State College of the State University of New York, an innovative open-admissions program.

Frank Mirer (Cambridge, Massachusetts) is an organic chemist doing research at the Harvard School of Public Health in the "toxicology of everyday life"—environmental contaminants and occupational health. He has been active in Science for the People and the environmental movement, and is presently aiding workers who are organizing to eliminate occupational hazards.

Geri Steiner (Brookline, Massachusetts), formerly a physiological psychologist is now a juvenile justice planner. The mother of two children, one a medical worker, she has a long-standing, active concern with political issues in science, education, and law among professional and community groups.

Vinton Thompson (Chicago, Illinois) is a graduate student in evolutionary genetics and a member of the Science for Vietnam Chicago Collective. He is building local community interest in and support for various liberation struggles, especially those in Vietnam and Africa, and has been active in the antiwar movement in Chicago.

DISCUS BOOKS

DISTINGUISHED NON-FICTION

A SELECTION OF RECENT TITLES

DISCUS BOOKS
DISTINGUISHED NON-FICTION

Wherever paperbacks are sold, or directly from the pub-
lisher. Include 15¢ per copy for mailing; allow three weeks
for delivery.

Avon Books, Mail Order Dept.
250 West 55th Street, New York, N. Y. 10019

◗ DISCUS BOOKS
DISTINGUISHED NON-FICTION

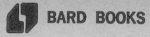 **BARD BOOKS**

DISTINGUISHED MODERN THEATRE AND FILM